PERILOUS FUTURES

PERILOUS FUTURES

On Carl Schmitt's Late Writings

PETER UWE HOHENDAHL

CORNELL UNIVERSITY PRESS
ITHACA AND LONDON

First published 2018 by Cornell University Press

Library of Congress Cataloging-in-Publication Data

Names: Hohendahl, Peter Uwe, author.
Title: Perilous futures: on Carl Schmitt's late writings / Peter Uwe Hohendahl.
Description: Ithaca: Cornell University Press, 2018. | Includes bibliographical references and index.
Identifiers: LCCN 2018012831 (print) | LCCN 2018015602 (ebook) | ISBN 9781501730665 (e-book pdf) | ISBN 9781501730672 (e-book epub/mobi) | ISBN 9781501726545 (cloth)
Subjects: LCSH: Schmitt, Carl, 1888–1985. | Political science—Philosophy—History—20th century.
Classification: LCC JC263.S34 (ebook) | LCC JC263.S34 H62 2018 (print) | DDC 320.01—dc23
LC record available at https://lccn.loc.gov/2018012831

CONTENTS

Acknowledgments

The idea for this book emerged during the first decade of the new century when American foreign politics took an unexpected turn under the influence of neoconservative thought and its central protagonist Leo Strauss. In this context Carl Schmitt was discovered in the United States as a critical voice in the heated debate about the fate of international liberalism and the call for regime change as a way of spreading democracy abroad. Schmitt's thought seemed to me to offer an answer to the vexed problems of American foreign policy. On closer scrutiny, however, I realized that Schmitt's work, including his late writings, does not fit easily and smoothly into the mold of a progressive theory of democracy. Confronted with Schmitt's late essays, I recognized that the link between Strauss and Schmitt is far more complex than one would have assumed by following the public debates of these years. This complexity was the challenge for this project. Where do we locate the late Schmitt on the theoretical map? It meant taking the late writings seriously as texts beyond their function in present controversies. Hence the central concern of this book was a close rereading of Schmitt's texts.

Parts of the first chapter were previously published in German in *Zeitschrift für Germanistik* (2016). The second chapter grew out of an article published in the volume *Solitäre und Netzwerker,* edited by Peter Uwe Hohendahl and Erhard Schütz (2009). An earlier version of the fourth chapter was published in *Constellations* (2011), and chapter 5 is based on an essay published in 2008 in the electronic journal *Konturen.*

This book benefitted greatly from the encouragement and advice of many friends and colleagues, among them Paul Fleming, Wolfram Malte Fues, Isabel Hull, Manuel Köppen, Max Pensky, Bill Rasch, William Scheuerman, and Erhard Schütz. They provided critical feedback and respectively challenged my position through their own writings. In other instances, extensive discussions about Carl Schmitt's controversial oeuvre helped me work out my own position. Their insights and judgments were greatly appreciated, even in those cases where I finally did not agree with them. Last, but not least, I want to thank Matteo Calla for translating the German text that became the basis of chapter 2 and Stephen Klemm for formatting and proofreading the entire manuscript.

Abbreviations

E   Carl Schmitt, *Ex Captivitate Salus. Erfahrungen der Zeit 1945/47*, 2nd ed. (Berlin: Duncker & Humblot, 2002).

G   Carl Schmitt, *Glossarium: Aufzeichnungen aus den Jahren 1947–1951* (Berlin: Duncker & Humblot, 1991).

GRO   Carl Schmitt, "The Großraum Order of International Law with a Ban on Intervention for Spatially-Foreign Powers: A Contribution to the Concept of Reich in International Law 1939–1941," trans. Timothy Nunan, in *Carl Schmitt, Writings on War*, ed. Timothy Nunan (New York: Polity, 2011), 75–124.

IVA   Carl Schmitt, *Das internationalrechtliche Verbrechen des Angriffskrieges und der Grundsatz "Nullum crimen, nulla poena sine lege,"* ed. Helmut Quaritsch (Berlin: Duncker & Humblot, 1994).

LER Carl Schmitt, *Die Lage der europäischen Rechtswissenschaft* (Tübingen: Universitätsverlag Tübingen, 1950).

N   Carl Schmitt, *The Nomos of the Earth in the International Law of the* Jus Publicum Europaeum, trans. G. L. Ulmen (New York: Telos, 2006).

PT   Carl Schmitt, *Political Theology: Four Chapters on the Concept of Sovereignty,* trans. George Schwab (Chicago: University of Chicago Press, 2005).

PT II Carl Schmitt, *Political Theology II: The Myth of the Closure of any Political Theology,* trans. Michael Hoelzl and Graham Ward (Cambridge: Polity, 2008).

TP   Carl Schmitt, *Theory of the Partisan: Intermediate Commentary on the Concept of the Political,* trans. G. L. Ulmen (New York: Telos, 2007).

PERILOUS FUTURES

INTRODUCTION

When the jurist and political theorist Carl Schmitt bitterly complained in his postwar diaries that he was unfairly treated by the victorious Allies, he could not have anticipated the impact his thoughts would have on legal and political discourse in the very countries that had banned him from the public sphere in postwar Germany. Although shunned in 1945 for undermining the liberal regime of the Weimar Republic and then openly supporting National Socialism, Schmitt has today achieved international recognition for his approach to and use of the political. Although his theories are still controversial, they have become part of contemporary legal and political theory, and their reception is by no means limited to the political Right. Clearly, Carl Schmitt has morphed from a specifically German figure to a global phenomenon. In this new intellectual and political environment, much of the older criticism of Schmitt's closeness to the Nazi regime has dropped out of sight, treated either as a minor offense or as irrelevant for the evaluation of his theoretical work.

Nonetheless, in this thoroughly transformed context, both his public role in Europe after World War II and his late writings must be reassessed because, looking at them from the vantage point of the twenty-first century, the relevance of his claims and arguments has changed. They have developed their own theoretical life, to varying degrees, without much regard for the original intentions of the author. It may be fair to say that Carl Schmitt's international influence today is less due to the value of his ideas as a coherent theoretical system than as the result of their adoption within a number of overlapping global political and social discourses. In other words, Schmitt is internationally present in a variety of heterogeneous legal, political, and social debates in which his thinking is used for different and conflicting purposes.

The purpose of this book is to explicate Schmitt's late work as part of a specific historical constellation and its importance for the present moment. By returning to Schmitt's historical roots, my aim is to interrupt the seamless appropriation of his work, while acknowledging the historical distance that separates us from the mid-twentieth century, when Schmitt was rethinking his own positions in light of the collapse of Nazi Germany and the rising hegemony of the United States. I hope to underscore the need to reconstruct Schmitt's work in order to better assess its present relevance, keeping in mind the tension between Schmitt's intentions and the later reception. I therefore avoid two possible methodological approaches: first, attempting to systematize Schmitt's late theory and, second, measuring it in abstract terms against the standard of competing contemporary political and legal theories. Instead, this book emphasizes the structure of his individual works, their rhetoric and composition as well as their language and style, thereby probing the text for its ambiguities and contradictions.

In doing so, this book also foregrounds the possibility of connecting and comparing Schmitt's late work with a variety of competing theories and ideological positions that are not necessarily compatible with Schmitt's own stance. It is precisely these ambiguities that a system- or dogma-oriented approach fails to recognize or acknowledge. Rather, such approaches tend to simplify Schmitt's teaching in order to create sharp borderlines and contrast it with competing dogmatic systems. This, of course, may be done either in the interest of identifying with Schmitt's position or with a polemic intent. Yet a polemic, as much as it may have been needed a generation ago, is not the purpose of *Perilous Futures*. It aims, rather, at a critical reevaluation of Schmitt's late work, an immanent reassessment that follows a process of close readings.

Why focus on Schmitt's late work? Until fairly recently, the majority of Schmitt scholars considered the late work as being less important, if not actually marginal. For them, "the real Schmitt" consists of his writings between the early 1920s and 1933, possibly extending to his study of Hobbes in 1938. It is as a theorist of the strong state and in his radicalized concept of the political that Schmitt is usually considered most relevant. By comparison, the late work seems to lack coherence, appearing to comprise isolated individual texts. In some instances, Schmitt seems to return to older concerns that he had since disregarded. The obvious example of this tendency is *Political Theology II,* in which Schmitt goes back to an older debate in order to set the record straight and to clarify his position. However, while it may be correct that we cannot understand this late essay without Schmitt's original 1922 essay, it would be misleading to read Schmitt's return to it as a mere continuation. In 1970, the stakes were quite different from those of 1922. In short, even as the late writings reconnect with Schmitt's earlier work, they also branch out, shifting emphasis and becoming involved in new conversations without always explicitly stating this. In the case of *Political Theology II,* for example, the relevant interlocutor is no longer Erik Peterson (who by then was dead) but Hans Blumenberg, who had offered a severe critique of Schmitt's position in his 1966 book, *The Legitimacy of the New Age.* It is a conversation about a necessary reassessment of the Enlightenment after World War II that Blumenberg had developed in his study. By extension, it is also a conversation about the legitimacy of the Federal Republic and its constitution, which had embraced the values of the Enlightenment. Schmitt's resistance to Blumenberg's thesis signaled his continued skepticism.

Similarly, *The Theory of the Partisan,* first published in 1963—
ostensibly a contribution to the growing field of literature on irregular warfare and therefore an isolated piece in Schmitt's oeuvre—is,
in fact, closely connected with ideas and themes that Schmitt had
first articulated in the early 1940s when he focused his attention
increasingly on international relations. Beyond the interest in the
changes that occurred in modern warfare, Schmitt looks at the fate
of colonial Europe in its late stage, acknowledging the futility of
defending the old political structures while supporting and prais-
ing these powers for their efforts to maintain order. In other words,
the essay is also a commentary on the changing international order,
its increasing volatility, and its lack of a clear-cut future. Moreover,
it is an unacknowledged conversation with the French Far Right
about the counterrevolution that could have happened had the OAS
(*Organisation armée secrète*) succeeded, thereby changing the political face of Europe. Schmitt's late works, although seemingly isolated from their contemporary environment, in fact resonate with
the problems and questions that surround them, even when this
connection is not foregrounded. The Schmitt of this era, while
extending and modifying his older positions, remains in touch with
the postwar period, very much insisting on his own point of view
as being still relevant for the new questions that Germany and the
international community face.

After 1945, Schmitt did not play an active role in German political life, yet his interventions were certainly noticed and his influence after a relatively brief period of silence grew during the 1950s
and 1960s. One could make the argument that it was precisely the
isolation imposed on Schmitt during the immediate postwar years
and his forced retreat to the small town of Plettenberg that later
enhanced his influence. He became the unacknowledged but influential voice of German and European conservatism, recognized as
such not only by old friends and political allies but also by a new
generation of German intellectuals, especially on the Right, who
were seeking to make sense of the fate of Germany after 1945 and
the chances of the new liberal order in the Federal Republic. One
of the most remarkable features of his postwar impact is the discussion his work generated on both sides of the political spectrum

of West Germany, for the most part within the constitutional framework, which questioned but also affirmed the legitimacy of the new
political regime. Unlike Schmitt, the majority of his students and
followers, especially the younger ones, applied the lessons they had
learned by listening to the master's voice to the problems of the im-
mature and still uncertain liberal democracy in which they lived
and struggled. In this way, Schmitt's late work contributed, at least
indirectly, to the consolidation of a political regime that he detested.

Schmitt's preoccupation with the idea of a new global *nomos*,
first articulated in *The Nomos of the Earth* (1950) and a number
articles during the 1950s, seems not have been at the center of the
Schmitt discussion in the early Federal Republic. For obvious reasons, this discourse focused on the difficult transition from a fascist
to a liberal political regime and therefore returned to Schmitt's critique of liberalism in the writings of the late 1920s and early 1930s.
This work could be used either to attack the Federal Republic from
the Right or, more strategically, as a tool to bolster the young republic from the Left. For instance, Reinhart Koselleck, in *Critique
and Crisis* (1959), relied on Schmitt for a historical critique of the
European Enlightenment, arguing that it was responsible for both
right-wing and left-wing radicalism in the twentieth century. Jürgen
Habermas, on the other hand, in his *Structural Transformation of
the Public Sphere* (1962), very much aware of Schmitt's critique of
the late liberal public sphere, offered a radically different analysis
of the Enlightenment, emphasizing its critical dimension as a corner-
stone for the development of a democratic regime.

Similarly, Schmitt's "European turn"—his interest in a new political
order that would replace the old European system—did not resonate
broadly in his immediate postwar reception in West Germany, although the internal discussion among intellectuals, especially on
the Right, suggests that Schmitt's position was acknowledged. It is
a discussion that eventually transcended the intellectual framework of the Cold War with its stereotypical division between Western freedom and Eastern totalitarianism.

The most concise form of this debate about Europe's postwar
future occurred in the exchange between Schmitt and his old friend
Ernst Jünger. While they shared an aversion to Anglo-American

liberalism and the domination of Europe by the United States, they strongly disagreed about the long-term future of the Earth and a viable new global order. The disagreement became visible for the first time in Schmitt's rather unfavorable response to Jünger's utopian novel *Heliopolis* (1949), at the end of which the hero is invited to join an extraterrestrial community where wars, as they are narrated in the main part of the novel, can no longer occur. Schmitt's politely negative response to this ending signals his marked opposition to the idea of a world state that has overcome war.[1] Jünger's 1960 essay, "Der neue Weltstaat" ("The New World State"), can be read as a belated response to Schmitt's criticism.[2] In it, Jünger insists on the viability of a universal political community that has outgrown the frame of the traditional *Machtstaat* (power-based state) with its emphasis on bureaucratic organization. The essay argues in favor of a new type of community that privileges the freedom of the individual, a form of conservative anarchism that resists centralizing bureaucracy. At the same time, however, Jünger holds on to the idea of a unified world state, which he defends against a position that looks very much like that of Schmitt, although his name is never mentioned.

Schmitt remained completely unconvinced, accepting neither the concept of a unified world state nor the utopian moment of a final stage in which political and military conflicts are no longer a part of our reality. His *Theory of the Partisan*, in particular, underscores the negative force of modern and contemporary history; namely, its potential catastrophic outcome in a global civil war. Schmitt's reading of international relations during the 1960s significantly differs from the mainstream by placing the emphasis on civil war rather than on the East-West divide, and on the end of this war rather than on the victory of the liberal West. (The implications of his arguments in *Theory of the Partisan* became more urgent only when the ideological and military problems of the American world order became more visible during the late 1990s.)

What marks Schmitt's late writings is their peculiar relationship to mainstream political thought. While they define their own position in clear opposition to the postwar mainstream in West Germany, they are in their own way very much in touch with global transformations, articulating responses that were not always immediately understood and appropriated. As the disagreement with Jünger shows, even within the Right, Schmitt remained a controversial figure.

Carl Schmitt died in 1986 and so he did not experience the fall of the Berlin Wall, the subsequent demise of the Soviet Union, and the rise of the United States as the sole remaining global power. The global extension of the *Pax Americana* under the auspices of international liberalism during the 1990s seemed to be the final proof that Schmitt's persistent resistance to a monopolar world order had been mistaken, that he had misjudged the inherent strength of liberalism. The intertwining of normative universalism and U.S. political and military power appeared to offer for the first time a sustainable peaceful global order.

From a specifically German perspective, the end of the Cold War and the unexpected success of reunification under the umbrella of international liberalism looked like a strong endorsement of liberal democracy as the self-evident foundation of a unified Germany. Hence there was no immediate need for a Schmittian critique. Schmitt's significance was felt again, however, when unfettered global neoliberal capitalism, beginning in the late 1990s, led to increasing social and economic inequality (which moderate socialist parties in Europe were unable to confront) and the slowly rising instability of the international political configuration. The growing strength of rightwing radical movements in Europe and the rising volatility of the international political constellation caused by international terrorism pointed to serious structural problems of the new world order. Schmitt's return to the international political discourse, in particular in the field of international relations, was enhanced by the (unexpected) intrinsic systemic problems of the international liberal order, which were most strongly felt in the capitalist West. It is not accidental, therefore, that interest in Schmitt's theory shifted emphatically to the anglophone world. The role of the American empire became an urgent subject for the renewed appropriation of Schmitt. Rereading Schmitt, especially his late writings, now offered a critical perspective on the dangers of globalization that international liberalism had overlooked or denied.

Ernst Jünger's vision of a peaceful world state appears to be more utopian than ever, and the trends moving us closer to a destabilizing economic order are perceived as threats both by the radical Right and the radical Left. Both sides have blamed globalization for the decline of Western democracies and, more specifically, for the loss of equality and solidarity among their citizens. Schmitt's international reputation grew simultaneously with the rise and disruptive force of an international neoliberalism that undermined existing social structures, adversely changing the life-world of a significant segment of the world's population. The global crisis of 2008 only underscored and suddenly made very visible a process that had begun in the 1990s: the loss of belief in a common social and economic project that would benefit the citizens equally.

The political consequences of this process finally became manifest in the 2016 election of Donald Trump. The election signaled a significant shift in the self-understanding of voters. Trump's victory proposed populist solutions to the crises confronting advanced democracies. This perspective also potentially changes the role of Carl Schmitt in the political discourse. The emphatic call for the people to completely identify with Donald Trump, and his close advisors resonates with elements in Schmitt's conception of democracy during the 1920s. At this writing, it is still unclear whether and how the new regime will make use of these elements. There can be little doubt, though, that the populist turn of America's politics has a bearing on Schmitt discourse.

As Schmitt's work is being used more frequently to approach pressing contemporary problems, interest in its historical dimension has waned and the line between affirmation and critique of his ideas (and the man behind them) becomes more difficult to draw. Accepting Schmitt's concept of a new world order does not necessarily include supporting his personal politics. Nor does a more a critical approach a priori result in a complete rejection of Schmitt's thought. Schmitt remains controversial, but at the same time there seems to be a growing consensus that his thought provides significant conceptual tools for the analysis of the present moment. So how reliable are these tools?

Perilous Futures responds to this question by going against the grain of much of the recent Schmitt scholarship and returning to questions of intent and historical context. Its engagement with Schmitt's corpus remains necessarily selective. It follows Schmitt's late writings from his thinking about the concept of *Großraum* (expanded territory) to his return to political theology in 1970. It begins in the first chapter by probing Schmitt's early response to the defeat of Nazi Germany and his status as an intellectual quasi-outlaw after he was forbidden to participate in public life until 1950.

During his "political exile" in Plettenberg in western Germany, Schmitt worked on a number of essays that were first published in 1950 under the title *Ex Captivitate Salus*. Less publicly but more importantly, he expressed his thoughts and feelings in his diaries, the so-called *Glossarium*, which was published posthumously (with good reason) in 1991. In style and content, his notebooks would have been unacceptable in the public sphere of the 1950s or 1960s. Even in 1991, their publication caused a scandal and did serious harm to Schmitt's reputation. While critics and scholars have used the content of these diaries for different purposes, their formal structure has been taken for granted. The peculiar nature of Schmitt's notes, which tells us much about their author's way of dealing with the most serious crisis of his life, has remained unexamined. In chapter 1 the close readings of the *Glossarium* and the slim volume of essays focus on the language and rhetoric. The analysis approaches Schmitt's grasp of his postwar situation through textual details that shed light on author's complex subjectivity or, more precisely, on his multiple subject positions, depending on the topic. While Schmitt's aggression and resentment toward enemies real and imagined are apparent features that have been frequently noted and cited, the internal connections between various aspects of the self deserve further scrutiny. As it turns out, Schmitt the diarist can speak as a native of Germany, specifically as a part of a defeated and "victimized" collective, but also as a misunderstood member of the legal profession or as a member of the Catholic Church. In each case, a different self-perception and public position emerge. As much as they differ in their form of self-assertion vis-à-vis their social and political environment, they share a moment of strong resentment and hostility toward the victorious Allies that exert control over the public space of Germany.

As a member of the German collective, as well as of the legal profession, the diarist presents himself as a victim of hostile outside forces, either the Allies or those Germans and Jews, even worthy ones, who had been in exile and judged him because of his National Socialist (NS) connections. It is only in his role as a Catholic Christian that the question of guilt and accountability emerges as a serious problem with which the diarist has to wrestle. Given the centrality of the issue of faith and the importance of a renewed theological position for the late Schmitt, the diaries sketch a tentative transition from his early to his late writings. On the whole, however, the *Glossarium* presents a defiant subject, unwilling to recognize the responsibility of the German collective for World War II (including the Holocaust); refuses to acknowledge his culpability for his active support of the NS regime as a jurist; and seeks the forgiveness and support of the Catholic Church for his ambitions. There is no sign that the writer is willing and ready to support the liberal regime of the young Federal Republic. In fact, he always denies its legitimacy. The most striking feature of the notes is the intricate intertwinement of the private and the public, of Schmitt's strong, hostile emotions, and his almost rigid rationalization of specific public positions and views. But there is no clear path to the future.

As far as Schmitt's theoretical reflections are concerned, the diaries look mostly to the past and fiercely defend the roles that Schmitt played before 1945. In this respect, the essay volume, *Ex Captivitate Salus,* and the 1950 essay "Die Lage der europäischen Rechtswissenschaft" provide more insights. While some of the essays and notes are concerned with private issues, others turn to a broader assessment of his contemporary historical and theoretical situation. By gaining greater distance from his personal struggle and focusing on the political transformation in general, Schmitt is able to define the years between 1914 and the postwar era in a way that allows him not only to establish a conceptual frame for this period but also to see his own fate as part of this age. Schmitt describes these decades as an age of global civil war in which a common ground of values and norms is no longer given. Everything had become partisan, including the law. This means that Schmitt as a jurist had no other choice; he was pressured to become just as partisan as everybody else by serving the NS regime. Thus, for Schmitt, the concept of culpability no longer applies. From a political perspective, however, the concept of a global civil war opens up a new theoretical space. On the one hand, it shifts the focus from a national to an international approach; on the other, it looks at how global civil war can be overcome. Put differently, it raises the question of a new and different world order, one that Schmitt raises in *The Nomos of the Earth* (1950).

This new, international perspective of Schmitt's late work is the subject of chapter 2, which traces his thinking back to the early 1940s when Schmitt, still under the umbrella of the NS regime, developed his concept of the *Großraum* in order to address the expansion of the German Reich at that time. While 1945 was a critical time in Schmitt's private and public life, in theoretical terms it was not a turning point. Some of the central ideas and concepts that Schmitt used in his postwar writings, especially in the field of international relations, go back to the late 1930s and early 1940s. In this context, the concept of *Großraum* is one of the crucial *Kampfbegriffe* (battle concepts) that Schmitt introduced in order to formulate a new framework for a foreign policy that transcends the limits of the nation-state. The new concept is linked to the idea of a spatial ordering of the globe comprising a small number of independent and more or less equal *Großräume* (expanded territories), which guarantees peaceful coexistence through a balance of power. In accordance with Schmitt's notion of concrete thinking, the new concept had a specific political function at that time. It supported German foreign policy before and during World War II. His thought touched on and was in part fed by government policies. For example, it was not only Schmitt who referred to the American Monroe Doctrine of 1823 to legitimize German claims but also Hitler and his foreign minister Ribbentrop. In this way, Schmitt's postwar revisionist conception of a new world order was closely linked to the policies of the Third Reich, even though this connection was completely cut after 1945.

Other prewar elements of the new global conception were, however, retained and became an important part of Schmitt's postwar understanding of international relations. The polemical target of the idea of balanced *Großräume* was the universalism of the British Empire and the United States, both of which were, to Schmitt's mind, maritime powers that used universal values and norms to defend their international position. In this context, the Monroe Doctrine plays a crucial role in Schmitt's thought, since it makes visible the point where American foreign policy shifts from a normative to a spatial principle. By claiming a specifically American space that was off limits for European powers, the doctrine provides an example of a spatial order that could be used by other powers as well. Insisting on the original, purely defensive meaning of the Monroe Doctrine (in contrast to its later imperialist function), Schmitt presents the idea of an expanded political territory in which common interests are shared without necessarily guaranteeing equality among the political communities brought together under one roof. The unspoken assumption here appears to be that there is always a regional hegemon, providing the political and military power to defend the territory against outside aggression.

For Schmitt there can be no normatively secured peace agreement among the *Großräume*; only general readiness for war secures international peace. The repeated polemics against the victorious Allies in his diaries touches precisely on this point. For him, a war of aggression (*Angriffskrieg*) is a legitimate tool of international relations. Following this logic, it was therefore unfair and even illegal to punish the Germans for World War II. Accordingly, in his 1945 legal brief for the German industrialist Friedrich Frick, who expected to be put on trial, Schmitt presents an extensive argument why the average German citizen could not be held responsible for the war crimes of the NS regime.

This aspect of his larger argument, the problematic force of German nationalism, does not play a significant role in Schmitt's late work and has already disappeared behind the curtain of a European outlook in *The Nomos of the Earth* (1950). In Schmitt's assessment of the older European order, the *ius publicum Europaeum*, Germany is surprisingly absent. Instead, his focus has shifted to the other Western colonial powers and their (imperial) conception of a global order built on colonial expansion. He conceives of these powers as imperial *Großräume* and in this respect, there is a relatively smooth continuity of ideas from the 1941 *Großraum* monograph to *The Nomos of the Earth*.

The standard approach to *The Nomos* is to focus on Schmitt's interpretation of the *ius publicum Europaeum* as the central category of his reading of modern European history between 1500 and World War I. This book takes a different approach: By emphasizing the role of European colonialism in the development of the modern global order, it shifts the focus to Schmitt's understanding of the historical context for the anticolonial liberation movement that followed World War II. This shift underscores two moments. First, it points to the parallel between Schmitt's celebration of the older European order and the protest against this order by the liberation movements; second, it scrutinizes the precise link between the *jus publicum Europaeum* and the material history of European colonialism, bringing forward the social and economic consequences that Schmitt's legal approach keeps more or less in the background. Seen from the perspective of the colonial discourse, Schmitt's narrative appears in a very different light. First, its contemporary relevance around 1950 becomes much more obvious and possibly explains why the book did not stir up public opinion, since by that time Germany had long lost its former colonies. Second, its deeply conservative agenda—the political and cultural defense of the grand European colonial project—becomes more legible.

Perilous Futures addresses both aspects and in chapter 3 confronts the narrative of *The Nomos* with the historical critique of colonialism as it developed during the 1960s and 1970s, primarily in response to defenses of the colonial project rooted in its supposedly progressive aspects. The first generation of revisionist historians pointed to the tremendous human costs of imperialism, which disappear in Schmitt's narrative. But even in their critique, many of these historians still clung to the logic of colonialism as a necessary and inevitable process, a viewpoint that also impacted Schmitt's interpretation. I argue that only because of this second step—challenging the logic of the colonial project and the very premise of a fundamental European superiority beginning around 1500—can Schmitt's reading of modern European history as the bearer of the rightful legal order (one that was then crudely destroyed by modern international liberalism) be rescued and possibly even turned against the conservative agenda of its author. In *The Nomos*, a Eurocentric perspective is self-evident and not in need of proof, since Schmitt invokes Christian medieval history as the apparent but not always acknowledged background to his own narrative. Early forms of colonization, for instance those in South America, had the ideological support of the Catholic Church. For Schmitt, the theological as well as legal transformation from medieval to modern European history provides the underpinning of Europe's centrality for the modern global order. In light of more recent colonial history, however, this certitude is no longer a given, which in turn places Schmitt's interpretation under pressure and its partisan, Eurocentric position becomes apparent. I challenge Schmitt's analysis with the logic of the decolonization movement, in particular with Frantz Fanon's support of the Algerian uprising, which contrasts with Schmitt's account of General Salan's role as a defender of French colonialism in Algeria in *The Theory of the Partisan* (1963). As Walter D. Mignolo has pointed out, at stake is the fate of the postcolonial order itself.[3] Must we, as Schmitt assumes, conceive of it as a continuation of an imperialist, Eurocentric model? Or can we think of it as the return to a state that preceded European domination? For Schmitt, as he explains in a number of postwar essays, the new *nomos* must overcome the universalism of international liberalism precisely by going back to a structure that defined the modern European order: a balance of independent powers. Yet this position is, I argue, by all means compatible with imperialism and not in itself a guarantor of a peaceful community of democratic nation states. As it turns out, Schmitt is closer to theorists of an American imperium than his defenders think.

The following chapter, chapter 4, continues the discussion of the new world order, but now from the perspective of modern warfare, especially guerilla warfare, as a growing threat to political stability and peace. In some respects, *Theory of the Partisan* can be read as

a continuation of *The Nomos of the Earth,* which would emphasize the crisis of the world order after 1918, the end of controlled
interstate war, as it was known in Europe between 1648 and 1914,
and the rise of global civil war. The crucial question the chapter addresses is the nature of Schmitt's contribution to the subject of
small wars. Given that Schmitt was not a military theorist, he could
not advance significantly new tactical and strategic insights—nor
did he claim to. Instead, he was keenly interested in the link between military strategies and political structures, making use of the
existing international relations literature. Broadly speaking, Schmitt
sees the partisan as a crucial element in a new, highly volatile world
order that is determined by revolutionary struggles caused by colonial liberation movements and social revolutions on the basis of a
communist ideology. Yet his response to this transformation is more
ambivalent than is generally acknowledged.

This ambiguity calls for closer scrutiny. Schmitt's fairly extensive
treatment of Carl von Clausewitz's role in the Prussian War of Liberation in 1813 is a good indicator that he cannot be simply assigned
the role of the confirmed conservative who wants to preserve the
form of traditional interstate war. While he follows Clausewitz's
thoughts about popular uprising as a revolutionary movement out
of sync with the idea of the Prussian monarchy, Schmitt also appreciates the force and political purpose of revolution and is aware
that these ideas were later picked up by Marx and Engels, and then
further developed by Lenin and Mao. His interpretation of this
connection is not unsympathetic, although he remains highly critical
of the concept of a just war as an instrument of politics. His critique of the just war tradition (in which he includes modern revolutionary movements) and his appreciation of the Leninist or Maoist
partisan are hardly compatible, resulting in an intellectual tension.
On the one hand, his critical reading of warfare connected to the
decolonization movements in Indochina and North Africa aligns
him with the defenders of European colonialism at a time when
even conservatives like Charles de Gaulle were retreating from a
procolonial position. On the other hand, his analysis of Lenin's and
Mao's theory of the partisan, especially when connected to Mao's

actual practice in China, shows an understanding and appreciation of the revolutionary logic in which the enemy is always conceived of as absolute.

For Schmitt, therefore, the partisan remains an ambiguous figure whose political role can change with historical circumstances. Yet it is apparent that he does not easily fit into the new rules of regulated (*gehegt*) interstate warfare. The more Schmitt emphasizes the revolutionary nature of the partisan, the more difficult it becomes to see the partisan as part of a stable global order. The partisan epitomizes crisis, as Schmitt recognizes in his reflections on the concept of the enemy. This is the historical moment when common ground between adversaries is no longer possible. For this reason, Schmitt embraces a solution that transcends the military theory on which he depends. Ultimately more interested in the outcome of history than in military strategy and tactic, Schmitt includes political theology in the discourse.

In 1970, Schmitt returned once more to the question of political theology. Chapter 5 explores both the specific historical context of this return and the nature of his argument. This late essay, *Political Theology II*, has received relatively little attention in the anglophone world because of its peculiar structure and unfamiliar historical references, which create obstacles for the uninitiated reader. *Political Theology II* is a belated response to the argument of his old friend, the theologian Erik Peterson, who had denied the possibility of any political theology in 1935 (instead arguing in strictly theological terms and without ever mentioning the political context) in reaction to the concordat between the Catholic Church and Hitler's Germany, an agreement that Schmitt (as well as his friend, Hans Barion, to whom the monograph is dedicated) had supported. By the 1960s and 1970s, political theology had become an urgent question again, but this time from the Left. Progressive theologians like the Catholic Johann Baptist Metz and the Protestant Jürgen Moltmann called for a deeper involvement of the Christian faith in political and social issues, in keeping with radical social movements of the time. And it was now the Right (including Barion) that spoke out against the lure of political theology, aligning with Peterson's prewar position. Within this controversial discussion, Schmitt renewed his own position, underscoring the need for a political theology but without underwriting the project of the progressive theologians.

Unlike left-leaning theologians, Schmitt is not interested in the Church becoming more engaged in social issues. His concern is the grounding of political discourse in theological concepts, and he does this on a number of levels. In historical terms, he defends the Roman bishop Eusebius and his role as an ally of the Roman emperor Constantine against Peterson's critique because, for Schmitt, it affirms the crucial alliance between church and state. Theologically, he argues that the political has been from the very beginning a part of Christian dogma. The concept of the Trinity, Schmitt tells us, contains the moment of conflict between father and son. In his dialogue with Peterson, Schmitt attempts to rescue the possibility and legitimacy of political theology *tout court*. But hidden within his critique is the ultimate motive for this belated intervention, one that becomes more legible in his argument with Hans Blumenberg's polemic against the category of secularization that was fundamental to Schmitt's thought.

For Schmitt, the modern age (*Neuzeit*) is marked by a loss of theological substance and thereby remains indebted to medieval Christian thought. By contrast, Blumenberg's reading of the modern age emphasizes the positive aspect of human self-preservation (*Selbstbehauptung*) against the theological burden of the late medieval period. Schmitt is unwilling to concede this revisionist turn, which would frame the Enlightenment in much more positive terms. For him, the historical process between the birth of Jesus and his Second Coming stood under the sign of the apocalypse. The historical process is therefore marked by crises and catastrophes that may be slowed down but cannot be stopped. Under these conditions, political order is the best that humans can achieve. Schmitt's answer to the Left is that the human condition, given the immanent structure of the Trinity, cannot be improved.

Even if we are inclined to take Schmitt's political theology seriously, the reception of his theory faces a major hurdle, since it seems to limit its affirmative appropriation to those who share Schmitt's fundamental beliefs. Even within the larger orbit of Catholic thought, this would be no more than a small subset because Schmitt's interpretation of the New Testament and the dogma of the Trinity are marked by gnostic elements that the Church classifies as heretic.

The final chapter, chapter 6, takes up the late twentieth- and early twenty-first-century reception of Schmitt, specifically his incorporation into the anglophone world that had banned him and his teaching as problematic and dangerous. In this discourse, Schmitt's writings—and his late writings in particular—have seemingly achieved classic status, especially in the field of international relations, even as he is still seen as a somewhat controversial theorist in his home country. Remarkably, this international anglophone Schmitt has been assigned a degree of relevance and power that he did not have in Germany after 1945. Chapter 6 examines both Schmitt's transformation in the English-speaking world and the shifts that occur during the process of textual and ideological appropriation. Without a specific confluence of historical events—the end of the Cold War, the demise of the Soviet Union, and the subsequent rise of the United States as the sole remaining global superpower—it is unlikely that Schmitt's writings would have found the same urgent response. His critique of liberalism resonated with the international Left in its growing opposition to American neoliberalism and its policy of enforcing a globalized economy. Both the Left and the Right could therefore refer to Schmitt in their critique of globalization.

This partial, post-Cold War embrace of Schmitt's understanding of international relations was enhanced by the radical interruption of September 11, 2001, which deeply and permanently changed the self-understanding of the United States. Almost immediately, the study of Schmitt moved from critical analysis to a wider, though by no means total, appropriation and application. This turn also implied an emphatic and engaged rereading of Schmitt's work, as well as a selective use of his thought. With only slight exaggeration, this Anglo-American reception and discussion has created a distinct and novel version of Schmitt, one at a considerable remove from the historical Carl Schmitt. It is this latter figure that I try to recover and challenge in the pages that follow.

1

THE OUTLAW

Carl Schmitt's Postwar Notebooks and Small Essays

This chapter examines Schmitt's postwar years; in particular, his response to the experience as a prisoner in Berlin and Nuremberg, as well as the precarious situation after his release in 1947 when he returned to his hometown, Plettenberg, in rural West Germany, far removed from the intensive public life of the big city. The central question posed in this chapter is: What was the meaning and significance of 1945 for Schmitt? There can be no doubt that it was a sharp caesura. Not only did he lose his post at the University of Berlin and was never allowed to return, he found himself treated as a war criminal who nearly went on trial in Nuremberg. At the same time, Schmitt, when he looked at his intellectual development and his work, tended to downplay the significance of 1945. It appears that in his mind the end of the Third Reich and the following restoration of a liberal political regime in West Germany were not decisive turning points for him. While Schmitt encountered more problems and setbacks after 1945 than most Germans and bitterly complained about his fate, his understanding of his own intellectual commitments is not tied to 1945 as an index of fundamental change.

Nonetheless, the military defeat of the National Socialist (NS) regime in 1945 confronted Carl Schmitt with serious personal as well as theoretical questions: How did one judge the rise and fall of the Third Reich? What was the appropriate response to the destructive forces that the Hitler regime had unleashed and the enormous loss of life as a result of these forces? And how would Schmitt explain his own role as an active participant of the NS regime? These were not only moral and historical but also legal questions. It characterizes Schmitt that he publicly responded to them primarily in legal terms. For him the military defeat and the decision of the victorious Allies to hold the German people and their leaders accountable for the war raised fundamental legal questions about the conduct of war, especially the responsibility of the state and its leaders vis-à-vis the international community. In other words, Schmitt placed the war in the broader context of international law (*Völkerrecht*) and sought to determine whether the German Reich, by declaring war on Poland and the Western powers as well as Russia, had violated international law. This assessment, however, had a very personal aspect as well. Schmitt had played an important role in the Third Reich, especially in the years between 1933 and 1936, in shaping the organization of the NS legal system. Should he be held accountable for these actions? Schmitt argued that as an ordinary German citizen he was not responsible for Hitler's war.

The occasion for Schmitt's sustained analysis of this problem was the request of the industrialist Friedrich Frick for a legal opinion because he expected to be put on trial for war crimes.[1] Schmitt's extensive and thorough brief covers the ground, as one would expect, in broad terms, starting with a discussion of the question of Germany's responsibility (*Kriegsschuldfrage*) for World War I, and subsequently providing an overview of the changes that took place in international law during the interwar years. Schmitt focuses his attention on the case of a war of aggression (*Angriffskrieg*), a war started by a nation-state that had not been attacked or threatened by another nation-state. In the treaty of Versailles, the German

Reich was declared culpable and therefore held accountable for the damages that its military actions had caused. Schmitt argues that this judgment was not in line with older international law, in which a sovereign nation-state had the right to declare war on another state without criminalizing itself. Further, Schmitt points out that the United States did not follow the line of argument presented by the entente and set up its own separate peace treaty with Germany that did not mention German culpability.

In Schmitt's mind, World War I was not only the turning point in the international evaluation of *Angriffskrieg* but also the model for his assessment of the Third Reich. By focusing on the problem of its military aggression, Schmitt underscores the continuity from Imperial Germany to the Third Reich, thereby downplaying the fundamental political and moral differences between the two regimes. The extraordinary excesses of Hitler's totalitarian regime become less apparent behind a veil of Schmitt's legal arguments. In the brief, the question of total war, which Schmitt does take up in other contexts, especially the war of annihilation (*Vernichtungskrieg*) against the Soviet Union and the extermination of the Jews, which of course was intricately linked to the German conduct of war in the East, are no longer part of the narrative. However, elsewhere in the brief Schmitt points to the peculiar character of the NS regime as different from either the monarchy or the liberal democracy of Weimar. The NS regime was characterized by the preponderance of the National Socialist Party, which had penetrated both the state and the social community. As a consequence, at least according to Schmitt, the responsibility for the war and its conduct is limited to Hitler and a narrow circle around him because they participated in the decision-making process. "Turning to the question of the search for the perpetrator and the circle of perpetrators of the international crime defined as 'war,' it follows that only those can be considered as perpetrators who were actual participants in terms of being part of the political decision making process" (*IVA* 65). Focusing his attention on the specific organizational nature of Hitler's regime as a system of competing in-groups, Schmitt comes to the conclusion that only those who had immediate access to Hitler should be considered as perpetrators. It is not enough to be part of the state hierarchy, because the structure of Hitler's regime made it difficult, if not impossible, to think of it as state-centered in the traditional sense, thereby also moving power and responsibility from the state to the NS Party.

Given the special purpose of the legal brief, the crucial question then is the situation of individual German citizens (among them Carl Schmitt). Under what circumstances can they become responsible and potentially culpable for Hitler's war? Schmitt presents two arguments. First, he repeats the older argument that there was no clear distinction between wars of aggression and other forms of war in the older international law by pointing out that even in 1939 the neutral powers did not use that distinction in their declarations of neutrality. Second, he claims that the individual citizen could not be expected to resist his or her government in the case of war. In fact, Schmitt suggests that this citizen can leave the judgment on whether a war is just or unjust to his or her government. "This practice was in accordance with the secular tradition, which dominated the practice of all nations of the European continent for centuries, and could be replaced only by new institutions" (*IVA* 74).

It is worth noting that Schmitt invokes the authority of Luther and Kant to support this point. According to Schmitt, the modern state does not grant the right to resist the state (*Widerstandsrecht*) that the medieval order explicitly recognized. The citizen who refuses to follow orders or resists orders is therefore logically treated as a traitor to his or her country. The point of this argument is obvious: The average (German) citizen was not in a position to resist the state in his or her assessment of the justification of a war. While this holds true even in democracies, we are told, it is especially pertinent in the case of Nazi Germany. For Schmitt this is not a question of moral judgment and conscience but an issue of protection and obedience. If the government cannot protect its citizens from reprisals, the citizens cannot be expected to resist orders that are unlawful.

Schmitt's defense of Frick as a German citizen draws on a number of different lines of arguments and legal traditions. He rejects in strong terms the criminalization of modern interstate war as hostile to the tradition of the *ius publicum Europaeum*. In addition, he draws on the laws regulating the relationship between citizen and state. Finally, he argues that because of the special nature of the Hitler regime the individual citizen was in a particularly weak position and had good reason therefore to be cautious in his or her dealings with the government. All these arguments could of course also be applied to the case of Carl Schmitt and his role during the NS regime. By building a defense for Frick, therefore, at least implicitly, he builds a defense for himself. However, the critical question is this: Was Schmitt no more than an ordinary German citizen without influence and power, as the defense maintained? In his notebooks, his *Glossarium,* Schmitt makes a similar claim, writing passionately against those who accused him.

Schmitt's Notebooks

In Schmitt scholarship, *Glossarium* has been harvested mostly for supporting evidence of Schmitt's opinions and resentment. But rarely have these diaries been studied as a coherent text, a text characterized by severe tensions and contradictions. The notes, written between 1947 and 1951, articulate an inner turmoil that shocked his readers when the diaries were first published in 1991. They show a side of Schmitt that his visitors in Plettenberg did not see. While the visitors received the impression that their genial host enjoyed the freedom of his forced retirement from public affairs, the notes document Schmitt's deep anger and resentment as well as his continued commitment to his well-known political positions. *Glossarium* offers an unflattering but critical portrait of Carl Schmitt in transition, a picture that we have to keep in mind when reading his late work.

The biographical facts leading up to the diaries are well known.[2] At the end of the war, Schmitt found himself in Berlin in a house in Grunewald after losing many of his possessions in an air raid that destroyed the apartment building in which he lived. Initially, he was not seriously bothered by the military occupation, although he was not called back to teach at the University of Berlin. Schmitt's problems began in September of 1945 when he was arrested by the Americans, probably at the request of Karl Löwenstein, a refugee and lawyer, who had followed Schmitt's career under the Nazis. It was Löwenstein who had written the first memo for the American forces concerning Schmitt's participation in the crimes of the NS regime. Schmitt was kept in a camp for civilians for more than a year and was exposed to repeated interrogations. The purpose was to clarify Schmitt's active participation in Nazi politics, especially in the field of Nazi law. In the end the interrogators were unable to prove Schmitt's direct involvement in Nazi policies as the advisor of Hermann Göring and Hans Frank. As a result, in October of 1946 Schmitt was released from the camp.

Yet the freedom did not last. Schmitt was arrested again in March of 1947, this time in the larger context of the Nuremberg trials, where the core of the Nazi elite faced accusations of war crimes and crimes against humanity. Schmitt's role as an important and highly visible legal advisor to Göring and Frank (both of them on trial) exposed him to the scrutiny of Robert Kempner, the deputy prosecutor, who interrogated him four times. In the first interrogation Schmitt was asked to explain his concept of *Großraum* (expanded territory) and its possible impact on Hitler's political and military strategy for Germany's expansion during World War II. In the second meeting, Kempner demanded to know whether Schmitt had supported the preparation of the war as an *Angriffskieg* (a war of aggression). While these meetings clearly focused on Carl Schmitt as a potential defendant, the third and the fourth meetings shifted the direction of the interrogation. Now Kempner wanted to find out whether certain ministers and state secretaries were, in Schmitt's opinion, accountable for the criminal nature of Hitler's policies. In this context Schmitt moved from potential defendant to potential witness. At this point, the question of the nature of World War II seen from the German point of view, and the character of a new imperial German strategy under Hitler, still occupied Schmitt in his diaries. Schmitt vehemently resisted the link between *Angriffskrieg* and war crimes that Kempner and his colleagues imputed in the trial. Schmitt was set free on May 13, 1947, without having been charged, and he returned to Plettenberg.

Although free, Schmitt found himself in a precarious position. He had been removed from his teaching post and therefore had no income. Moreover, he was not allowed to publish and was excluded from public discourse. Thus Schmitt was a man without a public voice in a radically transformed cultural and political environment that he experienced as hostile. While the immediate impact of the Allies on the civilian population was already decreasing in 1947, it was obvious that they controlled all major political decisions and carefully watched the first steps of the German people toward building new political and social institutions. By 1947 the tensions between liberal solutions in the West and Communist solutions in the Russian zone were visible. The unification of the Western zones in January of 1947 and the failure of the governors of the individual German states to agree on a common nation state in June 1947 were clear indicators of a growing ideological and political divide, which would lead to the foundation of two separate states in 1949.

With the restoration of the public media (newspapers, journals, radio) and the political parties, the future of Germany, her political structure, and her cultural revival became the central issue.[3] Yet it is important to note that in 1947, this future was still uncertain. Everything seemed to be in flux. The proposals and party programs ranged from liberalism, which emphasized individual freedom and stressed the dangers of collectivism, centralization, and authoritarianism, to democratic socialism on the left. The Social Democrats, under the leadership of Kurt Schumacher and Carlo Schmidt, favored socialist solutions, including the nationalization of basic industries. But they were highly critical of the Soviet model as a totalitarian solution. Nonetheless, their plans were still based on Marxist theory, assuming the centrality of the working class for the future of Germany. In the liberal camp, Wilhelm Röpke, for example, praised the synthesis of humanism and (restrained) capitalism in *Die deutsche Frage* (1945) and *Civitas humana* (1946).[4] He and theorists such as Walter Eucken and Alexander Rüstow pleaded for a third path that would avoid the pitfalls of monopoly capitalism in the West and state socialism in the East. This option could align itself with a revival of German Classicism and Goethe in particular, as it was propagated by the journal *Deutsche Beiträge*, which was supported by moderate conservatives like Ernst Robert Curtius, Rudolf Alexander Schröder, and Hans Carossa. Essential to this position was, of course, the emphatic distance from and critique of fascism and the Third Reich.

Given the severity of the German defeat and the increasing awareness of the crimes of the Nazi regime, any public defense of the Third Reich was out of the question. But there were different ways of accommodating those like Carl Schmitt who had collaborated. They could be absorbed into a broader, acceptable ideological framework on the right spectrum or they could be selectively integrated into existing programs and positions. For Schmitt, conservative and nationalist groups were of course of particular interest. But these intellectual communities had reasons to be cautious because of the still existing general oversight by the allied military administrations. On the whole, the German Far Right remained in hiding. In this respect the churches enjoyed a greater degree of freedom, since they could claim, with limited justification, to have resisted Hitler.

Indeed, in these years much of the energy to overcome the spiritual vacuum following the ideological defeat of fascism came from the Catholic and Protestant Church, although not necessarily from the administrative center of these institutions. One could build on the public record of known opponents, some of whom had given their lives for their Christian faith. From a theological perspective—and this became important for Schmitt—National Socialism was not primarily the enemy of the Weimar Republic but the last and final stage of a long process of secularization, which had to be reversed. On the Protestant side, Reinhold Schneider in his 1946 study *Die Heimkehr* (*Homecoming*) argued that it was the German Enlightenment (Lessing, Kant) and German idealism that were responsible for the rise of National Socialism and the following catastrophe. Obviously, such criticism leads to the demand that only a return to the foundations of the Christian faith can stabilize Germany and offer a spiritually secure future. Within the Catholic Church, this intellectual work was frequently organized around journals, among them *Neues Abendland* (*A New West*, founded in March of 1946) and *Die neue Ordnung* (*A New Order*, founded in October of 1946). As it turns out, in these journals there was also room for authors with a problematic past like Schmitt.

In 1947, when Schmitt settled in Plettenberg, it was by no means clear which of the above-mentioned positions would dominate the still tentative reorganization of West Germany. But it was fairly predictable how Carl Schmitt would evaluate these competing intellectual tendencies. He felt closest to the Catholic groups and strongly articulated his opposition to liberal theories and programs, without showing much interest in socialist proposals.

The publication of Carl Schmitt's notebooks, *Glossarium,* in 1991 caused a scandal in the German public sphere.[5] Even friends and admirers asked in private, and sometimes even in public, whether the publication of Schmitt's diaries from the years 1947 to 1951 improved the still somewhat controversial reputation of the author. Typical is the response of Nicolaus Sombart, who had been close to Carl Schmitt in his early years: "After a careful review one has to ask the question if the editors of this bundle of notes did their idol a bad service. These notes were written in his worst time when his life had reached the lowest point. Would it not have been better to leave them in the archives? In the way they have entered the public sphere they are an annoyance that causes embarrassment to his friends and confirms the worst prejudices of his enemies."[6]

Whether the publication of Schmitt's most intimate feelings and personal assessments negatively affected the interest in Schmitt's theory during the 1990s is a different question, for by that time it had already separated itself from the persona of the author. His theoretical work had developed its own complex and complicated history. The shocked reaction to the diaries was in part due to their tone, the brutal frankness of Schmitt's judgment of his friends and his enemies, the intensity of his hatred as well as the contempt for his political environment (especially the new political elite), and the unmistakable signs of self-pity combined with severe censure of his opponents. The portrait of the author emanating from these notes had a negative force that also disturbed Schmitt's friends. Although the events and personal relations mentioned in the diaries predated publication by more than forty years, the notes remained a posthumous provocation that caused a vehement reaction within the German public, although the discussion of Schmitt's theoretical work had already transcended the phase of heated controversies. The publication of the diaries, however, reminded the readers of the difficult case of an eminently gifted German political theorist who had collaborated with the NS regime. In these notes the years after the defeat of the Third Reich and the anxieties of a tentative new beginning had left their permanent imprint. It was obvious that the author not only resisted the new liberal regime but also despised it.

Public reaction to the book was swift and harsh. The initial readings of *Glossarium* mostly confirmed what Schmitt's critics had expected. They had always seen him as a dangerous mind that subverted the young Federal Republic. A good example is, again, the opinion of Nicolaus Sombart: "Notwithstanding his erudition and his presentation of an incredible display of knowledge, in these notes Carl Schmitt remains the prisoner of systematic delusion."[7] This statement offers a succinct summary of the substantial political changes that had occurred between the late 1940s and the early 1990s. For Sombart, the *Glossarium* was primarily a document of Germany's collective mental history, of its errors and later corrections. Richard Faber's 1994 essay comes to a similar conclusion. For him Schmitt remained first and foremost a refractory collaborator with German fascism who continued to defend his support of National Socialism even after the war and therefore attacked those who opposed his position: "In particular, Schmitt dislikes those refugees who returned to Germany, especially the Jewish refugees, among them his teacher Erich Kaufmann whom he had disavowed during the Nazi years. Schmitt's personal lack of shame is without limits. His attacks on former friends who, unlike Schmitt, did oppose National Socialism . . . document this lack."[8] Faber mentions George Bernanos, Waldemar Gurian, Theodor Haecker, Jacques Maritain, and Ernst Niekisch. He goes on to describe Schmitt's position as fascist, right-wing Catholicism, which invokes the Roman Empire and the Roman Catholic Church as its defining historical and institutional moments.

While it would be possible to disregard Faber's completely negative evaluation of Carl Schmitt as the opinion of a political adversary, this would be much more difficult in the case of the Strauss scholar Heinrich Meier, whose long review in the weekly *Der Spiegel* seeks to define Carl Schmitt as a historical phenomenon. But even Meier, a confirmed conservative, cannot gloss over the scandalous aspects of Schmitt's diaries. *Glossarium,* according to Meier "gives us, so to speak, the whole Schmitt, it shows his sparkling brilliance as well as his shocking brutality."[9] Later, Meier points to Schmitt's "abysmal self-righteousness" with respect to his self-assessment. This leads him to the question: "Are Schmitt's anti-Semitic tirades less pernicious because their energy is grounded in a fundamentalist anti-Judaism?"[10] Without a doubt, for Meier, Carl Schmitt remains a deeply problematic figure and he suggests that a reexamination would be productive only if all aspects of his persona and his work were taken into consideration.

In his review in the daily *Süddeutsche Zeitung,* Jürgen Busche comes to a similar conclusion. He does not mean to dismiss Schmitt without further consideration. The title of the review, "Carl Schmitt—the Assistant" (*der Gehilfe*), clearly a reference to Schmitt's collaboration with the Third Reich, is far less aggressive than Faber's essay. Busche advises a cautious approach to Schmitt, for "The *Glossarium* . . . is a violent totality with subtle detail. It is a horrible and an inspiring book."[11] Although the reviewer does not see himself in the camp of Schmitt's confirmed opponents, he feels that he cannot remain silent about the shocking aspects of the diaries. For him it is less the bitter attacks on friends and enemies than Schmitt's fundamental inability to examine his relationship to power that is disturbing. "He [Schmitt] remained throughout his life in a subaltern position toward power. He was the assistant (*Gehilfe*). More he could not be. And he insisted on the fundamental neutrality of his talents."[12] When Busche highlights Schmitt's claim to be no more than the "*Gehilfe*," the shocking and scandalous moments of Schmitt's career become more accessible. Nonetheless, Busche refuses to accept Schmitt's claim to have acted in good faith and describes him as a "deeply troubled mind."[13]

Yet even in a case where the reviewer is clearly trying to present Schmitt's diaries in a positive light, moments of concern and resistance can be observed. Henning Ritter, writing for the conservative daily *Frankfurter Allgemeine Zeitung,* says, "Anyone who reads through these notes with the expectation to find an explanation how it [the author means the relationship between the intellectual and the center of power in the Third Reich, *puh*] happened will be disappointed,"[14] because Schmitt did not change his position even after the end of the war. While Ritter—the son of the philosopher Joachim Ritter, who had been in close contact with Schmitt after the war—is fundamentally sympathetic, he refuses to condone the bitter attacks against Thomas Mann, Karl Jaspers, and the eminent jurist Gustav Radbruch, and he is put off by Schmitt's vicious remarks about his old friend Ernst Jünger. At the end of the review Ritter seems to be more distant from Schmitt than at the beginning. He calls the notes the expression of an existential panic.

Style

The scandalous effect of the diaries is closely related to Schmitt's style, which contrasts starkly with the diaries of his friend Jünger but also with the diaries of Thomas Mann.[15] Schmitt's notes are clearly not the rough draft of a literary diary that is composed with the intent of later publication, nor are we confronted with mundane notes that have the function of keeping a record of the daily experience, as is the case in the diaries of Thomas Mann. Schmitt's style is provocative in that it does not accommodate the feelings of readers. Readers are confronted with a monologue, sometimes an internal dialogue to which they are not invited. Frequently the tone of the notes is aggressive, especially when the author responds to accusations that he considers unjustified. The same is true for Schmitt's assessments of individuals and groups. Schmitt means to belittle and discriminate the opponent.[16] Although Schmitt assigns to himself the art of politeness, this self-characteristic does not apply to his diaries. In fact, their tone is marked by extreme openness. In his discussion of the jurist Karl Schulte he uses the term "poisonous gnat" (*Giftmücke*; G 166, June 17, 1948). When Schmitt expects to find enemies, his language uses discriminatory terms. These elements influenced the early reception of the *Glossarium*. Occasionally the aggressive tone preoccupied the early readers and drew their attention away from other moments of self-articulation and self-fashioning.

Still, Schmitt has more than one tone. When the author deals with his own situation there is a noticeable change. These existential remarks share with other parts a pointed and aggressive language, but their aim is different. Their purpose is self-preservation in a concrete historical and biographical situation that the writer experiences as hostile. In these instances a broader topic is taken up and developed, but then, frequently unexpectedly, the argument becomes personal and focuses on Schmitt's own life. What begins, for example, as a discussion of the Catholic thinker and journalist Theodor Haecker leads to the point where the writing subject sees himself within this Catholic environment and arrives at the following assessment: "This is the secret key word of my entire existence as an intellectual and public writer, namely the struggle for an authentic Catholic radicalization" (*Verschärfung*; G 165, April 16, 1948). What Schmitt seems to have in mind is the promotion of a decidedly Catholic position in the public sphere, combined with an insistence on the importance of a political theology. Whether this formulation actually defines Schmitt's agenda does not matter in this context. What does matter is the formal aspect, the way the theoretical discussion turns into an existential concern. By applying the term "Catholic radicalization" to himself and in fact regarding it as the decisive "secret key word," he arrives at a concise self-definition. In this definition, theory and subjectivity completely merge.

As a rule, Schmitt does not like to be defined or judged, but in the case of an observation that Ernst Jünger offers in *Strahlungen*, he makes an exception, because Jünger praises Schmitt's special capacity to come up with concise definitions (G 168, June 22, 1948). This observation becomes the occasion for Schmitt to think about the difference between his public and his private life; that is, between a well-ordered public career and a rather messy private life, a contrast that another observer had mentioned to Schmitt as well. These reflections then become the first step in a serious confrontation with his identity. Here Schmitt distinguishes between essential and superficial aspects of his life. "Still deeper [in the self, *puh*] one would find a desert from where a scream has reached the ears of other humans, a scream that is comparable in world literature only to the voice of Annette [von Droste-Hülshoff] in her *Geistliches Jahr* [*Spiritual Year*]" (G 168, June 22, 1948). What is remarkable in this self-assessment is the reference to a literary work. Again Schmitt defines himself by referring to an object outside—a poet with whom he identifies. In this instance the determining rhetorical figure is the analogy instead of logical subordination as in the case of a theoretical discourse.

Whereas Schmitt's attempts to reflect on his present situation and the core of his subjectivity are cautious and frequently tentative, his assessment of individuals and groups tend to be firm and unambiguous. Especially when he considers them as enemies, he does not mince words in his diary. His remarks about Jews, for example, are characterized by a tone that combines aggression with self-righteousness: "The Jews are an elite in close proximity to the Christian elite, a more or less accurate replacement (*Platzhalter*) when the Christian elites get lost in legalism. Because the Jews have a better understanding of the logic, tactic, and practice of an empty legalism than the Christian people, which continues to believe, against the law, in love and charity" (G 154, May 24, 1948). The reference to the contrast between law and love set up in the New Testament (Rom. 7:7) is hard to overlook. It justifies the anti-Semitic attack. Even more outspoken is the following frank and emphatic definition of the Jews as the enemy par excellence: "The Jews always remain Jews. While communists can improve and change. . . . Especially the assimilated Jew is the true enemy. There is no point in proving that the paroles of the wise men of Zion are false" (G 18, September 26, 1947). Schmitt's language is absolute; the content of the statement is supported by its emphatic articulation and is not in need of proof. For this reason historical arguments such as the proof that the documents attributed to the wise men of Zion are false become superfluous.

Still, in terms of their style, the notes cannot be reduced to confrontational language. The diarist is by all means capable of variations and modifications. In fact, he makes regular use of different tones. Changing the rhetoric is part of the pattern. One approach consists of moving to another language. This occurs not only when he quotes in another language (which happens rather frequently) but also when he speaks in his own voice. Thus, in addition to French passages, we find passages in English and Latin, not to mention the occasional Greek words. Although Schmitt is in some respects an ardent German nationalist, he is not a purist who remains fixated on the exclusive use of German words and sentences. In particular, he feels close to Latin because of his Catholic background as well as his expertise in older international law. Thus he likes to quote from the Latin edition of Hobbes's works or the writings of Francisco de Vitoria. In some instances he continues to use the foreign language when he continues the discourse. In these instances the diarist identifies with the author he quoted. Schmitt takes on the voice of Hobbes or de Vitoria. As some of the early readers of the diaries have noted, these variations are part of a complex form of self-fashioning.

Formal Structure

Although Carl Schmitt more than once articulates serious reservations with regard to the form of the diary (G 96 and 130), he began a new diary in August of 1947 and continued writing until August of 1951. From the lower density of his notes in 1951, it becomes apparent that the form of the diary has lost its crucial importance for the author. At this time, there were other outlets for his thoughts and opinions. It seems that it was primarily the social and intellectual isolation after his release from prison in Nuremberg that motivated him to keep a diary. The notes became the locus where Schmitt would address not only his experiences but also his assessment and criticism of the outside world. Therefore the structure of the diaries is largely determined by a defensive posture. One can think of these notes as a secret court where Carl Schmitt is the defendant, the defense lawyer, and the judge at the same time. Clearly, the public is not admitted to the proceedings. Even friends are suspected of betrayal and are mentioned and quoted only when they offer testimony to the effect that their author is not guilty of the crimes of which he is accused.

But who is the subject of the diaries? This question can be answered only when we distinguish between the subject as a diarist and the observed and interrogated subject; that is, the subject whose experiences are noted and commented on, the subject whose thoughts and ideas become the object of analysis, and the subject whose social and political acts and interventions are under investigation. Schmitt is very clear about the role of the diarist. In his critique of Ernst Jünger's *Strahlungen,* the war diaries that were published in 1949, he rejects the format of the literary diary that is written with an eye to publication. More specifically, he accuses Jünger of including too much private material. "There is too much talk of private things, too much Burgundy wine, too many orchids, too many epicurean experiences and also too many assessments of the present situation" (*G* 113, April 18, 1948). The Schmittian diarist denounces the moment of self-reflection in the context of everyday life and the careful, differentiated observation of the environment. This is not just a matter of defining the diary as a genre—which is clearly the case—but also of questioning the character of the writing subject (the diarist). How does the writing subject define itself? Who is the "I" responsible for the many chronologically organized entries? Schmitt's critique of Jünger assumes a private subject, which is constituted through sensual observations of the environment as well as a mode of sustained self-reflection. Schmitt questions the value of this approach because he questions the legitimacy of this form of subject formation. For Schmitt the diarist is not expected to focus on individual moments of his or her life or reflect on special moments of this life. Possibly we can go even further and say that the diarist should not be concerned with the unfolding of an individual life, although in the case of the *Glossarium* Schmitt's strong claim to defend certain problematic parts of his individual life are difficult to overlook. Yet this aspect does not reflect the intent of the author and remains possibly outside his own self-observation. Instead, Schmitt understands his own subjectivity as a theoretical or philosophical entity, as connected with the larger ideological issues that engage the fundamental questions of the present time. This happens in different forms and on different levels where the writing subject articulates himself by using rational arguments or aggressive polemic and other forms of persuasion.

At the same time, Schmitt's critique of Jünger's diaries makes apparent what the writing subject keeps at a distance: the openness for sensuous impressions and for stylistic complexity and refinement, which underscore the aesthetic character of Jünger's writings. In other words, for Schmitt, the aesthetic, both in its immediate sensual and in its poetic form, remains outside the scope of a good diary. For this reason Schmitt's notes have a more casual but also a more abstract character. Nonetheless, even the diarist Schmitt is not without a biographical and historical context that impacts his writing. The notes respond to a very specific existential situation after his release from prison in 1947. He is free but not allowed to teach, to publish, and to speak in public. Moreover, his financial situation is precarious, since he does not receive a pension. The diary deals with this situation indirectly, without concrete references to Schmitt's daily life. Schmitt's social and economic condition, for instance, is rarely addressed. The diarist does not elaborate on his role as husband and father, although these relationships were important to him, as we know from his letters.[17] Schmitt's house in the small town of Plettenberg is not described. Neither his study nor his library is treated as spaces that matter to him. The same applies to visits and visitors. We know from his letters how important visitors were for Schmitt because he had been banned from the public sphere.[18] The diary occasionally mentions visitors but without going into details. The same is true for travel experiences; the sensual side of people and spaces does not matter. The diarist would never sketch the atmosphere of a town he visited.

Still, this abstractness must not be confused with objectivity. The diary is focused on the subjectivity of Carl Schmitt and seeks to articulate the situation of an individual who is struggling to cope with his social isolation and a significant loss of social as well as professional status, resulting in intellectual and emotional upheaval. The entries definitely lack the aesthetic polish that conveys distance from the self. Would one conclude therefore that the diary is essentially a conversation of the writing subject with himself, a dialogue that leaves no place for a second person? The following passage suggests that this may well be the case: "Nobody can catch up with me because I am moving at high speed, but I am not fleeing from my enemies. How should they be able to catch up with me?" (*G* 190, August 15, 1948). It is worth noting that Schmitt's attempt to describe his difficult private situation refers to his central political concept friend/enemy. Hence not surprisingly the next sentence mentions the "essence of enmity," thereby abstracting from the concrete situation of the diarist. The writing subject tries to find a roof under which he can gain security and the possibility to assert himself.

The efforts to define his subjectivity in religious terms in particular lead to formulations that project a broad frame. Schmitt makes use of the term "Catholic radicalization," which he borrowed from the poet and journalist Konrad Weiß to define his own locus in the world of religion (*G* 165, June 16, 1948).[19] By defining himself as emphatically Catholic, the diarist characterizes himself not only as Christian but as a person finding peace specifically under the umbrella of the Catholic Church. In more than one passage the close link to the institution of the Church plays a significant role. The broader institutional context provides enclosure and security for the subject, which means that even in the case of a dialogue with himself, the diarist is never alone. Instead, the writing subject conceives of an institutional space in which the conversation takes place. The conversation makes use of a number of separate but linked discourses, among them the religious (Catholic), the legal, the political, and the philosophical. Sometimes the diary engages with scholarly works or literary texts, respectively with writers and thinkers in general. Sometimes the diarist engages in a dialogue with a specific person (who can be addressed). In other instances the diary is focused on the interpretation of a quotation from an important legal or religious text.

More than one critic has noticed and remarked on the extraordinary erudition of the diarist. But the mere mention of the multiple cross-references and allusions to uncommon authors and works fails to explain their function; namely, the combative moment. The writing subject finds himself in combat most of the time. For this reason his enemies are more important than his friends (although they are occasionally mentioned). For example, the diarist finds words of praise for the critic Gerhard Nebel, who was a frequent visitor in his house, while Ernst Jünger, with whom Schmitt had been a close friend and ideological ally since the early 1930s, is seen as a hostile presence and receives bad marks. Among the enemies we find the philosophers Karl Jaspers and, occasionally, Martin Heidegger, but also the jurist Robert Kempner, a leading prosecutor at the Nuremberg trials, who had interrogated Schmitt,[20] and Thomas Mann whose prominent role in postwar Germany irritated Schmitt. While the number of enemies in the *Glossarium* is large, the number of trusted friends is very small and not stable. Schmitt has a tendency to see himself as the victim of persecution, a constellation that is then thoroughly discussed in the diary.

The notion of persecution turns out to be a suitable guide for connecting the different aspects of the experiencing and suffering subjects. This idea relates the private and the public spheres, the personal experience and the public role in the world of scholarship and politics. In Schmitt's conception, the public side extends to the nation and finally to the fate of humanity. Carl Schmitt sees himself as a victim in his role as a German citizen, as a jurist, a political theorist, and, last but not least, a Christian, specifically a member of the Roman Catholic Church. For the diarist this persecution is fundamentally unfair and unjustified because it is directed against the member of an innocent collective, a collective that the diarist is called on to defend.

This sense of victimization and irritation was particularly strong in the fall of 1947 because the wounds caused by the repeated interrogation in Nuremberg were still open. It is not accidental that in this period the question of suicide comes into the foreground more than once. Both the life of the individual and the existence of the political collective appear as façades behind which a darker reality can be found; namely, the threat of death. In this context the diarist invokes Kierkegaard and his impact on the history of the European mind. But then the discussion of Kierkegaard's influence is brought to bear on personal circumstances, as the following entry shows:

> Life-time does not create the same disturbance as life-space. Why? Life-time already contains death. . . . I do not see more than the will to

survive. This then is superman: the man with the will to survive, more is not left. Whom does he survive? The competitors of the threat to life? Those who are also threatened or those who threaten others? Possibly both sides, possibly only those who are also threatened. What do they survive? The threat to their lives. That is all they want to survive." (G 18, September 27, 1947)

Yet even in this radical statement the experiencing subject retreats behind the collective of those who are threatened; that is, the collective of the defeated Germans, of the accused jurists, and of the endangered Christians. In the same vein the entry of October 20, 1947 invokes the "we" when the diarist discusses the acceleration of life experience: "Today we do not live any longer in terms of days or hours but in terms of small parts of seconds and splinters of moments" (G 34). What is not explicitly mentioned here is the fact that the altered experience of time changes the common experience of the collective as well as the continuity of institutions. For the will to survive—that is, to survive at any price—is in need of an institutional frame, as Schmitt notes, but the organization and structure of this new order are not in the hands of the defeated Germans, who are still controlled by the former enemy. The diary returns to this point again and again. The experience of collective defeat is regarded as defining also for the fate of the individual.[21]

Whenever the diarist reflects on the fate of the collective he paints a very dark picture of the present. "The poor Germans, today they are the Ophelios of the Leviathan. . . . As Germans we are pushed 'beyond the line' into a perfect otherworld, thrown out of the world, pushed into the state of an outlaw . . . the disinherited of the Leviathan" (G 29, October 9, 1947). Noteworthy is the reference to the world of theory and scholarship, in this case to Hobbes's *Leviathan*. In other words, a theoretical discourse serves as a means to articulate the situation of the threatened self. While the basic pattern remains in place, the specific frame of interpretation can change. In his entry of October 7, 1947 the diarist explicitly invokes a Christian horizon: "I have to confess a sin. Toward the end of August 1946 in my morning desperation in the camp when the first rays of the sun touched my plank bed, I have addressed the sun and said to it in a loud voice: 'You swindler'" (G 27). This rather obscure passage becomes more legible only later when the diarist explains his use of irony as a means to assert himself in the interrogations. Yet how seriously can the reader take a confession that does not make sense without a reference to Kierkegaard's concept of irony? It is apparent that the confessing subject, supported by an extensive library, is simultaneously pursuing a personal, scholarly, and literary discourse.

When the diarist speaks as a jurist the close connection with books and authors is to be expected, since this role includes the interpretation of the literature of this discipline. The jurist Schmitt presents himself as a member of a profession in which he developed and argued for specific legal positions. In this context it was his prominent role as one of the leading constitutional jurists of the Third Reich that got him into trouble after 1945. Again, he sees himself as the victim of persecution (G 17). Schmitt believes that he is misunderstood and therefore attacked from two sides: on the one hand by the positivists who are unable to understand and appreciate his political theory (political theology), and on the other hand by nonjurists who misunderstand his legal terminology and are inclined to misinterpret the metaphorical nature of his language.

Yet another entry shows that the stakes are higher. The diarist has to deal with more than misunderstandings. Looking at his own fate, the subject compares himself with Plato and concludes that the jurist Carl Schmitt, when moving from legal theory to the political arena in 1933, did better than the Greek philosopher in Syracuse (G 18, September 26, 1947). The entry of October 3, 1947, is equally defiant. Here the diarist chooses polemic: "How is it possible that all these excited detractors like Radbruch and Schwinge do not see that their indignation over me is identical with Hitler's rage against degenerate art" (G 24). By comparing Schmitt's critics, both of them leading constitutional jurists, to Hitler and his unjustified rage against modern art, Schmitt implies that their criticism is not only misplaced but positively mean and stupid. In addition, the diarist proves his own superiority over his enemies.

How much the German and the constitutional questions are linked in Schmitt's mind becomes apparent when the diarist discusses the concept of "just war." He holds this concept responsible for the extreme character of World War II. The polemic against the idea of a just war is also a defense of German military operations between 1939 and 1945. Here it is the expert of international law who stubbornly defends the German collective and complains bitterly not to be acknowledged by the Allies or the refugees who returned to Germany after 1945. The diarist exclaims: "(Suffocate under the deception of the ideology of cosmopolitan war. Is there no human ear to hear my voice?) Poor *justicier,* that is what you are" (G 29, October 8, 1947). The diary allows the writer to rearrange the factual relationships in such a way that the experiencing and suffering self can live with the new situation, even when it has to admit to itself that it is entirely powerless.

The deep frustration over the loss of power becomes noticeable even though it is not openly articulated. In this situation the diarist withdraws to a core space that he considers unassailable, the theological. Just as Schmitt provided his political theory in the 1920s with a theological base, in *Glossarium* the diarist presents himself as a Christian and member of the Roman Catholic Church. Although the diarist occasionally claims that he was foremost, if not exclusively a jurist, there are numerous entries where the borderline between law and theology is porous and both disciplines are used to define Schmitt's intellectual identity. But there is an interesting difference. When the diarist engages theological questions, including his own identity as a Catholic Christian, the tone becomes more subdued, occasionally even self-critical.[22] Is a Christian allowed to write a diary? The answer is yes, but only when the Christian diarist recognizes the need to defend himself against unjust accusations. Yet even in this extreme situation the diarist acknowledges the danger of following a path of sin, since "our deeds are our beloved daughters, our too beautiful women to whom we are drawn, whose beauty we admire as did Lucifer and father Adam" (G 13). The diarist looks at his own acts of writing with suspicion, but at the same time, it becomes apparent how much he clings to a theological definition of the human condition because such a definition seems to provide spiritual support in a chaotic secular world.[23] Within this framework the Christian diarist considers even the pleasure in nature when taking a walk in the valley of the Lenne River as a problematic activity because it is self-centered rather than open to God because the human subject takes on the position of God the creator (*G* 26). In this rigor against the natural self, the Christian diarist turns out to be in conflict with the secular self that relies on the law and the power of the state.

When the diarist reflects on the use of irony in the philosophical sense as discussed by Kierkegaard, he arrives at the conclusion that as a Christian he is not allowed to rely on irony to cope with difficult or extreme situations. He must criticize himself when he used irony in the battle with his (numerous) enemies. Still, there is the characterization of the (unnamed) opponent as a Caliban, who "will be driven even deeper into wickedness" by Schmitt's use of irony (*G* 28, October 7, 1947). In short, the self-criticism simultaneously affirms the superiority of the Christian self over his (non-Christian) opponent. This means that the Christian self can only gradually approach its moral goal without ever reaching it during its lifetime. Similarly, the diary underscores that the sensual nature of the human individual always subverts the direction of the Christian self toward the metaphysical goal. Thus the diarist notes: "Each moment of breathing belies your word, since each act of breathing is an unconditional surrender to the physical existence and the total terror that it exerts over spirit, soul, and body. But I am still allowed to touch the cross; great consolation" (*G* 33, October 14, 1947).

Depending on the thematic context, Carl Schmitt's notebooks can move back and forth between the above-mentioned positions of the subject. But there appears to be a hierarchy: The Christian self has the highest place and the German self the lowest. For this reason the theological discourse is given a higher dignity, which then informs the legal and the national discourse. This means that ultimately both law and politics are impacted by theology.[24] However, we can also observe the opposite: The discussion of legal and political issues influences Schmitt's theological self-definition.

Aspects of the Subject

As we have seen, Schmitt's subjectivity confronts the reader in three modes: the faithful Catholic Christian, the learned jurist who was dismissed from government service, and the victimized German citizen. Sometimes it is not easy to separate these aspects because they remain intertwined. Furthermore, the diarist—the writing subject—frequently transcends the confines of these roles and branches out into broader spheres of general knowledge, among them modern physics, art, literature, and history. Still, these parts, while showing his uncommon erudition and broad intellectual interests, remain detached from the core elements of Schmitt's subjectivity and are not perceived as existential components. Although many entries touch on his role as a member of the defeated and victimized collective of the Germans, the relationship between theology and law remains the deepest and most urgent concern. The fierce opposition to the persecution (of the German people) invokes a legal defense that is ultimately grounded in theology. In two early entries the diarist explicitly refers to his role as a jurist. On September 23, 1947, the diarist notes: "I have always spoken and written as a jurist and for other jurists. It was my misfortune that the jurists of my time had become positivist legal technicians, ignorant and uneducated; at best admirers of Goethe and neutralized humanists. For this reason the non-jurists who were listening in could focus on every word and tear me apart like a desert fox" (G 17). This passage interprets the link between legal language and persecution as a misunderstanding by laypersons, since the positivist jurists are unable to help them with the correct interpretation of Schmitt's legal theory. In other places, however, the diarist presents different and more aggressive interpretations, especially when the jurist Schmitt feels attacked by other jurists (among them former refugees or representatives of the Allies). In all instances it is crucial that the diarist invoke Schmitt's role as a jurist, which is regarded as distinct from a position of power or that of an observing intellectual (humanist). An entry dated October 3, 1947, on the other hand, highlights the link between theology and law by mentioning Theodor Andres Marcos and Hans Barion, both experts of canon law. "These two canon lawyers are jurists of theology; I am a theologian of law (*Jurisprudenz*); the result is failure in an age of fundamental secularity, heavy and clumsy (*gusseisener*) concepts and a delicate as well as hyper-careful *potestas indirect*" (G 23). In this instance the diarist describes Schmitt as jurist grounded in theology, but there are other instances where the writer is more careful and defines himself as a Christian layman who borrows concepts from theology and applies them to law. In any case, as a jurist Schmitt distances himself from two positions; namely, legal positivism and natural law. Therefore the distinction between legality and legitimacy, a distinction that Schmitt developed in his 1932 monograph *Legalität und Legitimität,* remains an important conceptual instrument for the jurist Schmitt to defend himself against critique from hostile positions.

Nonetheless, the theological foundation of legal and political theory remains an unresolved question for the diary. Some of his essays from the early 1950s tentatively approach the problem from a different angle, but only twenty years later, in *Political Theology II,* does Schmitt return to this question and offer a definitive solution. Here and there the diary touches on the question, for example in its response to Ernst Troeltsch's remarks on theocracy (G 234). Yet the writer places more emphasis on his own religious position and the role of the Roman Catholic Church. As it turns out, the Christian faith that the Christian self professes and to which it emphatically clings during these dark years, is bound up with the Catholic Church, while the various forms of Protestantism are seen as alien and problematic. Even more strongly the diarist articulates his distance from Judaism, because he sees the Jews as responsible for the death of Christ. The diary explicitly calls this death a ritual murder.[25]

Why is the connection between personal faith and the institution of the Church so very important for Schmitt during these years? More than once the diary responds to this question. In light of the continuous persecution and victimization that Schmitt believes to experience, the Catholic Church becomes the most important sanctuary. An entry of January 26, 1949, underscores this link. After once more stressing the harsh and ruthless victimization, the diarist notes: "When the Catholic Church becomes our asylum, she proves her ability as a church, as the dialectical synthesis of the perceptible and the imperceptible" (G 216). In this context the diarist also clarifies the link to the national discourse. A few weeks later the diary invokes the authority of the pope to discuss the possibility of asylum for German nationals. "The only asylum that was granted to a German, was granted by the Vatican" (G 217, February 13, 1949). What is critical for Schmitt when looking at the Catholic Church is her refusal to underwrite the agenda of the victorious Allies. Instead, the Church remained politically neutral.

As it turns out, not only are the Catholic and the German questions closely related, but so are the national and the legal discussions. Justice for Germany and the Germans is a central issue for the diarist; he opposes the moral and legal pressure coming from the Western powers and their ideological allies in Germany. As one would expect, the resistance is developed with the tools of constitutional and international law.[26] The diarist claims that both the liberal critique of *Angriffskrieg* and the return to the concept of just war are mainly instruments to discriminate against the German side. "The new dogma of just war turns justice into booty; it is also robbery" (G 229, April 4, 1949). At stake is no less than a fundamental revisionist reading of World War II. The diary questions the criminal nature of the German military operations. "But who is turning us into criminals? Those who judge us on the basis of criminalizing *Angriffskrieg,* a strategy which they themselves invented. A judge who judges by the rule of criminalization that he has created is already judged" (G 229). The diary uses this approach, which tries to exonerate the German side through a formal conceptual argument, several times. The point is that in older international law the sovereign state has the right to declare war without restrictions. Its use does not exclude the possibility of guilt (*Schuld*) but it is not criminal per se. The diarist's insistence that the German people were unfairly persecuted rests on this argument.

This juridical assessment also influences the conception of German history, notably the years of National Socialism. When reflecting on the concept of the tragic in Schiller's work, in particular on the tragic quality of the Demetrius fragment, the diarist touches also on the link between World Wars I and II.[27] He notes that Hitler

was meant to be the son who carries out the revenge for the lost Great War. This Caspar Hauser and *soldat inconnu* was adopted as the false

Demetrius by Mother Germania. Between 1933 and 1941 she said again
and again:
Even if he is not the son of my heart
He shall be the son of my revenge.
Yet faithless Mother Germania could not carry though her role when
she realized that things were moving toward the abyss. He [Hitler] however pulled down the house with his fall. Only the Catholic and Wallo-
nian Joseph Goebbels from the left bank of the Rhine remained faithful
until the end. (G 239, May 1, 1949)

By interpreting the connection between World War I and World
War II as a causal relationship in which the second war becomes
an act of revenge for unjust German sufferings in and after the first
war, the catastrophic outcome of the Third Reich turns into a
Schillerian tragedy rather than a crime that leads to the Nuremberg
trials. Only a few days prior to this entry the diary, referring to Re-
nan and Toynbee, reflects on the end of French and English national
history, subsequently discussing the German military defeat in terms
of the loss of a distinct German national history. In Schmitt's view
it was the decline of the West European powers that pulled Germany
down as well. In light of this pessimistic assessment, the diarist shows
little confidence in the beginning revival of liberal democracy
under the supervision of the Western Allies. The new political leaders are called "the poor little guys in Bonn" (G 222). According to
Schmitt, their task is to extend the political status quo—the continuation of German dependence—instead of creating a truly new
order. And looking at the recent political division of Germany the
diarist speaks of bootlickers both in the West and the East "who
have found a new master whose enemies they are allowed to abuse"
(G 212, December 24, 1948).

Ex Captivitate Salus: Global Civil War

Schmitt's *Glossarium* remains a provocation even today, two generations after its composition. Taken by itself, it is a document of Schmitt's
stubborn resistance to the social and political changes that were
occurring between 1945 and the foundation of the Federal Republic

in 1949. The notes document his despair, his rage, and most of all his determination to defend his views and positions in an imaginary court where he is the defendant as well as the judge. For this reason they tend to look back. There are only glimpses of a future life. Similarly, there are only glimpses of future theoretical projects. Still, some of the topics that preoccupied the diarist turn up in Schmitt's late work. His fierce commitment to the Catholic Church, for instance, comes to the fore not only in *Political Theology II* but also in *The Nomos of the Earth*. His frequent complaints about the victimization of the German people, on the other hand, do not determine his late writings.

Schmitt's essays from the same time are a better indicator of his later work than the diaries. Prima facie, the small essay volume *Ex Captivitate Salus* (1950) is also mostly concerned with Schmitt's fate after 1945.[28] It is a defense against his opponents and enemies, among them Eduard Spranger and Karl Mannheim. But there are glimpses of new theoretical insights that will be used to develop the themes and positions of Schmitt's late work. While the *Glossarium* focuses on the persona of Carl Schmitt, *Ex Captivitate Salus*, consisting of essays, reflections, and personal statements, shifts the focus to an abstract level where the persona of the author is still visible and sometimes explicitly named but now carefully framed in theoretical and historical terms. This strategy is most effectively applied in the title essay "Ex Captivitate Salus" of 1946, which engages Schmitt's position as a constitutional and international lawyer who was part of the legal and political system of Nazi Germany. Yet there is no mention of National Socialism in the entire essay. The particular circumstances of Schmitt's role between 1933 and 1945 disappear behind a theoretical construct that reframes Schmitt's thoughts and decisions (for which he was later held accountable) in the context of civil war. By presenting the period between 1933 and 1945 as a period of (global) civil war, Schmitt's agency takes on a fundamentally different character. It is that of a lawyer functioning under the conditions of civil war. That he represented the German side is secondary to the more fundamental situation, the pressure on the legal theorist under the condition of civil war.

What are these conditions? Schmitt does not explain why the first half of the twentieth century can or must be understood as an age of civil war. There is no explanation of how the civil war started and who was responsible. He only states the fact and describes the consequences. Civil war is defined as a state in which there is no common ground between warring political factions. Instead, each of them claims to be the rightful owner of law and morality, which means that the opponent makes false claims, which must be categorically denied and eradicated. Therefore under the conditions of civil war the character of war fundamentally changes: "Civil war is especially cruel. It is a war among brothers because it is carried out within one political community (*Einheit*), which includes the enemy, and within the same legal system, and because both warring sides absolutely claim this common ground (*Einheit*) and absolutely deny this ground to the other side" (*E* 56). Without further explanation Schmitt transfers this definition, which would apply to a civil war within a nation state, to the international constellation of the twentieth century, although it would be much more difficult to claim an original common legal and moral ground between fascist and liberal political regimes. Yet this transfer is crucial for Schmitt's model in which the alteration of warfare and law are critical moments of a global transformation.

What are the consequences, and how do they impact Schmitt's own role? The essay is concerned with two aspects in particular. First, it examines the changes that occur in the arena of war. Schmitt emphasizes the uncommon brutality of civil war compared with traditional interstate wars. The extreme cruelty is the result of the expected outcome. The goal is no longer the mere defeat of the enemy but his destruction. As Schmitt notes, the intertwinement of law and war "poisons the fight. It intensifies it to the level of extreme brutality by turning the means and methods of jurisprudence into means and methods of annihilation" (*E* 57). For Schmitt it is precisely the legalization of war that results in total war, since both factions are convinced that the enemy is culpable in terms of its own law. The transition from conventional to absolute war is one side of the coin. The other is the transformation of the legal system.

Revolutionary and People's Tribunals (*Volksgerichtshöfe*) have a different function than traditional courts of law. They are not created to serve justice but to instill terror. They are, Schmitt tells us, open and explicit instruments of political power. The methods are legal discrimination; public or secret proscription lists serve the same political purpose. They are designed to discredit the opponent and applied to take away his or her legal standing. In short, the law is used to undermine the rule of law. Under the conditions of civil war the concept of law has become essentially partisan. Schmitt speaks of a complete *Entrechtung* (delegitimization) of the opponent, who stands outside the law.

It is apparent that the essay deals with Schmitt's own situation. In the first paragraph he refers to himself as a constitutional and international lawyer whose thoughts and decisions were impacted by the particular conditions under which he was living and had to act. But if the reader expected self-critical reflections about Schmitt's complicated involvement in the legal and political system of Nazi Germany, he or she would be disappointed. There is no discussion of National Socialism and Schmitt's actual role as a legal advisor and writer for Hitler's cause. Schmitt uses the notion of an impact of special historical conditions for a rather different purpose—as the first step in a broad narrative about the age of civil war and its impact on the legal profession. It is worth noting that in this context the difference between fascist and liberal political regimes disappear. Both sides are guilty of discrimination, since they use the law for political purposes. This means that the individual Carl Schmitt who decided in 1933 to join the Party disappears behind the generalized abstract role of the jurist in the age of civil war. The essay claims that it was the professional role that defined the limits of thought and action. Where the law had lost its standing above the parties, the lawyer could only be partisan himself. Possibly against his will, he becomes an instrument of power.

The theory of the civil war as the nemesis of constitutional law and the constitutional lawyer provides the frame for Schmitt's inquiry into the history of modern international and constitutional law. It is from there that the essay seeks to rebuild the general conditions for the rule of law and, by extension, prepare the exit from civil war. Schmitt's personal fate—his decision to support the Third Reich as well as his exclusion from public life after 1945—is recast in such a way that it becomes a legitimate stance in dark times. Schmitt speaks of a "tragic dialectic of law" (*E* 59) and seeks to answer the implied question by way of a historical narrative that goes back as far as the sixteenth century. It is the story of the origin and evolution of the *ius publicum Europaeum* and its theorists, among them Francisco Vitoria, Jean Bodin, Hugo Grotius, and Thomas Hobbes. In particular, Schmitt elevates Bodin and Hobbes as the founding fathers of modern international law (*Völkerrecht*).

The point the essay wants to drive home is the similarity between the early modern age and the present. Both are times of deep political disturbance and civil war. The confessional unrest of the sixteenth century corresponds to the ideological wars of the twentieth century. The rise of European international law, Schmitt tells us, was the answer to the civil war. The new law brought an end to civil war and prepared the ground for the expansion of Europe. Schmitt celebrates the *ius publicum* for two reasons. On the one hand, it becomes the basis for the development of the modern secular nation state, and on the other, it allows Schmitt, when he considers his own professional status, to seek the proximity of great jurists such as Bodin and Hobbes. He underscores the deeper nature of the similarity, which goes beyond mere analogy. As he explains, "There are identities of the spiritual existence that one can trace back to the personal fate, even to the soul of those humans who are seeking to master this condition through their thinking and their concepts and who have to endure the entire burden of such an effort" (*E* 63).

By embracing Bodin and Hobbes as those international lawyers whose lives were radically determined by civil war, Schmitt not only finds himself in good company but also lifted to a level of existence at which the accusations of his enemies cannot reach him. Schmitt counts on the spiritual support of his illustrious colleagues. While Jean Bodin represents the type of lawyer who is involved in the political struggle of his age, Thomas Hobbes represents the theoretical mind that looks at the struggle from a distance. While Bodin fights for a position of neutrality that transcends dangerous theological disputes, Hobbes, as an early enlightener and agnostic, seeks to establish a new concept of the political. Thus, by intertwining his own biography with that of his famous colleagues, the essayist seeks to establish for himself a legitimate ground beyond the strife of the postwar period. At the same time, the concept of the *ius publicum* offers the answer to the larger problem that Schmitt had examined. He seems to believe that the restoration of the *ius publicum Europaeum* would also restore the political order of postwar Europe.

Looking back at the sixteenth and seventeenth centuries, Schmitt argues that the theoretical position of Bodin and Hobbes was closely related to their biographies. To what extent can this argument be applied to Schmitt? Does Schmitt's late work grow out of the personal crisis of the postwar years? Without any doubt the essay *Ex Captivitate Salus* reads the history of European international law as a frame for an appraisement of Schmitt's personal crisis, but the reverse is relevant as well. Working through his own problems, especially trying to deal with accusations and criticisms, becomes the starting point for reorganizing his thought and rethinking his theoretical position. But this transformation does not follow the lines presented in *Glossarium*. The narrative of the development of international law from the sixteenth to the twentieth century in the essay has two significant new features. First, while the *Glossarium* underscores the continued central importance of the German question, the essay radically shifts from a national to a European perspective. It is telling that Schmitt does not invoke German authorities (possibly Kant or Hegel) and strongly emphasizes a European point of view. Second, the essay assigns theology and the Catholic Church a different role than the diary. Instead of highlighting the ultimate relevance of the theological question, the essay uses the familiar concept of secularization to describe the evolution of modern international law. In brief, the Church is replaced by the sovereign state and the legal profession replaces the theologians as definitive authorities for the political order. The ultimate consequence therefore is "complete profanation" (*E* 74). Yet this is precisely the point where the narrative turns around, where the progressive moment of secularization becomes a fundamental problem. What Schmitt fears in the late modern period is the transition from enlightenment to positivism and a technocratic understanding of law. "At the beginning [of modern law, *puh*] we find a demand to keep silence, which was articulated by the jurists and addressed to the theologians, who supported the idea of just war. At the end we find a demand directed to the jurists to apply a pure, that is a completely profane technocracy" (*E* 75).

The Future of Jurisprudence

As much as the theological question was on Schmitt's mind during the early postwar years, it was by no means his only preoccupation. Reflections on the role of theology in the modern world simultaneously open the question of the role of law, since for Schmitt the rise of modern law and the modern profession of law (*Rechtswissenschaft*) are closely connected to the decline of theology as the central discipline defining not only the religious belief system but also the cultural and social structure of the medieval world. In his essay *Die Lage der europäischen Rechtswissenschaft* (The State of European Jurisprudence), originally a lecture presented in 1943 but only published in 1950,[29] Schmitt argues that the autonomy of the legal profession was obtained in the sixteenth and seventeenth centuries by pushing back and limiting the demands and expectations of theology.

It is clearly this autonomy that Schmitt, looking at the European situation during and after World War II, wants to reinstate and strengthen against developments during the interwar years, which were defined by the rise of extreme forms of positivism in which there was no room left for the reflective work of jurisprudence. What he has in mind is the transition from the *Gesetzesstaat* (legal state) of the late nineteenth century to the administrative state of the twentieth century that uses *Verordnungen* (ordinances) and *Anordnungen* (decrees) as the most efficient instruments to organize administrative interventions. Although one could make the case that this describes the type of legal system adopted by the Nazis, where the law was replaced by ad hoc orders and rules, Schmitt does not explore the development between 1933 and 1945. In fact, the essay does not once mention the Third Reich and its abuse of the law.

While most legal scholars in Germany after 1945 defined the central task of jurisprudence as a thorough critique of the perversion of the legal system under Hitler, Schmitt keeps a noticeable distance from this topic. His focus is both broader and historically more expansive. What we have already observed in *Ex Captivitate Salus* we find here as well: an emphatic European turn. For Schmitt, seen from a greater distance, the problems that have beset the contemporary legal institutions are European rather than specifically German. In fact, as Schmitt argues, the development from the early modern state to the rise of the legal state (*Gesetzesstaat*) and positivism can be better studied in France than in Germany, where it occurred later and less consistently. For Schmitt the French case shows with greater clarity the modern connection between state and law, the rise of a centralized state that defines itself in terms of its legal system. The implicit danger of this development becomes apparent in the later transition when the legal state becomes the administrative state in which the law (*Gesetz*) morphs into ordinances and decrees written and pronounced by officials who are no longer controlled by independent legal institutions such as judges or academic professionals whose task it was to interpret the law. The increasing loss of autonomy is defined as a common European process that couldn't be stopped by the counterweight of the British case law tradition because it lacked the philosophical sophistication to cope with the positivist turn in the nineteenth century. Schmitt suggests that the rigorous revolutionary efforts of Napoleon to systematically codify the law left its traces not only in France but in many other continental states as well, which meant that the revolutionary impetus was spreading all over Europe, leading to the preponderance of the centralized state and its bureaucracy over older forms of law.

For this reason, Schmitt contrasts Napoleon with another figure who represents a traditional view of the law and the legal profession. This person is the famous German legal scholar Friedrich Karl von Savigny. Typically, Savigny is seen as a representative of the

Historical School of Law in Germany, which argued in favor of the value of legal traditions in opposition to the dominance of natural law in the eighteenth century. But Schmitt is less interested in Savigny's historicism and the exploration of Roman law as the foundation of the modern legal system than in his resistance to abstract rationalism and the role that jurisprudence was supposed to play in this project. In fact, Schmitt openly rejects Savigny's archeological interests in the restoration of Roman law. Instead, he underscores the search for the living and breathing sources of the law (*Recht*) that are grounded in the life-world (*Lebenswelt*) of the people. Differently put, Schmitt is primarily interested in the importance of a living and flexible tradition as an argument against the abstract positing of legal statutes. His entire argument rests on the contrast between the *Recht* (law as justice) on the one hand and the *Gesetz* (law as statute) on the other. While Schmitt sees the *Recht* as a complex and changing unity of received values and ideas, for him the *Gesetz* stands for the posited decree or statute.

What makes Savigny a valuable model for Schmitt? Why does he believe that the crisis of law that defines the present can be overcome by following the ideas of a nineteenth-century German jurisprudent whom later generations decried as an impediment to the development of modern German law? Schmitt is aware of these arguments and does not mean to defend Savigny's legal politics. Rather, he reads Savigny's program as offering an important point of resistance to the tendencies set in motion by the French Revolution and its consequences in the nineteenth century that in Schmitt's mind ultimately destroyed the equilibrium between state and jurisprudence. While the early modern period had not yet quite overcome the supremacy of theology, the nineteenth century then witnessed the accelerated rise of the centralized secular state as an increasing threat to the autonomy of the legal profession. For Schmitt the reception of Roman law in the later middle and the early modern age created the common ground on which the European legal profession could stand and successfully operate. It produced the common vocabulary and a set of shared concepts and arguments that would interconnect regional traditions. Therefore Savigny's emphasis on the importance of Roman law as a shared European experience made him a central figure in Schmitt's struggle with the crisis of his own time.

There can be no doubt about the conservative aspirations of this essay. Schmitt underscores the need for restoring the autonomy of jurisprudence for the well-being of the state and the social community. By this he means not only the centrality of the law but also—and equally important in his opinion—the independence of the legal profession, since it is the legal profession that reflects on and supports the spirit of the law. The thrust of this argument overlaps with specific concerns in West Germany at that time about overcoming the legal system of the NS regime, including its officials (Carl Schmitt being one of them). But these efforts, which were among other things articulated in the new constitution (*Grundgesetz*) of the Federal Republic, had a distinctive liberal tendency that Schmitt did not share. For him the emphasis should be placed on the tradition of the law rather than on new *Gesetzgebung;* that is, the creation of new statues. In fact, he warns explicitly against the "empty legalistic technocracy" (*LER* 32) that dominated the late phase of European positivism. In other words, he reads the postwar era not so much as a struggle against the continued impact of National Socialism in Germany (as Horkheimer and Adorno would do) but as a confrontation with a technocratic state.

In his carefully calibrated final note Schmitt stresses the possibility of a new life of jurisprudence under the umbrella of Savigny's ideas: "European jurisprudence does not have to die together with the myth of the law (*Gesetz*) and the law giver. We have to remember the history of our suffering, for our strength is rooted in the record of our affliction" (*LER* 32). Clearly, Schmitt sees the legal profession, broadly speaking, as a victim of state interference, yet it is also seen as overcoming the state of victimhood. The autonomy of jurisprudence, as Schmitt makes clear, does not rest in the liberal myth of *Gesetz* and *Gesetzgeber*. In this statement both his precarious personal situation as a legal scholar barred from his profession and his belief in the healing force of the European tradition are cautiously articulated. However, it is worth noting that he neither admits his failure during the Third Reich nor supports the renewed liberalism of the young Federal Republic.

Personal and Theoretical Lessons

What is the lesson that Schmitt draws from the complex and twisted history of international law? There is both a personal and a theoretical lesson. In biographical terms, Schmitt defines himself as the last representative of the older European international law. "I am the last self-conscious representative of the *ius publicum Europaeum*" (E 75). In theoretical terms, the negative outcome of this history (among other things its fascist reinterpretation) calls for a reassessment of secularization. Hence the grounding of law is an open and urgent question, which means that the concept of a political theology has to be reconsidered. In *The Nomos of the Earth* Schmitt will approach the historical aspect by giving a fuller and more detailed account of the development of international law based on the concept of secularization. The unresolved theological problematic resurfaces much later; it is only in 1970, in *Political Theology II*, that Schmitt seeks to revisit the relevance of theology for the political sphere.

In 1950, Carl Schmitt was convinced that future theoretical work, including his own writings, would present itself as a continuation of older and established ideas and concepts rather than a break with the past as German liberals imagined it. This conviction was based on his belief that Hitler's totalitarian system was unable to entirely suppress intellectual freedom. The rather complete separation between the inner subject and the outer subject of the citizen, between the thought of the individual and the actions of the submissive political subject, a separation that had been part of the German tradition, allowed for a space in which free scientific and scholarly work could actually occur. Schmitt speaks of a well-known German "retreat into the private interiority [*Innerlichkeit*]" (E 18). Hitler's totalitarian movement, Schmitt argues, could not penetrate and change the churches and Marxist organizations.

Moreover, the German educated middle classes (*Bildungsbürger-tum*), as much as they were weakened under Nazi rule, were not completely destroyed (*E* 18). In brief, Schmitt presents a strong claim for the endurance and power of the inner emigration. In fact, he claims that he was part of these forces of resistance and quotes the following lines from his 1938 study of Thomas Hobbes: "If in a country only the public sphere remains in place that is organized by the power of the state, the forces of silence and peace grow" (*E* 21).

Intellectual and spiritual continuation is possible, Schmitt tells us, because the totalitarian state was not powerful enough to destroy the cultural and intellectual tradition. A revival therefore was possible as soon as the Nazi regime had collapsed and the hidden elements of spiritual freedom could come to the fore again. This strong belief explains Schmitt's deep and persistent irritation over the initial control of the public sphere by the Allies, since this control showed little interest in the intellectual work of the inner emigration. In fact, the controllers were suspicious of this movement because they assumed that some of its prominent figures, like Ernst Jünger, Gottfried Benn, and of course Carl Schmitt himself, had been collaborators. It is important to underscore this self-refashioning on the part of Schmitt in order to understand the direction of his postwar writings and publications. Schmitt refuses to accept the historical break of 1945 as a determining factor for his work. He might consider 1938 a turning point, when he began to articulate his distance from the NS regime, although he did not openly criticize this regime.[30] In fact, he (like Heidegger) rejects 1945 as a major historical turning point because the end of World War II did not end what he believes to be the defining conflict; namely, a global civil war.

What and who, then, could be a model for this work? The most obvious example is Thomas Hobbes, especially when he is moved closer to Christian theology than usual. But for Schmitt the English thinker is also connected with the idea of the secular sovereign state and the clear separation of church and state. In *Ex Captivitate Salus*, Schmitt tries to work with a more unlikely example, the French liberal Alexis de Tocqueville, whose concept of history seems to offer a way out of the conundrum of the postwar configuration. What makes Tocqueville attractive for Schmitt is his intellectual distance from the historical profession of his generation, including its historicism, and to the present class conflicts of his time (where he finds himself on the losing side). Schmitt praises his diagnostic force and his keen insights into the larger forces that determine the historical process, but without promulgating laws of history. Rather, Schmitt appreciates the astute observer who is willing to balance and compromise. Looking back from the catastrophic end of World War II at the mid-nineteenth century, Schmitt admires Tocqueville's prognosis "that humanity will irresistibly and without question continue on the path to centralization and democratization that it has followed since a long time. But the far-sighted historian is not satisfied with merely stating a general tendency of the future development. He names simply and distinctly the historical powers that support and enforce this development: America and Russia" (*E* 28). This judgment confirms Schmitt's own assessment of the postwar constellation.

There are explicit moments of identification in Schmitt's analysis, possibly the most important being with Tocqueville's awareness of his defeat as an aristocrat and a liberal, although Schmitt was neither an aristocrat nor a liberal. Speaking out of a position of defeat makes the French theorist attractive for Schmitt, the defeated German jurist. It means that Schmitt as a critical observer and writer takes himself out the political struggle. He claims distance from the active historical forces. There is also a noticeable moment of resignation that is absent from Schmitt's writings of the 1920s and early 1930s. It is not accidental that at the end of the essay the New Testament figure of the katechon, who slows down the progression of time, makes an appearance. The increasing importance of the katechon signals a shift in the political theology of Schmitt's late work.

Carl Schmitt's return to the public sphere in the 1950s was slow and not without setbacks. Although some of the most stringent sanctions were lifted—for instance the prohibition against publishing—he experienced not only encouragement by his friends and former disciples, who tried to find employment for him and attempted patiently to ease access to journals and publishing houses, but also rejection and criticism from institutions and individuals. As it turned out, Schmitt's comeback was more difficult than that of his friend Ernst Jünger and the poet Gottfried Benn, who had also emphatically supported the NS regime in 1933. But Jünger and Benn were writers; they were not part of the state apparatus and their work had no immediate impact on the legal and political system. It was Schmitt's official role that made his reentry so difficult. The fact that his influence had decreased after 1936 and that he had distanced himself from Hitler's policies was important for his friends but did not make a significant difference for the broad public, not to mention foreign observers. Even the Catholic Church remained ambivalent. On the one hand, Pater Eberhard Welty offered to let him stay and work at the Dominican Academy Walberberg and even gave him the opportunity to publish an essay in the journal *Die neue Ordnung* as early as 1950. On the other hand, the same journal published a polemical essay by a former assistant of the liberal jurist Hans Kelsen in response to Schmitt's essay on Vitoria. It appears that, at least from Schmitt's perspective, the Catholic revival did not quite work out.[31]

But notwithstanding Schmitt's numerous complaints about his isolation and punitive marginalization, friends came to his aid, providing psychological as well as financial support. They created contacts, among them to journals and publishing houses that allowed Schmitt to organize his comeback in the German public sphere. Especially after the foundation of the Federal Republic with its new capital in Bonn, the German Far Right got more breathing space and could slowly and cautiously restore its network. Naturally Schmitt did benefit from this change of the political atmosphere. It is no accident that *The Nomos of the Earth* was first published in 1950, not by Schmitt's old publishing firm but by Greven Verlag, where one of his old contacts could prepare the ground. Another index for the gradual change of Schmitt's public status was the attempt by the editors of the journal *Merkur,* which would become one of the most prestigious journals of the early Bonn Republic, to win Schmitt as a contributor for their project. The moderate liberalism of the *Merkur* was quite distinct from the Christian conservatism of *Die neue Ordnung,* which shows that the revived interest in Schmitt's work was not limited to the Catholic camp.

As long as the liberal definition of democracy, as it was stipulated in the Basic Law of the Federal Republic, was not openly attacked and rejected, there was room for discussion and thereby room, at least to some extent, for Schmitt's theories. Here the crucial but difficult task was to differentiate between his theories and his political and theoretical support of the NS regime. While this was not easy for first and second generation students such as Ernst Forsthoff and Ernst Rudolf Huber, who had been equally compromised because of their proximity to the Third Reich, for the third generation the new political regime was already the basis for discussion and political action. They were inclined to see Schmitt's involvement in the Third Reich as an episode that did not define the author or his work. Of course, this acceptance did not extend to the liberal center and the Left. The members of the Frankfurt School for example kept their distance and occasionally reminded the public of Schmitt's dangerous opinions. For this reason, during the 1950s and 1960s Carl Schmitt remained a highly controversial figure in West Germany (not to mention the Communist East), but he was again part of the public discourse. Especially the conservative media and their journalists were eager to renew the contact and to support a dialogue that would restore Schmitt's status as an influential public voice. And Plettenberg, where Schmitt had resided since 1947, became a kind of pilgrimage site (*Wallfahrtsort*) for conservative intellectuals. Here, the private space of the author's home became the center of a conservative public sphere that was still seeking shelter from the hostile intrusion of the new (liberal) state.[32]

2

TRANSITION

The Concept of Großraum *and Global Politics*

Although the events of 1945 severely ruptured Carl Schmitt's personal life, they did not bring about an equally decisive break in his thinking. In the essays he wrote between 1945 and 1949 Schmitt carries forward ideas and concepts that he had developed and applied during the 1930s and early 1940s, albeit placing them in a transformed context. This means that to interpret Schmitt's late writings we must to look back to the late 1930s and examine Schmitt's concept of *Großraum* (expanded territory), an idea that has played a surprisingly significant role in recent debates within political theory. These debates rarely mention the concept's background and even more rarely elucidate it. Instead, scholars have frequently addressed Schmitt's theory of space as if it could be detached from its original purpose. But Schmitt's own postulate of concrete thinking sought to derive theories from their particular historical conditions, and Schmitt's theory of *Großraum* grew directly from his reading of German foreign policy between 1939 and 1941. Further, Schmitt's understanding of the U.S. Monroe Doctrine (1823) influenced the political and legal purpose of *Großraum,* and the tension between the American and German concepts casts considerable light on Schmitt's thinking. Only in this light can we examine the present debates, in particular the question of whether Schmitt's theory remains useful for critical political theory.

Carl Schmitt introduced the concept of *Großraum* in the late 1930s in the interests of establishing a distinction between his own thinking and a normatively informed conception of international relations at the time that demanded political and military intervention for the sake of securing international peace. Schmitt famously held one such policy to be the principal cause of particularly destructive wars under the auspices of the League of Nations, in which the defeated state was considered the transgressor. By contrast, the concept of an expanded political territory contained for Schmitt the possibility of guaranteeing the more or less peaceful coexistence of peoples, renouncing normative viewpoints and in the process precluding discrimination against political adversaries. This concept was developed by Schmitt most thoroughly in *The Nomos of the Earth*—a text that was already essentially written before 1945 but not published until 1950.[1] This has led to the impression that the text is a postwar work reflecting on the consequences of German defeat, but while it is clear that Schmitt cautiously changed some of his positions after 1945, he was notably willing to continue to defend positions he had held in the early 1940s even after World War II. Strong evidence of this is that Schmitt's *The Großraum Order of International Law* (*Völkerrechtliche Großraumordnung*), first published in 1939, was republished after the war in unchanged form (appearing posthumously most recently in 1991).[2]

The foreign policy of the Third Reich is the context for Schmitt's concept of *Großraum* in the 1940s, referencing a definitive position within Germany's controversial foreign policy at the time. In this regard, the interpretation of the U.S. Monroe Doctrine played an important role, since as with Hitler's use of the doctrine, it allowed for the principal ban on intervention in the European continent. As a new *Großraum* with Germany at its center, Europe could in this way be protected from non-European intrusion. In short, Schmitt's interpretation of the Monroe Doctrine had the effect of neutralizing the United States.

The present interest in Schmitt's concept of *Großraum* cannot be directly related to the historical discussion of the term, since it would need to both unequivocally distance itself from National Socialist foreign policy and refer to a globalization discourse that can no longer assume the validity of the older geopolitical concepts taken up by Schmitt in the 1940s.[3] In light of globalization's full manifestation in mass media, financial capital, and international politics, the notion of expanded territories as politically autonomous presents a challenge, since it resists the idea of an all-encompassing global order. Loosely speaking, Schmitt's concept allows for two possible uses: on the one hand, as a not-to-be-dismissed objection to a normative or hegemonically defined world state, and on the other, as the positing of a pluralistic global order reliant on a balance of major powers. In the first case, the perspective is regional (i.e., specifically European), in the second unambiguously global, yet without the assumption of universally grounding political action in a universal moral norm. The aversion to moral ideas in politics in both instances is apparent. This aversion is based on the notion that moral norms have destructive consequences when introduced to politics, and should remain separate. The conditions and possibilities of a global political order thus present themselves differently today than in the mid-twentieth century.

National Socialist Foreign Policy and Carl Schmitt

In order to more precisely distinguish between the older meaning of *Großraum* and its current use, it is necessary to reconstruct the concept's original context. Schmitt developed his theory against the background of German foreign policy, whose expansionist aims revealed themselves largely after 1939.[4] This foreign policy was no longer primarily concerned with renewing the political sovereignty of the German nation-state, but rather with creating a new European political order centered around the German Reich. It is no coincidence that Schmitt readily seized on the concept of the Reich, wielded positively by the National Socialists, and deployed the term against the narrower concept of the nation-state. In accordance with National Socialist foreign policy, Schmitt thought that the goal of the new order could only be reached by excluding non-European powers that could intervene in the name of international law, particularly the United States. Toward this end, Hitler argued against Roosevelt's demand that Germany refrain from further offensive measures following the annexation of Czechoslovakia and founding of Slovenian satellite-states, claiming that he would refuse the intrusion of any power not territorially adjacent. On April 28, 1939, Hitler denied Roosevelt's request with reference to the Monroe Doctrine, saying, among other things, that "we Germans employ exactly the same doctrine for Europe, in any case for the interests and territories of the greater German Reich."[5] Around the same time, the German foreign minister, Ribbentrop, outlined the German Monroe Doctrine to the U.S. secretary of state as primarily constituting a claim to a region (in Eastern Europe) in which the interference of other powers would be denied.[6] According to this interpretation, only the Soviet Union, as a neighboring power, but not France, Britain, or the United States, had a right to intervene.

The formulation of a German Monroe Doctrine served the obvious goal of lending aggressive German expansion the appearance of legitimacy. The expanding Reich refused to tolerate the intrusion of other powers as it occupied itself with reordering its living space (*Lebensraum*). Forcefully stated by the Third Reich, the German Monroe Doctrine came down to a simultaneous legitimization of then existing relations of power and a delegitimization of any intervention that would refer to universal norms of international law. According to the new doctrine, the decision concerning the legitimacy of political and military actions rested solely with Germany. Decisions concerning the foundations of existing relations could only be reached through negotiations or the use of force. Hitler thus first sought an arrangement with the Soviet Union to safeguard his own as well as the Russian expanded territories and a pact with Japan, which had for its part articulated its own Asian Monroe Doctrine. In the case of Japan, the Monroe Doctrine and

Großraum were also closely interrelated, insofar as the doctrine safeguarded their own claims to expanded territory. For German foreign policy, the Monroe Doctrine stood for a politics of continentalism, the demand for a regionalism directed at the "universalism" of Britain and the United States. A German commentator sympathetic to National Socialism like Giselher Wirsing contended that its use would avert world wars.[7] As was also the case for Schmitt, the difference between the original and later, imperialistic Monroe Doctrine therefore played a strategic role, since overturning U.S. expansion with reference to the original function of the Monroe Doctrine depended on this historical distinction. Put differently, the United States' originally defensive use of the doctrine stood in opposition to Germany's expansive use. Whether or not the 1823 doctrine allows for these reinterpretations is somewhat ambiguous.

In the context of German foreign policy during the early years of the war, maintaining the neutrality of the United States remained an important goal for propaganda as well as diplomatic reasons, with an aim of isolating Britain after the fall of France and imposing peace. The opposition between universalist and regionalist politics played a crucial role in this line of reasoning. Should the United States decide for universalism in a continuation of Wilson's politics, one could assume that the United States would support Britain. Carl Schmitt's commentary from the autumn of 1940 formulates this decision emphatically: The United States must decide "whether they want to enter into an alliance or even a fusion with the British empire and tradition of universalism."[8] Schmitt's explicit reference to "unadulterated" territorial thought underscores the possibilities available to U.S. foreign policy—neutrality or intervention on the side of Britain.

Following the defeat of France, Germany, insofar as it sought to pursue expansionist politics, had two options. With the Soviet Union's tolerance, it could turn against Britain or, in the hopes of an understanding with Britain, advance on the Soviet Union itself. While the German navy supported an expanded war against Britain, Hitler essentially opted for expansion toward Russia, banking on the neutrality of the United States as well as an understanding with Great Britain. This plan was further complicated by the Japanese factor, that is, the rising tension between Japan and the United States with regards to imperialist plans in Tokyo. Germany's open support for Japan would have threatened the U.S. neutrality on which Hitler's hope for an understanding with Britain relied. Although there were various schools of thought within German foreign policy at the time, advocacy for expanded regional territories was beyond dispute. Moreover, Hitler reserved the right to change the appraisal of existing territorial configurations and replace the German acceptance of the status quo with a policy of conquest, or more specifically, extermination. Thus the pact with the Soviet Union was considered temporary, as a step towards Germany's European and possibly global dominance. Compared to this project, the foreign office's plans to secure the German *Großraum* in Africa through renewed colonization held only a secondary importance.[9] In Schmitt's terminology, Hitler conceived of Germany principally as a land power. As a consequence, Russia was its actual enemy. Already in May of 1940, Hitler was reported to be planning a campaign against the Soviet Union.[10]

Schmitt's Understanding of the Monroe Doctrine in the Context of German Politics

Though Schmitt's understanding of Germany's position after 1933, and specifically German foreign policy around 1940, doesn't meld seamlessly with the official party line, it nonetheless touched upon basic ideas propounded by the government. Above all, he expected less from Britain and emphasized more strongly the opposition to and potential confrontation with Roosevelt's foreign policy insofar as it assumed the continuation of basic tendencies of Wilson's policies. Based on his criticism of liberalism and its political order, parliamentary democracy, which went back to the 1920's, Schmitt's polemic in the 1930s and 40s concentrated on the western powers that he held responsible for the breakdown of European international law, particularly Britain and the United States. In *The Nomos of the Earth*, Schmitt argued that traditional European international law would be destroyed by the introduction of moral categories in the appraisal of wars, as had occurred at the end of World War I. According to Schmitt, in place of traditional European international law emerged a universalist international law, favored by the United States, which moralized international politics. Critiquing this historical development occupied Schmitt's intellectual energy. The task was to counter this universalist international law with a law that didn't refer to abstract norms, but instead arose out of concrete historical and geographic circumstances. The foundation for this new international law was established by Schmitt's concept of *Großraum*. Schmitt needed to develop this newly legitimate international law in keeping with a global territorial order in which rules and values followed from existing relations of power. In terms of German foreign policy, this implied that Schmitt favored a primarily anti-American and anti-British position, while Stalin's leadership, insofar as it remained expressly limited to Russia and conceded its universal revolutionary goals, remained compatible with his conception of expanded territories. For him, the actual threat was the possibility of an interventionist U.S. foreign policy no longer limited to the defense of U.S. interests but purporting to speak in the name of mankind. By contrast, there is little doubt that Schmitt viewed the eastward expansion of the German Reich positively, as a logical extension of the German living space.

To legally safeguard his conception of politically expanded territories, Schmitt (but not him alone, as we will see) invoked the doctrine of nonintervention by non-U.S. powers in the politics of the American continent announced in 1823 by U.S. president Monroe.[11] What interested Schmitt in the Monroe Doctrine was the conceptual means to create a political space inaccessible to other powers—a quasinormative force nonetheless derived from a particular historical constellation. An act viewed by Schmitt as original land appropriation (*Landnahme*) is extended in time by the refusal to grant rival powers the right to ground their own claims through dynastic or other means. For Schmitt, the Monroe Doctrine is in principal incompatible with a universalist conception of international relations, as exemplified for him by the (implicit) conflict between the League of Nations and traditional U.S. foreign policy. That the League of Nations was forced to incorporate the Monroe Doctrine into its statute (Article 21) demonstrated for Schmitt that the doctrine combined two distinct and conflicting forms of legal thought.[12] Furthermore, it proved to him that Europe had been forced to concede the conception of its own territorial order to the United States. In the process, however, the original sense of a division between the western hemisphere and the European powers who had withdrawn from it was reversed, for now it was this western hemisphere that overshadowed Europe. For Schmitt, determining the boundary between the defensive and offensive use of the Monroe Doctrine was of particular importance. While he held the defensive use of the doctrine to be legitimate for U.S. politics, its offensive interpretation presented him with the possibility of increased intervention if self-interest could be defended in terms of universal values.

Schmitt's engagement with the Monroe Doctrine goes back to the late 1930s, initially in *The Großraum Order of International Law,* and subsequently in the essay "Großraum versus Universalism" ("Großraum gegen Universalismus," 1939), which Schmitt included in the volume *Positionen und Begriffe (Positions and Concepts,* 1940) shortly thereafter. The doctrine is for Schmitt the case of a simple, successful territorial order that serves to exemplify the basic principles of a political order of territories more generally. Thus Schmitt sought "to produce the core of a *Großraum* principle of international law in all of its simplicity and greatness" (*GRO* 84). It is precisely the proximity of law and politics, disturbing from a strictly juridical perspective, that attracted Schmitt to the doctrine, because it allowed for a transition between the political and the legal sphere. Even more important to Schmitt was the difference between the true Monroe Doctrine and its late nineteenth-century distortion in the service of imperialist U.S. foreign policy. Schmitt considered the first, defensive doctrine to emphasize the basic principal of self-defense, resistance to foreign interventions, and the solidarity of states within an expanded territory. The doctrine differed from the traditional European ordering principle, which proceeded from dynastic lines. In this respect the U.S. doctrine introduced something new to international politics: a principle that, precisely owing to its vagueness and ambiguity, challenged decisionistic interpretations, a possibility explicitly referred to by Schmitt (*GRO* 86). From a German perspective, the doctrine had the potential to reserve the interpretation of a German order of expanded territories exclusively for the German government. Schmitt stood in friendly opposition to the U.S. doctrine, even identifying with it insofar as it represented the collective interests of the American people. As Schmitt asserts: "Here is the core of the great original Monroe Doctrine, a genuine principle of *Großraum,* namely the connection of politically awakened nation, political idea, and a *Großraum* ruled by this idea, a *Großraum* excluding foreign interventions" (*GRO* 88).

The U.S. doctrine's applicability to the German situation in 1939 can be easily comprehended. Schmitt did not advocate for a special German Monroe Doctrine but rather an autonomous expanded German territory: "This *Großraum* thought . . . may not be arbitrary but is reasonably translatable based on the state of political reality. Its applicability to Central and East European space is not abolished through the fact that since 1823 the state of affairs in Europe and in America have fundamentally changed" (*GRO* 88). If it could be realized, a German Monroe Doctrine would prohibit liberal Western powers from intervening against Germany, since "already the war of 1914 to 1918 was a war of intervention of this liberal democratic legitimacy" (*GRO* 89). In light of the fact that Schmitt expressly considered the ideals of freedom central to Western democracies to be obsolete, his political aim is clear. The appearance of the internal political order within the *Großraum* remains undecided insofar as it is post- or anti-liberal. In this context, the Monroe Doctrine served to secure this new order against normative moral critique.

An interesting consequence of Schmitt's idea is that the United States, precisely owing to its deviation from the authentic Monroe Doctrine, developed into a capitalist/imperialist power, employing universalist principles in the service of its own dominance. "Theodore Roosevelt, Woodrow Wilson and the current President Franklin D. Roosevelt, in transforming a specifically American spatial conception into a transnational and trans-ethnic world ideology, have attempted to use the Monroe Doctrine as an instrument for the domination of the world market by Anglo-Saxon capital" writes Schmitt.[13] It is telling that Schmitt first describes these political consequences in the essay "Großraum versus Universalism," in which he openly polemicizes against the liberal conception of international law and advocates for "the right to life and living space" for Japan, Italy, and Germany. In this regard, Schmitt's support for the foreign policy of the Axis powers is beyond dispute. While he has a tendency to downplay Japan and Germany's expansionist goals with reference to the principle of living space, Schmitt chiefly directs his critique against the U.S. blending of economic interests and universalist principles, which allowed for economic and political hegemony while prohibiting (Japanese) militarism.

It is essential to recognize that, unlike liberalism's universalist theory, neither the original Monroe Doctrine nor the concept of *Großraum* presents an abstract ideology for Schmitt. As a result, the ideological character of *Großraum*—its potential to serve as a rationale for claims to power—remained hidden from public scrutiny. The concept of delineating territory (*Raumabgrenzungsgedanke*) took on the character of a natural order guaranteeing the (uncoerced) coexistence of peoples. Such naturalism first revealed its potentially aggressive features with the preparatory work to Schmitt's concept of the political from the 1920s and its concretization after 1933. The distinction between friend and enemy as the fundamental definition of the political (not merely a particular political constellation) not only defined the world's expanded political territories as potential political opponents, but also offered the possibility of greater cohesion and integration within a particular *Großraum*. Schmitt hoped that the prohibition on intervention central to the notion of expanded territory would further allow for the coexistence of *Großräume* (expanded territories) unaffected by normatively compelled intervention (moral and just war). But this claim is undermined by the possibility that both the right to self-defense as well the justification and potential expansion of living space implies conflicts that could escalate to a war of extermination.

Großraum and the Monroe Doctrine are closely related in Schmitt's theory, the doctrine specifically serving as the concept's legal justification. This explains not only Schmitt's intensive interest in the U.S. position (an interest he shared with official Nazi foreign policy), but also his interest in the doctrine's interpretation and reception. Schmitt sought above all to uncover the original concept of the doctrine and divorce it from its later history, when the revisionist interpretation of the doctrine around 1900 offered U.S. foreign policy legitimization for expansionist politics.[14] During this later period, the Monroe Doctrine and U.S. interventionism were combined, a combination that Schmitt wished to rebut for political reasons. On the other hand, there's no mistaking that Schmitt saw in the original Monroe Doctrine not only the U.S. retreat from European politics and the prohibiting of European intervention, but also the implicit constitution of expanded political territory under the leadership of the United States. Here Schmitt discovered mandated hegemonic claims on other American nations that were not contained in Monroe's statements from 1823. Monroe's message did not include a regulation on relations between American nations, such as a formal coalition or a restriction on their sovereignty.[15] The fact that unequal relations could later develop between the United States and the Latin American nations did not follow from the doctrine as such. Precisely this point demonstrates that Schmitt misunderstood the purpose of the doctrine, because he was primarily interested in the question of an expanded territorial order. He certainly failed to understand the new ordering of the Americas after they broke their colonial fetters, as demonstrated by the attitude of the United States at the Panama Congress of 1826.[16] When he speaks of a "genuine principal of *Großraum*" (*GRO* 88), Schmitt (willfully) misreads the function of the original Monroe Doctrine— an expanded political territory that could limit the sovereignty of adjacent nations was not the aim of the doctrine. Schmitt's idea of *Großraum* belongs unmistakably to the twentieth century and refers specifically to the political configuration of Europe (and East Asia) around 1940. It is therefore essential to understand Schmitt's concept within the concrete situation informing its emergence, and place it in the context of the Third Reich's own policy of *Großraum*.

In the context of international law, Schmitt accomplished a decisive step with the inception of expanded territory, insofar as he distanced himself from the concept of the nation-state that had informed his work in the 1920s and early 1930s. In place of the state as primary political entity stood the Reich as the political core of a *Großraum*. This suggests that Schmitt's understanding of *Großraum* is related to more than just geographical size. Nor is it simply an economically expanded territory, a notion that already existed in the 1920s. Instead, what Schmitt is after is a qualitative shift, one that should open up a new spatial dimension (more than simply a contrast to a small territory) while presenting a concrete constellation. His conception aims explicitly against the modern territorial state with its abstract structure and its division between private and public spheres. By contrast, the Schmittian *Großraum* emerges as a space that could be filled and structured completely by political authority. With reference to the geographer Friedrich Ratzel, Schmitt spoke of "coming to terms with space (*Raumbewältigung*) as the decisive trait of life" (*GRO* 122). The vitalist element is not insignificant here, as it creates a connection to the concept of self-preservation and self-defense. Schmitt is returning to the concept of Reich as a new form of political authority, tying it to that of expanded territory: "The concept of the *Großraum* serves us well to overcome the monopolistic position of an empty concept of state territory and to raise the Reich to the decisive concept of our legal thinking" (*GRO* 124).

The concept of Reich is the key to Schmitt's political and international/legal thinking in the 1940s; he views the Reich as the political nucleus of the *Großraum* that surrounds it, determining its political structure. As Schmitt defines it: "*Reiche* (empires) in this sense are the leading and bearing powers whose political ideas radiate into a certain *Großraum* and which fundamentally exclude the interventions of spatially alien powers into this *Großraum*" (*GRO* 101). His definition combines two elements: a reference to the superior power position of the state addressed as Reich (its hegemony), and an overarching political idea corresponding to *Großraum*.

However, the content of this idea remained completely indeterminate, its availability apparently more important to Schmitt than its content. Unlike universal ideas and norms, it had the sole function of forming a particular political territory, since the ban on intervention existed not only at the level of political violence but apparently also at the level of worldviews. Every legal and ethical universalism was excluded by a conceptual construct that itself did not subsist without a universal element; namely, the general claim that worldviews themselves possess only a spatially limited meaning. On the meta level, empires (*Reiche)* and their *Großräume* were presented as equals. Accordingly, Schmitt spoke of a "fenced-off co-existence [of *Reiche*] on a sensibly divided Earth" (*GRO* 101). The new international law conceived by Schmitt exhibited a clear imperialistic structure in the context of a pluralism secured by the ban on intervention. In this sense, Schmitt spoke of a "developing effect [in] a new international law" (*GRO* 101).

The colloquial use of the term "Reich" by historians—referring to an historical empire—is inadequate as a legal definition of adjacent political territories. For this reason, Schmitt chose to differentiate his notion of Reich from the concept of the state recognized by international law. The object of his critique was the sovereign state as a supposedly autonomous entity with equal status on the international stage. That the equality assumed by international law is not a de facto given, and more, in actuality relies on inequality (namely the fact that particular state has a different character specifically as a Reich) contains within it the solution to the problem for Schmitt: not to cling to an abstract concept of equality but rather to make existing differences between major powers and lesser powers into the basis of international law. In this way, the normative and factual levels of the argument are brought into unity.

Older European international law (*Völkerrecht*), in which the concept of the state finds its legitimate place, relies, for Schmitt, on a balance of European powers in which the smaller states in the alliance play the role of counterbalance. There is no determinate order, but rather one that is adjusted according to circumstance. This successful international law, according to Schmitt, collapsed under the pressure of the moral verdict against the war of 1914–1918, raising the question: What should stand in its place, if we do not want to pursue the path to a universal global legal order? Schmitt discusses two possibilities: a law based on the concept of the *Volk* (people), and a territorially oriented international law proceeding from a global division of power. It is the undeniable transition from a European to a global perspective that leads Schmitt to the construction of *Reiche* and expanded territories. The plurality of states demanding equal recognition for all sovereign entities, as the argument goes, proves antithetical to the development of a durable and lasting order. More precisely, it is not so much the concept of the state that Schmitt is averse to as the new global configuration in which the old European national order has lost its raison d'être. For this reason, he believes that global *Großräume* should replace nation-states.

If we examine the inner structure of these *Reiche* or their relation to one another (independent of the ban on intervention), much remains open. With regard to Germany's situation, which was undoubtedly central to Schmitt's interests, it remains unclear as to how exactly Schmitt envisioned the relation between the *Deutsche Reich* and adjacent nation-states. From a positive reference to Adolf Hitler, we can in any case ascertain that Schmitt agrees with some of the goals of Nazi foreign policy (*GRO* 99). That Schmitt emphasizes the difference between the weak Weimar Republic and the strong Third Reich as a gain for Germany, lies close to the conception of a strong Reich surrounded by weak and dependent states, together forming a *Großraum*. Because of the ban on intervention, this expanded territory would remain relatively secure, in both a political and economic sense, from the outside world. As is known, Schmitt was opposed to a liberal economic policy reliant on global networking and open markets. The Schmittian conception of a plurality of *Großräume* is specifically directed against the form of economic globalization sought by Britain and the United States. Put differently, the type of globalization occurring in the twentieth century is accepted only in part; namely, insofar as expanded political territories could take the place of nation-states. In this regard, the *Großraum* served, according to Schmitt, a protective function against the intrusion of external powers—even though the cost was dependence on and subordination to the will of a hegemonic Reich. Schmitt explicitly notes (*GRO* 110) that one couldn't conceive of relations between *Großräume* according to the model of international relations offered by existing international law, although he fails to state how these relations are in reality to be conducted concretely. Is this purely a question of power that cannot be addressed in terms of norms?

If it is a question of power, then maintaining peace is precarious, as is the case in European international law, where peace is not preserved through universal norms but rather via a balance of power relations. In the words of Schmitt: "It goes without saying that the coexistence of such sovereign institutions of power proceeds not from a substantially given actual peace, but rather from the continual permissibility of war. This means that the peace here is only 'not war'" (*GRO* 115). Does the global existence of *Großräume* alter this fundamental situation? Can it lead to a substantial peace? The question is not answered by Schmitt in those places where he is frequently preoccupied with the issue of discrimination against Germany following World War I. Perhaps we can read this polemic against the Western powers as an indirect reference to how lasting peace can be achieved; namely, through the abolishment of international/legal discrimination against war, which is to say through the legal recognition of wars between expanded territories defined as enemies in the Schmittian sense. If this supposition is correct, then Schmitt is offering a solution to the question of peace related to old European international law and correspondingly rejecting the idea of universal peace through a prohibition on war. In this regard, such a return to the previous status quo is no longer possible by 1939: As Schmitt maintains, European international law rests on the distinction between European states and overseas colonies. Colonial land holdings were practically a prerequisite for participation in the group of major international powers. Schmitt's concept of the *Großraum* appears to take leave from this constellation. Accordingly, he did not speak out in support of the reclamation of German colonies in Africa. Instead of colonialism, Germany's *Großraum* would materialize through regional expansion, above all in the east.

That Schmitt's reflections rest on the conceptions and goals central also to National Socialist foreign policy has been frequently noted.[17] Likewise, the form of presentation and argumentation in the reprinted and revised study *Völkerrechtliche Großraumordnung* (The *Großraum* Order of International Law) relates to its particular historical situation, its tone substantially determined by the German perspective during the years 1939 to 1941. At the same time, it bears noting that Schmitt does not show explicit interest in the specific aims of the Third Reich's foreign policy. These aims must be considered as a background, a background that remains to be elucidated. What is more, we should recall that neither the concept of *Großraum* nor the idea of a German Monroe Doctrine were foreign to the Third Reich. Hitler referred repeatedly to the Monroe Doctrine to justify his aims, and in particular to refute U.S. and British interests. His eastward expansion policy utilized the Monroe Doctrine to portray Britain and the United States as the true aggressive powers. German foreign policy at the time needed to calculate the probability of the United States intervening in the war under the leadership of Roosevelt, and to consider propagandistic means of strengthening the isolationist tendencies in the United States.

In autumn of 1940, following the occupation of the Netherlands and Belgium to the west, Denmark and Norway to the north, and the defeat of France, the restructuring of Europe posed itself as a concrete task for National Socialist foreign policy. From the beginning, there was no doubt that the Third Reich would expand significantly through the incorporation of formerly Polish, Czech, French, and Belgian territories, in part through immediately executed decisions, in part through plans deferred to the future (namely, in the case of France). These annexations, undertaken on behalf of the German *Volk,* functioned to strengthen Germany's national core, while the remaining territories were to become dependent satellite-states within Germany's *Großraum.* The autonomy of these states would be retained only formally, with important political decisions to be conducted in Berlin. Germany's specific influence on a given territory was to depend on the particular conditions in that territory, at the same time taking into account potential differences between the foreign office, the Wehrmacht, and the SS. In no case was a return to the status quo expected after the war, but rather to differently envisioned forms of affiliation within the Reich.

The plan in the east was essentially different from that for the states in the west and north, where Nazi policy was much more severe and unambiguously dedicated to subjugation.[18] Maintaining Polish and Czech statehood was never under consideration. National Socialist policy regarded the Polish territory in particular as a future German settlement area, part of eastward colonial expansion. The goal was a racially distinct territory that was to be transformed through a systematic "Germanization" policy: the expulsion of foreign ethnic groups and methodical settlement by Germans. "The infamous and fantastic-seeming 'Eastern General Plan' elaborated by the Reich Main Security Office (RSHA) in April 1942 stipulated the resettlement of the entire 'racially undesirable' Polish population to Siberia within a time span of thirty years."[19] It is apparent that Germany's policy in the East was openly and decisively determined by racist political ideas. Speeches by Himmler and Frank in the years 1940–1942 leave no doubt concerning the goal of developing a new "pure" German settlement area east of the Reich. Where this project was to encounter significant resistance owing to great population density, as in the case of the protectorate of Bohemia and Moravia, a systematic policy of assimilation was proposed.

The particularities of National Socialist foreign policy find no echo in Schmitt's discussion of *Großraum*. Nevertheless, they are compatible with Schmitt's conceptions insofar as he merely developed a general blueprint to be filled in various manners. Accordingly, in the fourth edition of *Völkerrechtliche Großraumordnung* (1941), there is no indication that Schmitt wished to distance himself from German foreign policy. However, it must be added that the idea of racial expulsion typical of Hitler and National Socialist policy is not to be found in Schmitt's writings. In this regard, he was closer to the old conservative elites (which he supported until 1932) than to the National Socialists. For German foreign policy in the late 1930s and early 1940s, the development of a German Monroe Doctrine as presented here was part of a strategy dedicated to securing expansionist goals, not the basis of a new German world order. Schmitt, by contrast, discovers in the U.S. doctrine the foundation in international law for a novel global order. His concept is conceived pluralistically, without fundamental regard for concepts such as human dignity, freedom, and equality. To be sure, it cannot be ruled out that these concepts were to be realized in particular expanded territories, but there can be no universal guarantee and even less a claim to applicability in the relations between a Reich and its satellite-states or between adjacent expanded territories. Schmitt's conception of international relations would have opposed the foreign policy of the Nazi regime only if the latter would have declared its claim to world dominion openly and without limitation.

Schmitt's Theory of *Großraum* in the Context of Contemporary Debates

For the Schmitt reception after 1945, particularly on the left, Schmitt's proximity to the Third Reich (as Crown Jurist) has been a complicated and vexing problem to be denied only through suppression (i.e., by minimalizing it, or making a fundamental distinction between the author's culpability as a person and his theory). We are not concerned here with the biographical attribution of guilt or moral discrimination, but the historical and systematic significance of Schmitt's theory of *Großraum*. Its historical proximity to the foreign policy of the Third Reich is difficult to deny, even if it does not theoretically encompass all of the policy's elements. Hitler's plans for the eastern front, calling for the military annihilation of his adversaries and the subsequent resettlement, which is to say extermination, of populations that cannot be assimilated, followed another logic. In short, Schmitt's pluralistic world order and Hitler's conception of total German world domination are not compatible with one another. At the same time, it was possible for a representative of the Third Reich to refer to Schmitt's interpretation of the Monroe Doctrine in the interests of fending off U.S. or British intervention. The strict regionalization of international politics through a generalized ban on intervention by foreign powers was understood only as a formal principal that could be filled with a variety of contents, such as with the ban on intervention in the case of Germany's foreign policy concerning Czechoslovakia and Poland. The claim to an expanded German territory, that Schmitt wholly supported between 1939 and 1941, in this case serves as preparation for an aggressive war.

Irrespective of Schmitt's own intellectual involvement in the foreign policy of the Third Reich, the fundamental theoretical question remains: What advantages does *Großraum* offer international law? Schmitt expected the concept to have a pacifying effect on international relations, in particular to prevent the possibility of total war. In the juxtaposition, taken up by Schmitt, between total wars emerging from the liberal idea of necessary intervention and those based upon regional conflicts between expanded territories, the morally motivated just war stood under the suspicion of becoming total through the escalation of moral claims. Regional wars emerging out of conflicting interests, by contrast, were for Schmitt containable. The truth of Schmitt's thesis depends on whether we accept as logical and inevitable the connection between universalism and total war, as well as limited war within a pluralistic regionalism. This is, however, not the case. Not every war of intervention (as a "just war") escalates into absolute war, just as, conversely, a war between expanded political territories itself has the potential for total escalation. The war between the Third Reich and the Soviet Union, as a war of annihilation planned by Hitler, escalated into total war because the continued existence of both regimes hung in the balance.

The notion that a pluralistic order of expanded territories would be more peaceful than an international community built upon liberal principles rests upon assumptions left unexamined by Schmitt. Among these is the assumption that in political reality, a balance of great powers more effectively guarantees peace than a universal order built upon humanitarian (moralistic) foundations. Another is that moral viewpoints, such as those applicable to the coexistence of individuals, cannot be transposed into international relations. Applying such perspectives, Schmitt explains, leads to greater calamity than their absence. We can therefore assume that Schmitt understood international relations as an amoral complex of rules to be determined exclusively from the perspective of power (national exigency). This appears not to be the case, for if it were, it would be impossible for Schmitt to theoretically differentiate between a "normal war" and a war of annihilation. National aggression undertaken with the goal of annihilating the enemy and eradicating his statehood (Hitler) is a possibility available within the concept of *Großraum*. The fact that Schmitt appeared to exclude this possibility, instead trusting in a balance of great powers, suggests that something other than questions of pure power play a role. But how are we to explain this uncertainty? It appears that Schmitt incorporated ethical considerations in his judgment of international relations, ethical considerations that remain invisible as tacit presuppositions. These include not only a people's claim to a living space and the right to self-defense, but also the belief that value is contained in the actually existing balance of great powers itself. This value would be based on the idea that great powers and their expanded territories find security in such an order—not a durable, but rather a precarious security, nonetheless tolerant of even significant differences between the internal political order of these powers. Discrimination would be disallowed, since a particular form of statehood, such as an authoritarian monarchy or a liberal democracy, could not claim the right to organize the global order according to their own ideas and norms.

Schmitt appears, however, not to have adequately considered the perils and limits of his conception of *Großraum*, possibly because his polemic was chiefly aimed at devaluing liberal universalism. In this regard he exaggerated his own rejection of morality and also the devaluation of humanism as pure ideology. Schmitt's expanded territorial order, which globalizes the old European order of states, cannot solve two problems. First, there are no criteria for regulating claims to global domination, except for the probability that the remaining threatened great powers would unite against the aggressor. Second, the potential conflicts between expanded territories determined by conflicting forms of government contain the danger of humane indifference, since the internal politics of a foreign great power (including the policy between a great power and its satellite-states) would preclude discussions beyond the immediately affected populations and states. In light of the recent historical experience of totalitarian regimes, these blind spots in Schmitt's expanded territorial order are deeply problematic. The attempt, out of a clear and sharp differentiation from the foundational ideas of liberal international law, to conceive of a global order promising greater security, cannot do away with the question of the (radical) abuse of power. The Schmittian thesis that total war is primarily a logical consequence of military interventions based on liberal universalism bypasses the historical reality of the twentieth century, either overlooking or misinterpreting the (complex) causes of the two world wars. Put differently, *Großraum* as the theory of a new global political order cannot exclusively trust in a balance of great powers but rather requires a political ethic if it is to guard against singular claims to world domination as well as totalitarian systems—normative elements that it cannot help but make explicit. The difficulty of such an ethic rests nonetheless in the fact that it cannot depend on universal ideas (like humanistic liberalism) but must take into account and build on the structural and ideological differences between individual expanded territories (*Großräume*). How can we come to an understanding concerning political acts of power in light of the existing differences between political cultures? Schmitt's theory offers us nothing more than hints. The modern European system of states functioned between 1648 and 1914 on the basis of a relatively high level of cultural homogeneity (including the United States as former European colonies). Thus Schmitt makes, among other things, the intrusion of foreign powers that were not part of the European sphere such as Japan and the Ottoman Empire into European concerns responsible for the collapse of European international law.

Notwithstanding the particular concrete circumstances underlying its development as theoretical support for German foreign policy between 1939 and 1941, Schmitt's conception of an order of expanded territories quickly encounters its limits, especially with regards to its faith in a balance of powers. Its implicit assumption that great powers will behave according to similar real-political principles (guided, that is, by necessity) begs the question of whether such behavior can be generalized. Schmitt's theory therefore assumes that political elites, at least, are relatively homogenous. Precisely where Schmitt speaks of global civil war (*Weltbürgerkrieg*) as the specific political configuration of the twentieth century, however, is it clear that such homogeneity cannot be assumed, since global civil war is a situation in which the state of war can no longer be ended according to diplomatic-political rules. For ideological reasons, enmity becomes absolute under the conditions of global civil war. The ideological opposition of the parties involved leads, according to its own logic, to wars of annihilation. In order to end the state of global civil war, a position external to the conflict is required that can relativize the opposition of those involved, just as in the religious conflict of the seventeenth century it was the absolutist state that occupied a neutral position securing peace. Such a position cannot be found within the global civil war itself.

Schmitt's theory of *Großraum* contains no provisions that would override absolute enmity or total war. It attempts to prevent such an occurrence solely through a balance of great powers assumed to behave in the interests of rational self-preservation. Schmitt's conceptual arsenal remains effective only where he discusses the limits of a just war, such as in his discussion of aerial war against civilian populations in which civilians are not only harmed as collateral damage but are expressly the target of the attack in an attempt to annihilate a segment of the population (N 320–21).[20] In this instance, Schmitt can show how an attempt to punish an enemy labeled as criminal can lead to the legitimation of behavior wholly opposed to the concept of morality. It is a case where the demand for justice transforms into its opposite, potentially leading to total war. Nonetheless in *The Nomos of the Earth* Schmitt does not provide an answer to the question what kind of ethics can secure a restriction of war, for the mere abstract negation of the model of just war (in its liberal justification) does not produce an adequate justification for contained war (*gehegter Krieg*) as part of an order of expanded territories. Though it may be probable that under the conditions of a global order of expanded territories, the forms and procedures of international relations would themselves be transformed, it is nonetheless no more plausible that such a structural transformation would lead to a qualitative improvement. The faith in a Monroe Doctrine applicable on a global scale as a concrete territorial order remains an illusion, since the mere prohibition on interventions neither guarantees the legitimacy of an expanded territory's inner structure nor secures stable relations between the principal and dependent powers—at least not without additionally assuming a shared political ethic. Schmitt relinquishes the possibility of elaborating such an ethic in the present, since he sees no chance for a theological justification. The concept of "divine monarchy," which Schmitt once again defended against Erik Peterson in *Political Theology II*, remains for Schmitt, unlike for Peterson, in principal conceivable but inapplicable in the present, since a close relationship between state and Christianity (the Church) assumes, first of all, the globalization of Christianity uncontested by other religions, and second, the monarchy as the sole legitimate form of state. In light of global civil war as Schmitt's present reality, the notion of divine monarchy appears, however, as a utopia reconstructed from the past.[21]

Schmitt's theory of expanded territories and the version of the Monroe Doctrine it endorses are unable to solve the problem of the discrepancy between a mere positing of actual power relations and their justification, unless pure political and militaristic decision is accepted as such legitimation. In this case the further question arises: How is this discrepancy to be filled, or, in other words, how must a political ethic be designed so as to transform a plurality of expanded territories into a meaningful global order, an order, for example, that would be better than a unitary world state?

I would like to distinguish between a dogmatic-normative and a pragmatic-normative approach. Dogmatic safeguarding through basic concepts relies on categories such as justice, relative equality of territory, and protection of citizens, each concretely differentiated when applied to each particular territory. The pragmatic approach would depart from a functional description and interrogate the implicit norms and values of the described configuration. In this procedure we can make room for diverse moral values without being bound to their contradictions. Instead, at this level the leading perspective would be to assess the functional success of the total system, which is to say the existence of a lasting and relatively faultless international order on the global as well as regional level (within a *Großraum*). In this way, boundaries would be set concerning the use of violence by a superior power within its expanded territories, so as not to provoke neighboring powers and lead to intervention. Put differently, consideration for the functioning of the global order, which benefits all of its participants, excludes wars of annihilation between expanded territories as well as between great and dependent powers as long as all participants place more value on the balance of powers/expanded territories than on regional advantages (expansion, subordination of smaller neighbors, etc.).

This approach presupposes a minimal ethic of self-preservation, which assumes and acknowledges the same ethic in political opponents and allies. It is incompatible with the supposition that opponents or neighbors are fundamentally evil and must therefore be attacked (a central argument made by Schmitt). Yet the system as a whole remains unstable under these conditions for two reasons: first, because there can be no compulsory objection to breaking the rules (attempts at world domination are always possible and, in particular circumstances, even attractive), and second, because respect and regard for one's neighbor (within and beyond the *Großraum*) is left to the discretion of each territory. Nothing guarantees that parties will be treated equally—for example, that foreign interests will receive the same recognition as one's own.

The stability of the unstable international relations inherent in a pluralistic order of expanded territories therefore demands additional values that exceed the minimal principal of mutual recognition of self-preservation. These cannot be specifically posited norms, but rather values already implicit in the successful functioning of the system. To these belong the recognition of cultural differences, respect for particular concrete conditions and circumstances as well as respect for those affected by violence, even readiness for international aid where the material distribution of goods is uneven. Conversely, a global order of expanded territories must be ready to address elements that would disrupt its healthy systemic functioning. Great powers that want to expand their position of strength in the interests of global dominance are obviously undesirable. In accordance with the classical concept of balance, breaking the rules will be answered with the threat of economic sanctions or actual diplomatic or military violence against those striving for hegemony in the interests of restoring order. In addition, solidarity between other powers and the attacked is necessary to prevent the annihilation of states or power groups. Still, it must be understood that what is advocated here are not universal norms demanding intervention, but values that protect the weaker state. It would be difficult to find such considerations in Schmitt. The reason for this is presumably the assumption that it suffices to reveal and guard against liberal universalism as a concealed claim to hegemony. Such a critique leaves unanswered, however, the question of precisely how a global politics of expanded territories can be effectively realized.

In this regard, it cannot also be overlooked to what extent Schmitt's own worldview changed between adopting the concept of *Großraum* in the late 1930s and publishing *The Nomos of the Earth* (1950). Out of an affinity with the expansionist policies of the Third Reich, Schmitt's critique of U.S. hegemony would emerge a decade later, to be developed further two generations after that by Schmitt exegetes like William Rasch.[22] For Rasch, Schmitt's late work, not least of all the conception of expanded territories and ban on intervention, contains the essential critique of U.S. hegemonic foreign policy. The upshot of this interpretation is that the policies of the George W. Bush administration can now be read as the culmination of the liberal program.[23] With Schmitt, then, humanism is held responsible for U.S. interventionism. In particular, Habermas and Rawls appear as the liberal theorists of the status quo, which is to say, U.S. hegemony. This interpretation is all the more notable given that Bush advisors such Richard Perle, William Kristol, and Paul Wolfowitz, as well as their predecessors such as Irving Kristol, Norman Peretz, Charles Krauthammer, and Michael Novak, all came from the ranks of neoconservatives who based their position on, among others, Leo Strauss and more indirectly Carl Schmitt.[24]

The decisionist character of George W. Bush's policies has been emphasized many times.[25] Although Rasch has conceded the conservative and counterrevolutionary character of the Schmittian project without reservation,[26] he believes nonetheless that he can resolve two problems with the help of Schmitt's theory: first, he wants to offer evidence for the claim that humanism and liberalism necessarily lead to a politics of exclusion and enmity, and second, he wants to show that a politics recognizing of difference can be developed from Schmitt.[27] In support of the first claim, he refers to the connection between humanism and Christianity; that is, humanism's structural dependence on Christianity, which proceeds from a logic of exclusion (of nonbelievers). But the secularization thesis underestimates, as Blumenberg has shown,[28] humanism's critical distance from Christianity.

The problem of modernity has been how to assess and evaluate various forms of distance (Schmitt's answer is that in the end all that remains in contemporary politics is decision and the preservation of one's own). The Schmittian critique of liberalism remains ambiguous in that it does not adequately differentiate between its alleged logic of exclusion (its Christian heritage) and the application of universal norms, which, according to Schmitt and Rasch, imply the mastery of the weak by the strong. The mixing of interests and moral-political norms, particularly in the case of the United States, is, however, not synonymous with a logic of exclusion in the name of human rights. In the case of Rasch, epistemological and ideological critique remain insufficiently differentiated. That norms can be abused—and in the case of the United States, repeatedly were abused—is not a fundamental objection to normative perspectives. Such objections must instead arise from political-social relations themselves. In this regard, the classification of Habermas and Rawls as affirmative theorists of the status quo leads no further, eluding engagement with a subsequently developed postmetaphysical liberal theory (as was already the case with Schmitt, which resulted in a theoretical caricature of liberalism). It needs to be noted that Habermas was decisively opposed to the Iraq war. Rasch therefore rightly asks: How must a critical engagement with the hegemonic policies of the United States look? The call for a fundamental principal of nonintervention supported by Rasch cannot be the answer, since, as we have seen, such a perspective also allows for the subordination of weaker states within an expanded territory (for Schmitt, a political given). The downside of such politics is the rejection of every responsibility for genocide. Nevertheless, it is undoubtedly crucial to separate the United States' dominant position of power from the protection of human rights (understood as defense from coercion and suffering) and to examine critically its claim to speak on behalf of mankind. But the contribution of Schmitt's theory to this task remains admittedly limited.

3

THE FATE OF EUROPEAN COLONIALISM AND CARL SCHMITT'S NEW WORLD ORDER

Schmitt's theoretical transition from a position that remained rather close to the official conception of German foreign policy during the early 1940s to a still-tentative theory of a new global order based on the concept of *Großraum* (expanded territory) was complex and difficult. The initial alignment of Schmitt's theory with National Socialist (NS) policies based on the shared use of the concept of *Reich*, which Schmitt eagerly picked up, became weaker and was replaced by a European perspective for which the fate of the German Reich became less important. In this process, the Monroe Doctrine, which Schmitt used to defend German expansion during World War II, dropped completely out. Schmitt did not return to the doctrine in his postwar writings, although it would have been a useful tool for a continued critique of U.S. liberalism.

The German use of the Monroe Doctrine remained too close to NS policies to be acceptable in postwar discourses. The concept of *Großraum,* however, which dated to late nineteenth-century political geography, was sufficiently abstract to overcome the ban on NS terminology after 1945. This concept enabled Schmitt to perform a double move: it provided the framework for a rereading of European history, perceived now as a gradually changing constellation of great powers, and it prepared the way for his conception of a pluralistic new world order. The fact that the concept had a different function in Schmitt's work of the late 1930s and early 1940s became invisible after 1945, once Schmitt cut the theoretical link between the concept of *Großraum* and the idea of a new German Reich. His previous interest in German expansion was transformed into the notion of a greater European order built on mutual recognition and a pragmatic understanding of power relations. While Schmitt completely withdrew from German power politics, he continued his critique of liberalism and its universalist propensities, perceived as the ideology of the United States, the new hegemon of the West.

With the publication of *The Nomos of the Earth* in 1950, Schmitt, who had been more or less excluded from the public sphere after 1945, regained national visibility in Germany. In more than one way this work challenged the new mainstream of German political theory. The author pays only scant attention to the politics of the Third Reich and its catastrophic military defeat, and he shows little interest in the restoration of liberal democracy in West Germany, the dominant concern of other political theorists and commentators during the 1950s. Instead, he views liberal democracy as a challenge to—rather than the foundation of—the emerging new world order. Clearly, with his claim that the legitimate *ius publicum Europaeum* was lost, Schmitt established himself as an outlier in the new Federal Republic of Germany, in some respects a voice from the past, bringing back topics of the old German Right and in other respects a forceful proponent of developing an oppositional model of the new global order. While it is safe to say that this model had no major impact on the general political discussion of the early Federal Republic, it was received and discussed by a small group of younger intellectuals, thereby influencing the political discourse of West Germany when these students took over positions of influence. Intellectuals and academics such as Reinhart

Koselleck, Hermann Lübbe, and Odo Marquard would not only revise the understanding of the German past but would also reconsider the definition of modern democracy, without being dogmatic followers of Schmitt's theory.[1]

From the perspective of the German Right, weak as it was in 1950, *The Nomos* reset the discourse on the German past, although German history receives only scant attention. Yet it is precisely the European emphasis of the conception of the past—more specifically, the structure of an older European legal order, the *ius publicum Europeum*—that changes the debate, because it focuses on the common European ground (of which Germany was a part until 1918) rather than the German exception that would become the central concern of the debate among German historians. In fact, one of the significant themes of the study is the harmful revision of the concept of interstate warfare after 1918. For Schmitt, the Treaty of Versailles, with its emphasis on Germany's responsibility for the Great War, was a serious violation of the old European order in which sovereign states had the unquestioned right to declare war, a strictly political decision in which moral considerations played no role. The fact that liberal theory tends to criminalize war and wants to set up international agreements to outlaw war, makes it a dangerous ideology in Schmitt's mind. We have to note that this interpretation stood in apparent opposition to the political agenda of the new regime in West Germany. Here the revival of liberalism (broadly speaking) stood in the service of combating totalitarianism and restoring peaceful democracy.

As the thrust of *The Nomos of the Earth* makes clear, Schmitt had very different ideas about the shape of the new world order than the framers of the new West German constitution (*Grundgesetz*). One unexpected element of this work is its extensive discussion of European colonialism. This discussion primarily refers to the colonies of Spain, Portugal, England, France, and Belgium; the brief colonial history of Germany plays no significant role. In other words, Schmitt does not consider a return to German colonial possessions or present an argument in favor of past German colonialism *tout court*. The stakes are different and higher. The emphasis is placed on the European character of colonialism. Schmitt argues that the acquisition and possession of colonies outside the European space was a defining and essential element of the first global political order. Europe, Schmitt insists, created this first global order through colonial expansion.

While the factual aspect of this argument was possibly not very controversial in 1950, Schmitt's use of the thesis certainly was provocative, since he suggests that this older European order had not only been very successful in its own time but that it was also politically superior to the present order, which was the result of the changes that had occurred after 1918. The older European order still deserves recognition, Schmitt maintains, and should be considered in any discussion about the future world order. Schmitt's approach to the colonial question foregrounds the legal aspect, giving much less attention to the economic side. Moreover, he underscores the political significance of the colonial enterprise for the European states at the expense of its impact on the indigenous populations. There is no mention of slavery, for instance. Even in the context of the present complex and diverse discourse on colonialism Schmitt remains an outlier. In certain respects, he stays very close to a traditional defense of colonial expansion, in others his peculiar legal focus makes him insensitive to major issues of the more recent discussion.

European Colonialism Reconsidered

What makes the assessment of Schmitt's position more difficult today than it was seventy years ago is the shifting understanding of the historical record, which was contested from the very beginning. As Francis Brooks points out, "From the earliest years there have been those who have denounced as 'the destruction of the Indies' what Spaniards did. Fray Antonio de Montesinos in his famous sermon of Advent 1511 is the first one of whom we have record. Fray Bartolome de Las Casas gave the genre definite form."[2] A so-called white legend of legitimate occupation and submission of indigenous peoples was used from the very beginning to justify the historical facts against a "black legend" that underscored destruction and reckless exploitation. On both sides, however, it was assumed that that the process of colonization was inevitable because of the material and intellectual superiority of the European invaders. The argument could be formulated in religious and moral terms (mostly in the sixteenth and seventeenth centuries) or in technological and biological terms (in the eighteenth and nineteenth centuries) without breaking up the basic dichotomy between conquerors and conquered. In either case the outcome was considered as logical and inevitable. The overall historical process confirmed the actions of the Europeans.

This assumed necessity of the outcome is precisely what Carl Schmitt uses to construct the form and evolution of the *ius publicum Europaeum*. The justification of the legal order depends on the inevitability of European expansion. Put differently, the expansion is not a marginal phenomenon but a central feature of the postmedieval European order. Schmitt's own understanding of this process after 1945 places him squarely within the parameter of the "white legend" that maintains the cultural and, specifically, the religious superiority of the Spanish Conquista.[3] Had he revised his study in the 1960s or 1970s and made use of new revisionist historiography on colonialism—for instance of the work of William McNeill or Carlo Cipolla[4]—he could have argued that the outcome of the historical process was inevitable. Revisionist historiography, which began in the 1960s and dominated the field until the 1990s (for instance Jared Diamond, 1998),[5] attacked the "white legend" by pointing to the material side of the colonial enterprise, but it did not challenge the fundamental logic of the process. The historians undermined the self-understanding of the colonizers by documenting the brutality of the actual occupation without making room for the real complexity of the encounter between colonizers and colonized populations. In short, Schmitt could have adopted the criticism of the revisionist without losing his basic argument that it was the innate superiority of the Europeans which led to colonial expansion and thereby to the legitimizing emergence of the *ius publicum Europaeum*. In one respect, however, the adoption of the gun-and-germs thesis would have changed Schmitt's position significantly: The theological and moral defense of colonialism would have been much more difficult.

With the second stage of revisionist colonial historiography, starting in the 1990s, this basic dichotomy begins to break up, creating space for a more complex and nuanced narrative, which portrays colonial subjects as having agency, rather than as inferior beings either to be discriminated against or admired for their endurance.[6] In this context Schmitt's emphasis on the original *Landnahme* (actual occupation of the land) by the Europeans, as the decisive moment of the colonial experience with lasting legal consequences, would lose much of its persuasive power. From the very beginning, subaltern resistance must be accounted for as well, including the global liberation movements after World War II.[7]

The more radical second phase of revisionist colonial historiography challenges the European model at a deeper level by suggesting that looking at the world in the late fifteenth century would not disclose apparent European superiority over the rest of the world.[8] As Francis Brooks argues, "Throughout the world of the fifteenth century we can identify eight exploring cultures: the Polynesians, Japan, China, India, Islam, Latin Christendom, the Aztecs, and the Incas. Each of them was a contender for the role of world unifier."[9] Therefore expansion becomes a question of probability and specific circumstances, an open process in which a new European order evolves between 1500 and 1900. While Eurocentrism (which is essential for Schmitt's approach to colonialism) cannot be denied at the factual level, it loses its preordained validity. In other words, the global order of the twentieth century does not have to be seen necessarily through European lenses as the logical result of an inevitable historical process. By challenging the necessity of European colonialism, the liberation movements after World War II appear in a different light. They become as much part of the historical process as the occupation and domination by the European powers, a question of circumstances, specific conditions, and available intellectual as well as material resources. One of the crucial changes is that European colonial rule loses its self-evident nature, which had been inscribed by law and social practices, increasingly showing the ideological character of the system. Still, the legitimacy of the colonial order had to be challenged, and the elements of the ideology had to be scrutinized and exposed. For this reason the intellectual confrontation with this order was an essential part of the struggle.[10]

The Case of Algeria—Fanon vs. Schmitt

In the heated postwar discussion Algeria played a prominent role on both sides. It was not only Frantz Fanon who used Algeria as his prime example to demonstrate the need for political emancipation but also Carl Schmitt who defended the colonial order by supporting the resistance of the French colonial military to liberation. The case of Algeria is instructive because it was, in more than one respect, a special case.

Its geographical proximity to France as well as the fact that it was legally a part of France set Algeria aside from other French possessions in Africa.[11] Moreover, it was a settler colony with more than a million of white settlers (the *Pieds-Noirs*), who considered Algeria their homeland. For the majority of the indigenous population, the French settlers remained colonial invaders. Yet the increasing desire after World War II to remove the *Pieds-Noirs* from Algeria met the determined resistance not only of the settlers but also of the French Army, which was determined to defend French Algeria at any cost, since the higher ranks of the army were convinced that French Indo-China had been lost because of the weakness and the corruption of the government in Paris. The acceleration of hostilities in 1957, when the paratroopers of General Jacques Émile Massu took over, hardened the enmity on both sides. "Massu effectively gave both groups what they wanted. Combining military and police powers, he masterminded a massive operation in which the pursuit of relevant facts through the internment, torture and sometimes murder of suspects was a necessary element."[12] While this strategy was initially successful, it only led to the absolute determination of both sides to win the struggle at any cost in the long run. Most importantly, it did not defeat the liberation movement, the *Front de Libération Nationale* (FLN). On the French side, it raised the larger question as to whether colonies were still useful in the context of a modern advanced industrial society, a question that neither the settlers nor the army were interested in answering. For this reason, the liberation movement had to develop its own ideology.[13]

It was Frantz Fanon, although not a native of Algeria, who emphatically supported the struggle against the French colonial administration through his writings. He joined the revolutionary organization that carried out the protracted partisan war against the French Army. Unlike Gandhi in India, Fanon argued in favor of violence when and where the colonizers were unwilling to grant freedom and independence to the colonized people. In this configuration, he is the archetypical opponent of Schmitt's more positive evaluation of French colonialism in Algeria in his late work. In *Theory of the Partisan*, Schmitt takes the side of General Raoul Salan, one of the ardent defenders of a French Algeria, at a time when even a national hero and conservative statesman like Charles de Gaulle had decided to support the liberation of Algeria. This posture is remarkable, since Schmitt had been an outspoken critic of Western colonialism in the 1930s, which he viewed as part of Western imperialism. In particular, he had criticized the United States and England for their neocolonial efforts motivated by economic expansion.[14]

Schmitt's early critique (1925–1933) of Western colonialism has to be seen in the context of a nationalist German resistance to foreign interventions. Germany, he writes, is exposed to a treatment by the Western powers that reminds him of the role assigned to colonies or protectorates. More importantly, Schmitt recognizes a new form of domination that was unknown to the older international law. As he argues in his essay on the status of the Rhineland in 1925:

> It characterizes [this new situation] that a legal form of domination has emerged, which consists of combining a right to occupy with a right to intervene. The right [of another state] to intervene has the purpose that the intervening state decides about certain undefined concepts that are nonetheless essential for the political existence of the other state, such as protection of foreign interests, protection of independence, public order and security, and the observance of international treaties.[15]

The point of Schmitt's remarks is a broader shift in the understanding of international relations that also touches on the development of the colonial system after World War I. England and France, Schmitt points out, did not simply annex the former Turkish possessions and German colonies. Instead, they created a system of mandates and protectorates that redefined the form of domination. While this new model seems to acknowledge the increasing striving for independence of the indigenous population, it covers the moment of actual submission by way of abstract legal agreements. In 1925, Schmitt suspects that there are two main reasons why the old colonial powers chose this path: the first has to do with migration (the colonial subjects do not gain citizenship), while the second is related to economic questions (the new masters do not pick up the debts and financial obligations of the previous master). Whether Schmitt's assessment was correct is of less importance here than the more general thesis: The result of the new international model is that terms such as "sovereignty," "freedom," and "self-determination" have lost their traditional meaning. The new model undermines the actual power of the controlled state. What Schmitt does not explicitly say but what is part of his broader argument, is that the distinction between colonies and mandates has become vague and uncertain.

These observations lead Schmitt to a broader reassessment of international relations after the war. The crucial insight is that the older system of colonial empires has lost its usefulness because of new forms of supremacy over other countries that can work without the typical institutions of colonial rule. This means that the concept of empire is not tied to the acquisition of colonies. In particular, by analyzing U.S. instances of informal domination, Schmitt comes to the conclusion that contemporary imperialism is in a process of transformation. His response to this process is conflicted. As long as he views Germany as a dependent state without full sovereignty, he is critical. Once he thinks of Germany, in the later 1930s, as a new empire (*Großraum*), he discovers political opportunities that throw a different light on the model. He begins to see the advantages of the U.S. position defined by the 1823 Monroe Doctrine. In this context, the answer to the colonial question appears to need revising as well. Schmitt's reversal becomes apparent in *The Nomos of the Earth* when he openly defends European colonial expansion in the early modern age and dismisses opposition to colonialism as anti-European ideology, without offering a more sustained argument for his assessment. It is likely that the liberal critique of colonialism offended his sense of historical fairness, which is part of his own defense of Spanish colonialism in the Americas. With respect to Schmitt's evaluation of the Algerian conflict, there is no proof that he was familiar with Frantz Fanon's writings. Had he included Fanon's arguments in his discussion, they would have supported the position he wanted to develop in *Theory of the Partisan;* namely, the absolute character of the new colonial warfare.

Although Fanon supported violent resistance to the colonial oppressors, the military argument is not at the center of his writings. Fanon's assessment of the situation in Algeria during the 1950s begins with the permanent traumatic damage done to the colonized people by the colonizers, whether they are aware of it or not. The colonized subject remains alienated from his or her own country. The continual pressure to conform to the ideas and practices of the colonizers leads either to complete retreat and silence or to depression over the loss of their native ground. As a psychiatrist (in the service of the French government), Fanon is particularly sensitive to the mental and emotional aspect of the suffering and deformation. Still, his understanding of resistance is not limited to this element, and he upholds a number of normative concepts that define the political struggle. This becomes particularly clear when he addresses the French attempts to defuse the tension by offering a compromise that would leave the colonial structure in place but grant more political participation to indigenous elites and assure existing minorities (who might be afraid of the Muslim population) of French protection. Against these two strategies Fanon posits the need for human autonomy and freedom (with no scaling of privileges), political self-determination (i.e., the removal of the colonial system), and equality vis-à-vis the colonizer. Neither economic nor cultural advantages (better education) can persuade Fanon of the benefits of colonial rule for the colonized population. Fanon does not compromise on the fundamental points. As he notes: "The real people, the men and the women, the children and the old people in the colonized country, take it for granted that existing, in the biological sense of the word, and existing as a sovereign people are synonymous. The only possible issue, the sole way of salvation for the people is to react as energetically as it can to the genocide campaign being conducted against it. The reaction is becoming progressively more absolute."[16] What makes Fanon a radical is his determination not to tolerate coexistence between Algerians and Frenchmen. "Every Frenchman in Algeria oppresses, despises, dominates. . . . Every Frenchman in Algeria is at the present time an enemy soldier. So long as Algeria is not independent, this logical consequence must be accepted."[17] For Schmitt this position would align Fanon with Lenin and Mao, especially in view of Fanon's repeated emphasis on the importance of local traditions as necessary resources in the struggle against colonial oppression.[18]

Fanon's firm commitment to the Algerian revolution demonstrates the sharp demarcation between the goals of the liberation movement and the implacability of the European powers during the 1950s. In this divide, Schmitt, who had been a critic of the colonial system in the 1930s, unexpectedly becomes a defender of the old colonial order, primarily in *The Nomos of the Earth* and to a lesser extent in *Theory of the Partisan*. This raises fundamental questions, not only about the interpretation of the *ius publicum Europaeum* but also, and more importantly, about his concept of the new global order—its spatial conception as well as its definition of political power relations. It is precisely Schmitt's emphatic defense of the older Eurocentric global order—which unfortunately for Schmitt, came to an end in 1914—that forces him to confront colonialism as a vital part of this order.

Schmitt's Position in *The Nomos*

Considering that *The Nomos of the Earth* was written partly before 1945 and finally published in 1950, Schmitt's relatively open defense of European colonialism comes as a surprise. He could have employed literary strategies available to keep this problematic part of European history in the margins; for instance, he might have moved the beginning of the new political order in Europe to a later date (for instance, 1648) or underscored the centrality of the balance of power among the European states. By openly pointing to the importance of colonies, especially in the Americas, Schmitt stresses the global character of the new order, in which Europe, or at least part of Europe, serves as the new center of the world. Schmitt's defense is especially remarkable in that it coincides with a broad and ultimately successful anticolonial emancipation movement in South Asia, Africa, and Southeast Asia. Schmitt, however, shows little interest in these movements, and when he addresses their struggle, as he does in the case of Algeria in 1963, he is not sympathetic to their goals.[19] In fact, he is more sensitive to the decline of the old European order than to the formation of the new global order in which the centrality of Europe is challenged. Still, by historicizing his argument he can avoid a clear and direct confrontation with the contemporary critique of the legitimacy of remaining European colonialism. Acknowledging the shifting historical ground of the debate allows him to keep his distance from the conflicted contemporary discourse on colonialism.

Schmitt's way of positioning himself in the debate is, I believe, largely due to his understanding of interstate war among European countries between 1500 and 1914. He is less interested in the acquisition and development of colonies per se than in the military and legal consequences of colonial occupation for relations among the European powers, specifically the nature of warfare taking place in Europe and of the wars that these powers carried out "beyond the line"—outside European borders. Differently put, Schmitt wants to explain the striking difference between European and colonial wars. While the European war is defined as *gehegt* (contained), colonial wars do not follow the same rules. Colonial wars never lost the more radical character of older warfare in which the stakes are higher for both sides. It is not accidental therefore that Schmitt, in *Theory of the Partisan*, observes the most serious challenge to contained warfare in the struggle of the liberation movements of the mid-twentieth century, for instance in China, Vietnam, and North

Africa. For Schmitt, it is the challenge of radical partisan warfare that now haunts (unfairly, he believes) the European colonial powers.

The drawn-out demise of classic colonialism, however, does not undermine Schmitt's conviction that the European occupation of land, considered as empty of political subjects and therefore free, was ultimately justified and reasonable. He spends considerable energy demonstrating that the defense of the "Indies" by the theologian and legal scholar, Francesco Vitoria (1483–1546), did not signal Vitoria's disapproval of colonial occupation in principle. Instead, according to Schmitt, Vitoria's critique of the inhumane treatment of the Indians should be seen as a separate issue, dealing with the military approach to the encounter between Spaniards and indigenous peoples. Central to his argument, Schmitt tells us, stands the assertion of the human qualities of the Indians. While Vitoria insists on their equality in terms of their humanity, despite being pagans, he allows for colonial occupation based on specific titles grounded in Christian theology. Schmitt underscores Vitoria's view that colonial rule not be derived from the supposed inferiority or inhumanity of the Indians; rather, it is based, as Schmitt (following Vitoria) stresses, on the missionary obligation of the Church.[20]

In short, Schmitt is not in disagreement with Vitoria's argument. Rather, he reserves his scorn for humanism and the Enlightenment, especially its distinction between the human and the subhuman, a distinction that allows (if not actively encourages) colonial occupation and oppression. For Schmitt, Vitoria's position by contrast remains defensible even today because it refuses to make a fundamental distinction between Christians and non-Christians in moral terms. This defense remains silent about the difference in political terms: It does not favor emancipation.

Nonetheless, Schmitt strongly opposes a view that sees Vitoria as a precursor of modern anticolonialism. To insist on this affinity is, Schmitt tells us, a misunderstanding: "Yet, it would be a gross misinterpretation to say that Vitoria had claimed that the great Spanish *conquista* was unjust, although this false assumption certainly is widespread."[21] Instead, Schmitt highlights the positive results of Spanish conquest—as seen through the eyes of the Spanish theologian. What is most important in this passage, however, is the gentle shift from Vitoria's point of view to Schmitt's. In the context of Christian missionary work, colonial occupation of "open" lands (i.e., those not occupied by Christians) becomes justified. Of course, this type of historical legitimization becomes problematic once the conquering state is no longer conceived of as Christian but as a modern secular state, in the wake of Hobbes's theory of the state, and a different set of arguments is needed to justify colonial expansion. Schmitt is aware of this change, although he does not foreground this moment. While he opposes a humanistic discourse that justifies colonial occupation based on different levels of civilization, Schmitt appears to be satisfied with the idea that "discovery" (*Entdeckung*) of a territory legitimizes occupation.

Once the argument that colonial conquest is part of a just Christian war against those who blocked missionary work was lost, the entire colonial enterprise, so central to the expansion of European state power, had to be reframed. As Schmitt concedes, this was ultimately less persuasive than the European colonial powers had expected. Now colonial possessions had to be evaluated in the context of the new international law (*Völkerrecht*), the *ius inter gentes* in which the consideration of religion as an institution had been eliminated (because of the confessional split) or at least moved to the margins. Therefore, Schmitt argues, "the struggle for the landappropriation of the New World and for land still free and outside Europe now became a struggle between European power complexes, which, in this specific sense, are 'states.'"[22]

In his reconstruction of the colonial discourse within the modern *ius inter gentes*, Schmitt is far less committed to the argument presented by theorists such as Hugo Grotius and Samuel von Pufendorf, because they neglect, as Schmitt reminds us, to distinguish clearly between European and non-European spaces and fail to understand the specific character of colonial space. "By contrast, the state jurist no longer could get close to the central question—the common land-appropriation of non-European territory—despite the wars fought among these powers."[23] Schmitt contends that while Grotius and Pufendorf recognize the concept of an original acquisition of land (*originäre Landnahme*), they misunderstand the precise legal and subsequently political nature of this act because they see it through the lens of Roman private law. In short, Schmitt criticizes modern international law because it misreads and misrepresents the conceptual basis of colonial expansion.

But this lack of conceptual coherence ultimately applies to Schmitt himself. His attempt to historicize the legitimization of colonial conquest by sharply distinguishing the older Christian approach to occupation from the later secular state-centered version also relativizes the justification for the European colonial enterprise. By shying away from an explicitly normative argument that contains a universal defense of colonialism, he presents an open flank to those who argue that the historical development has demonstrated the politically destructive quality of contemporary colonialism. For this reason, Schmitt is forced to naturalize European colonialism as an existing and therefore legitimate institution, treating any criticism of this practice as no more than anti-European ideology. Schmitt's defense of colonial appropriation uses the actual practice of the *ius publicum Europeum* as proof of the lawfulness of colonial occupation and possession.[24] Accordingly, an attack on colonialism is an attack on the very existence of European international law. But Schmitt seems to recognize that this argument could undermine the merit and advantage of European law, if we take the critique of colonialism as a destructive and oppressive practice seriously. Possibly for this reason Schmitt develops a different and more powerful argument in defense of colonialism: "World History is a history of progress in the means and methods of appropriation."[25] By insisting on a greater law of world history, colonial occupation becomes simply part of this grand process and loses its odium of which Schmitt is very much aware.

Schmitt's Defense of Contemporary Colonialism

Although the colonial liberation movement after World War II, beginning with India in 1947, left deep imprints on European history, politically as well as economically, Schmitt's *The Nomos of the Earth* maintains a noticeable distance from these events and their subsequent discussion by public commentators and political scientists.

Gandhi is not mentioned once in this study, perhaps because the methods of his struggle for India's autonomy does not fit Schmitt's frame. In *The Theory of the Partisan,* we might expect to find references to Frantz Fanon's writings in the discussion of Algerian resistance to French occupation. But Schmitt focuses almost exclusively on the conflict between General Salan, the leader of the French Army putsch in Algeria against the government of Charles de Gaulle, who had decided to grant independence to the colony; the struggle of the Algerian liberation movement serves merely as a background. What interests Schmitt is the threat of civil war between army and civil government, rather than the confrontation between the French Army and the Algerian resistance movement. The question as to whether the Algerian partisans have the right to attack French institutions and officials, not to mention civilians, is not posed.

The fate of Salan as the "tragic" defender of French colonialism, who is forced to take up arms against the legitimate government, is at the center of Schmitt's discussion, a perspective that amounts to an indirect defense of colonialism on Schmitt's part. Similarly, in the discussion of the French occupation of Indochina, Schmitt focuses his attention on Ho Chi Minh's subversive warfare, particularly its military as well as psychological strategies, which the French Army could not effectively counter and control. Partisan warfare in the service of a revolution is for Schmitt both fascinating and terrifying at the same time. This becomes most apparent in the section on Mao's war in China, since Mao succeeds because he remains in close contact with the land and the people he means to liberate. Mao is, in Schmitt's language, *tellurisch* (tellurian, or close to the ground). Schmitt's assessment shows clear respect for Mao's historical achievement, which is also true, though to a lesser degree, for Ho Chi Minh. Ultimately, however, Schmitt's sympathies lie with the European defenders of colonial possessions.

But there is more than sympathy. Looking at the colonial liberation movements from the perspective of warfare, Schmitt articulates his objections to the nature of partisan warfare. He correctly observes that these new wars were not compatible with traditional interstate wars. They had a tendency to radicalize and turn into absolute wars—wars in which a mutually agreed on peace settlement was no longer possible. In this critique, however, he is inconsistent in two ways. First, in his discussion of the Prussian general and military theorist, Carl von Clausewitz, and anti-French resistance in Prussia between 1806 and 1813, Schmitt sides not with Napoleon, who had defeated Prussia and therefore controlled their land, but rather with Clausewitz, whose revolutionary ideas he underscores. Second, in *The Nomos* he emphasizes without reservations that colonial wars were in principle exempt from the rules and conventions of European interstate war. This would, by extension, also apply to wars of independence. Liberation movements, when they could not succeed peacefully, made use of this exception for their own purposes. Still, once they had succeeded, as in the case of China and Vietnam, they reverted to building regular armies that would respect conventional rules of warfare. But Schmitt, even as late as 1963, does not fully acknowledge that the anti-European viewpoint of liberation movements was more than an anti-European ideology, mostly because there is no place in his argument for the suffering of suppressed populations.[26] To some extent, the notion that the pre-1914 order was for Schmitt primarily a spatial global order deemphasizes the human aspect of the relationship between colonists and colonized.

Colonies and the New World Order

It would be inaccurate to argue that Schmitt did not notice the decline and slow fall of European colonialism, but it is never quite clear whether he recognized the development in theoretical terms. As much as the decline of the *ius publicum Europaeum* and the gradual loss of European colonialism coincide, there is no sustained acknowledgement of a general postcolonial era in his vision of a new world order. The postwar divide between the United States and the Soviet Union was, in Schmitt's view, a highly problematic development that might lead to total destruction. Already in 1941, he had outlined a very different schema of a good world order, in which Germany would (finally) find its deserved place. His concept of *Großraum* is the basis for a pluralistic world order that relies on the balance among a small number of competing powers, each of them more than a nation-state but less than a single world state. In this vision, the notion of a hegemonic power within a specific space (*Raum*) plays a significant role, but there is no mention of colonies.[27] The new *Großraumordnung* is clearly still, spatially, a multipolar concept, a mix of greater powers and dependent smaller and marginal states. The United States and its hegemonic position on the American continent serve as a model for this *Ordnung*. Referring specifically to the Monroe Doctrine of 1823, which forbade the intervention of the European powers in the political affairs of the Americas, Schmitt envisions a new relationship between center and periphery, between hegemonic power and satellite states of different strength and importance. The new world order depends on the existence of a small number of greater powers that create and maintain order in their sphere of influence.[28]

The crucial question for Schmitt, then, is this: How will the post-European world order be structured? In a 1955 essay, he discusses three possibilities. First, the rapid development of military technologies following World War II could ultimately result in a single world state. Second, the old European order might be modified and then extended into the future, cementing the division between sea powers and land powers, which Schmitt had already discussed in *Land und Meer* (1942). In this vision, the United States would take over the role of England as the dominating sea power. Finally, the "third possibility also is based on the concept of balance, but not one sustained and controlled by a hegemonic combination of sea and air power. A combination of several independent *Großräume* or blocs would constitute a balance, and thereby could precipitate a new order of the Earth."[29] Schmitt calls this the most rational solution without (at least here) endorsing it as his favorite, though he had proposed precisely the same vision in 1941.[30] In neither iteration does he discuss the fate of the former colonies, however.

As early as 1932, Schmitt argued that advanced modern states like the United States no longer depended on colonies, in the traditional sense, to demonstrate their expanded power and influence. Instead, modern imperialism developed new models for constituting and cementing political domination. Formal acquisition (*Landnahme*) and occupation were no longer required to establish supremacy. In legal terms, dependent states are sovereign nations and therefore of equal rank with the hegemon. In reality, however, formal sovereign status is largely meaningless because the imperial hegemon creates new means of control, either through economic influence (including financial instruments) or through political influence (frequently articulated through bilateral international agreements). These contractual arrangements give the imperial power the formal legal tools to intervene in the affairs of the dependent satellite state. In short, according to Schmitt, a modern imperial power is defined by its lack of traditional colonies. It can in this way take a strong anticolonial position, using universal liberal arguments against colonial oppression, while maintaining a tight system of interventions—economic, political, and ideological. The United States has, he notes, "expanded the system of intervention agreements (*Interventionsverträge*), especially to the Central American states, to Cuba, Haiti, San Domingo, Panama, Nicaragua, etc. These states are connected with the United Stated through special kinds of agreements and find themselves in a position of submission, yet officially they remain 'sovereign' states."[31]

To prove his point, Schmitt uses the example of Cuba's precarious status vis-à-vis the country that supported its independence from Spain in ideological as well as military terms. The freedom that Cuba finally achieved in 1898 did not result in political or economic autonomy. Instead, the new republic found itself in the role of a junior partner of the United States, still in need of assistance and protection. As Schmitt explains, this is a pathway for the imperial power to exert a controlling influence, including military occupation, over a satellite state should it decide that the political and economic status quo is in danger—in the case of Cuba, passages in the new constitution that explicitly defined the U.S. right of intervention. In this way, Schmitt shows, modern imperialism presents the impression of a new world order in which all participating states seem to be free and equal, while in reality their status is hierarchical.

In the 1930s, Schmitt uses this argument to demonstrate the negative consequences of contemporary imperialism. During the

1950s and 1960s, however, the same arguments have a rather different function when the role of the United States in the Americas becomes the model for a new world order, but only if properly interpreted. In his 1941 discussion of *Großraum*, Schmitt distinguishes between the offensive and the defensive interpretation of the Monroe Doctrine.[32] While he rejects the expansionist use of the doctrine, which encouraged U.S. intervention in European affairs, he supports the defensive understanding that merely means to keep foreign powers outside the U.S. sphere of influence. Similarly, after World War II, the United States is recognized as a major global power and is given a legitimate sphere of influence in its rivalry with the Soviet Union. In sum, the Monroe Doctrine, understood correctly, offers the best model for establishing a stable world order built on the balance of great powers.

And although colonial possessions are not explicitly included in Schmitt's third vision for a post-European order, the *Großraumordnung*, it allows for both the extended dependence of newly independent colonies on their colonizers and the rise of a former colony, India for example, to the status of a *Großraum*.[33] (The rise of the United States to the level of a global superpower would be the most striking example of such a transformation.) But this evolution hardly guaranteed an alteration in the oppressed status of the former colony's indigenous population.

Carl Schmitt and the Contemporary Debate about International Relations

There is no consensus about Schmitt's place in present international relations debates. Some interpreters have read him as a fierce critic of liberalism and, by extension, of the West's tendency to impose its rules and values on the rest of the world. In this reading Schmitt is a necessary critic of U.S. imperialism. Other scholars have interpreted him as a conservative thinker with an unfortunate leaning toward the extremist positions of the Right and Far Right. In this reading, Schmitt is a brilliant but dangerous mind whose work should be read with suspicion because his theories undermine a fair and just world order. Schmitt's interpretation of European colonialism, however, does clarify the utility of his thought in current discourse.

Schmitt's approach is complex and not without contradictions and internal tensions. Moreover, his position evolved between the 1920s and the 1960s. While his early approach was marked by a decidedly nationalist and specifically German perspective, his postwar work shifted toward a European point of view. Furthermore, the later Schmitt is considerably more sympathetic to European colonialism than his early writings. What caused this shift? Was Schmitt redefining himself after the war as a European conservative instead of a radical German nationalist? I believe that it was a broader reassessment of international relations that influenced his change of perspective. A comparison with the writings of Niall Ferguson and Michael Ignatieff may help us better understand and evaluate Schmitt's development.

Such a comparison may at first seem unproductive because these theorists favor achieving a stable world order through a solution that Schmitt rejects: a benevolent U.S. empire as the guardian of international peace.[34] Ferguson is quite explicit in defending this controversial position: "Central to my argument is that there was such a thing as liberal imperialism and that on balance it was a good thing."[35] Ferguson understands the United States as a legitimate successor to the British Empire, as an indispensable great power that has the political (democratic), economic (capitalist), and ideological (liberal) resources to bring peace to a very conflicted world. While he does not idealize the history of the British Empire or the development of the United States as an imperial power,[36] he is convinced that the presence of a dominating single power is more beneficial than a plurality of competing nation-states too weak to create and maintain a stable global order. Of course, Schmitt would sharply disagree with this proposition, since the interventions of the hegemonic superpower would necessarily, he believes, destabilize the global balance of power.

Closer scrutiny, however, uncovers deeper similarities and affinities. Ferguson and Schmitt agree that, in the final analysis, a lasting world order depends on superior state power. Ferguson can acknowledge Schmitt's objections to political liberalism without yielding his position, since he is aware of the tension between the universalism of liberal theory and the concept of imperialism, which downplays universal norms. Ferguson invokes Harvard economist David S. Landes's expectations of an ideal "growth-and-development" government in order to demonstrate the need for a single great power: (1) secure rights of private property, (2) secure rights of personal liberty, (3) enforce the right of contract, (4) provide stable government, (5) provide responsive government, (6) provide honest government, and (7) provide efficient government (low taxes).[37] Three of these demands articulate fundamental beliefs of liberal theory, but the other four focus on the state and its use of power. Schmitt would have at least revised the order of these demands and most likely modified the first three points, but there is common ground where the centrality of state power is concerned.

Ferguson is also in full agreement with Schmitt on the complex but ultimately successful history of European colonialism. He explicitly describes decolonization as a failure: "In short, the experiment with political independence, especially in Africa, has been a disaster for most poor countries. Life expectancy in Africa has been declining and now stands at just forty-seven years."[38] Using primarily economic data, Ferguson seeks to demonstrate that for the majority of former colonies, the outcome of independence was a decrease in wealth, life expectancy, and security. This argument leads Ferguson to a renewed embrace of empire. While Schmitt would support this critique, especially the notion that decolonization results in international destabilization, he would reject Ferguson's conclusion that a U.S. empire is needed to guarantee world peace, favoring instead a plurality of greater powers with spheres of influence. Nonetheless, both take war into consideration as an intrinsic part of the new world order. Where Ferguson thinks in terms of necessary (U.S.) interventions in order to control and subdue rogue states, Schmitt thinks in terms of inevitable but legitimate wars between autonomous imperial powers when they disagree on questions of national interest.

In the end, the differences are less dramatic than might be expected. There are affinities and overlapping considerations that are hidden in Schmitt's critique of liberal empires. Schmitt is, no less than Ferguson and Michael Ignatieff, a proponent of empire, although not of a single world state. His concept replicates the older European order on a larger scale. Its elements are autonomous great powers separated by spheres of influence. The problem is that Schmitt's construct does not pay much attention to global economic interdependence, a factor central to Ferguson's argument. Global capitalism can no longer be conceived as a spatial structure, yet Schmitt remains invested in an earlier idea of largely spatial divisions. This makes it more difficult for him to come to terms with the structure of the emerging U.S. empire, which does not depend on colonies and can even exhibit a strong anticolonial position (as in the case of the administration of Franklin Roosevelt).[39] As Ferguson underlines, the U.S. empire, as it developed after World War II, dominates primarily through its economic power, which in turn is articulated through international institutions and agreements based on liberal concepts. For Schmitt, liberal theory itself is a threat to the imperial hegemony he supports when its norms and values are used by anticolonial liberation movements. Liberal values, especially when radicalized by colonized peoples, are dangerous to imperial power and should therefore be confronted and defeated.

While this constellation has no place in Ferguson's concept of empire, it is prominent in Michael Ignatieff's approach. Ignatieff shares with Schmitt the sense of a fundamental threat to global stability. For him, the defense of the United States is no longer possible exclusively in terms of its own liberal values. U.S. leaders, he tells us, find themselves in a situation that leaves them with difficult and problematic choices. Under attack from radical terrorist groups, the country must use defensive measures that are not compatible with its liberal credo. In the light of rising global chaos, especially after 9/11, Ignatieff reconsiders his commitments to humanism and an ethics of empathy. Now, he believes, state power, including military intervention, is needed to cope with the new conditions. While strongly asserting the liberal past of the United States, Ignatieff concedes the need for global supervision. He thinks of the United States as "an empire lite, a global hegemony whose grace notes are free market, human rights, and democracy, enforced by the most awesome military power the world has ever known."[40] International interventions, diplomatic or military, are the burden of the dominant global power in order to avoid or correct failure. But Ignatieff is less certain than Ferguson that the values of liberal democracy can be sustained in this process. There may be conditions and situations when the empire has to use violent force to achieve its political goals. Particularly in *The Lesser Evil,* Ignatieff develops a new and sharper definition of the U.S. empire as the guardian of global order and security, including exploring the limits of interrogation (torture). There is now a sharp division between "us" and "them," between friend and enemy. As Jeanne Morefield notes, "*The Lesser Evil* radically dehumanizes the 'they' in the process of convincing the 'we' that 'we' are doing the right thing."[41]

Nonetheless, it would be misleading to put Ignatieff ideologically in the same camp as Schmitt, for his anchor and point of departure is liberalism, whereas Schmitt's concept of *Großraumpolitik* is grounded in a radical critique of this very liberalism and its, at least in Schmitt's mind, inevitably bad political outcome. After all, Ignatieff holds on to the task of nation-building that Schmitt treats as the ultimate hypocrisy of the liberal empire. There can be no doubt that he would have been a severe critic of Ignatieff's project, in which the apparent tension between liberal values and the harsh use of imperial power is portrayed as a tragic struggle. As Morefield points out, "The overall effort of the narrative style is that we understand the liberal character of Western states as beyond dispute, as evidenced by the pained, self-justifying practices of liberal democratic debate in which citizens partake when faced with difficult issues of national security and intervention."[42]

Carl Schmitt's presence in the contemporary American debate evades easy location and placement. While his belated defense of European colonialism in *The Nomos of the Earth* does not impact this debate directly and significantly, his concept of *Großraum* as a gestalt of great power or empire involves him on both sides of this debate. He can be read as a critic of liberal U.S. imperialism but also as an imperialist with a different but similar agenda.[43] The notion that imperial power structures and hegemonic domination are

needed to sustain a new world order is one he shares with Ferguson and Ignatieff, although he would have criticized them sharply
for their positions. This could mean that the hope some Schmittians
in Europe and the United States sought in *The Nomos of the Earth*
to critique U.S. imperialism might have been misplaced.

To radically defend Schmitt's thought on international politics,
we must carefully select the objective of and the manner in which
such a defense would be mounted, since Schmitt's conception of European colonialism and its enduring impact on the global political
order is not without tensions and internal contradictions. Whether
Schmitt comes across as a severe critic of colonialism in the 1920s
and 1930s or underscores its positive aspects in the 1940s and
1950s, liberal internationalism is his opponent. A negative defense
of Schmitt would pick up on his energetic and radical critique of
late European colonialism, which argues the case of an autonomous
nation state (such as Germany in the 1920s), to object in strong
terms to the subversion of its full sovereignty and international
equality. This defense would focus on three areas in particular: first,
the ideological nature of the arguments by which colonial and similar arrangements such as protectorates are proposed and defended
even today; second, the legitimacy of the laws and rules by which
these arrangements are upheld in the context of international law;
and third, the political and military measures that are necessary to
sustain these arrangements—specifically, the question of partisan
warfare (including terrorism) as a form of absolute war.

Such a critique would emphasize the discrepancy between the
colonial power's claim to upholding universal values through its actions and its actual material interests. This is the locus where the
critiques of colonialism and liberalism merge, since liberal internationalism does not admit a contradiction between values and interests, claiming that the pursuit of the right (universal) values will
also result in reaching common material interests. The recent heated
discussion about the advantages or disadvantages of international
trade treaties would be a good example. It was the position of the
U.S. government during the Obama administration that transpa-
cific and transatlantic trade agreements would not only be in the best
interest of the United States but would also significantly benefit the

European Union and the Pacific states included in these treaties. But what is proposed as a legal contract between equals might turn out to be the imposition of a legal framework that primarily benefits the hegemon (in this case, the United States); formal legal equality might result in economic inequality. Schmitt's writings of the 1920s and early 1930s are very sensitive to this problem, since he writes from a nationalist German perspective, comparing the situation in Germany after World War I with that of a protectorate with diminished sovereignty.

In principle, this critique of colonialism focuses on the tension between the promise of legal and political equality and the actual dependence of the smaller states (colonies or protectorates) on the hegemon or the central power of the *Großraum* to which a smaller state belongs. This argument would also apply to the relationship between the central power of the *Großraum* and its satellite states. In either case, the standard of legal and political equality promised by twentieth-century international law is not upheld when the political relations are closely examined, revealing the true ideological nature of the value system. If, on the other hand, the claim to political and military superiority is openly and directly articulated without any reference to universal values, this argument must falter: its essential moment is its turn against universalism.

Once Schmitt's theoretical perspective moved from nation state to *Großraum,* his understanding and assessment of colonialism changed accordingly. It was the conception of Germany as a new *Reich* and *Großraum* that provided the arguments for the transition. He no longer viewed European colonial powers as problematic nation-states but as *Großräume* that are suitable if not essential for the global political order. This turn aligns with his positive defense of twentieth-century colonialism that we find in *The Nomos.*

The starting point of this defense is the desirable stability of the contemporary global political order, which Schmitt regards as threatened and undermined by unipolar global leadership—the United States, for instance. Schmitt's anti-liberalism is also present in this critique, but here it has a different function. Its purpose is to question the arbitrariness of the value system proposed for the global world order. Given the pluralism of existing value systems, the embrace of a particular one as the universal standard, Schmitt contends, is likely to create conflict and therefore instability. It is therefore advisable to acknowledge a plurality of value systems, leading to different political regimes (monarchies, democracies, authoritarian oligarchies, dictatorships, etc.) that can coexist peacefully as long as they do not attempt to impose their own values and form of government on other states or political communities. This means, for instance, that liberal democracies have to be discouraged from foreign policies that seek regime change in other regions. There are consequences to be considered, though. In this environment, questions of human rights, the suppression of minorities, and severe social inequalities must be removed from or at least marginalized in international relations, since they would interfere with the autonomy of the individual state or *Großraum* accused of violations. As long as a political regime contributes to global stability, in this vision, its internal affairs remain outside the purview of the international community.

Schmitt's emphasis on international stability guaranteed by a small number of great powers presents itself as a politics of realism. Its defense must argue, therefore, that the stability of the whole is more important than addressing problems resulting from the internal structure of these hegemons and their satellites. This approach certainly legitimizes inequalities within the political organization of an individual nation-state or *Großraum,* as well as inequalities between these great powers, which are to be understood as natural differences comprising and defining the whole. Indeed, the notion of a global order in which all human beings have equal rights and opportunities is implicitly rejected as a demand that would, by allowing social and cultural conflicts to move from the margins to the center, destabilize the global order. In this context, for instance, poor nations would have no right to demand access to the greater material resources of other nations, though neither would it exclude the possibility of negotiating compensations between rich and poor countries.

A serious defense of Schmitt's approach must stress the overwhelming advantages of a global stability achieved through balance of power politics in comparison to other solutions, such as a world hegemon that establishes and enforces rules and standards, thereby guaranteeing peace, or a plurality of smaller nation states linked and guided by an international organization like the UN. The assumption that Schmitt's pluralism of great powers would be more peaceful than any other solutions does not follow analytically from the theoretical conception itself; rather, we are dealing with an empirical assessment that looks at long-term historical developments. Schmitt argues that the European period between 1648 and 1914 was more peaceful than either the prior period of confessional wars (1520 to 1648) or the twentieth century. Apart from having to downplay the tremendous upheaval of the revolutionary period between 1789 and 1815, this argument relies on a relatively short period of global history. We could propose, for instance, the stability of the Roman Empire after the end of the civil war as a competing model. More critically, Schmitt stipulation of stability is never more than relative because it is always threatened by the military conflicts that reflect the realist assumption that international relations are fundamentally defined in terms of a struggle for power. Still, Schmitt's emphasis on stability sets him apart from the basic credo of political realism (Morgenthau or Mearsheimer) that highlights the centrality of states and state power in contrast to interdependent agreements and international organizations.[44] While Schmitt is certainly suspicious of liberal internationalism, he defends after all the concept of a European or global order, using the term *nomos*. As a legal theorist, he believes in the reality of legal structures as a form of power that has the effect of supporting and enforcing peace.

A defense of Schmitt therefore could argue that it is not the simply the factual balance of power that sustains international stability but a rational balance grounded in a *nomos*. But this *nomos*, Schmitt tells us, must not be perceived as an abstract norm. Instead, he seeks to reconnect the concept with the idea of Earth. As Schmitt asserts, "The Earth is bound to law in three ways. She contains law within herself, as a reward of labor; she manifests law upon herself, as fixed boundaries; and she sustains law about herself as a public sign of order. Law is bound to the Earth and related to the Earth."[45] By this forceful attempt to ground the law in material conditions and practices, Schmitt seeks to bridge the rift between abstract norms codified as laws and the material world of human labor and human conflict (i.e., politics). For Schmitt, the primary features of international law are linked to the original appropriation of land and the establishment of human communities.

Yet it is precisely this connection that erases the difference between the political act (of land appropriation, of colonizing, etc.) and the law that legalizes it. Something becomes law because it was successfully done. If the practice brings about the *nomos,* who and what guide it? Schmitt's model requires an ethics, but he does not spell one out in his positive defense of colonialism or in any kind of land appropriation that removes or suppresses another group of human beings. Moreover, a strong ethics would be needed to undergird a peaceful coexistence of great powers, beyond the political calculation that the complex pluralism of these powers would as such stabilize the global order. Schmitt's ultimate answer would be a recourse to a theological construct that also determines the historical background of his theory: the figure of the katechon from 2 Thessalonians, the ruler who can slow down the accelerating process of history and the coming of the Final Judgment. Schmitt's is a postlapsarian world of sin and evil, where enmity between men is the fate of humanity until the Second Coming of Christ. Nothing could be more futile, therefore, than to hope that mankind will improve and reach autonomy.

It is not accidental that Schmitt returns to the question of a political theology in his later writings,[46] since the search for a concrete political order in *The Nomos* raises questions that the abstract definition of the political cannot answer. But understanding and accepting the truth of Paul's letter to the Thessalonians presupposes a global Christian order—the way, according to Schmitt, that the older European *nomos* was determined by a common Christian religion. Yet this common ground is, as Schmitt recognized, no longer available. The political plurality of the late twentieth century is matched by a religious and ideological plurality.

This means that a secular solution has to be sought, one that can negotiate between diverse religious and other ideological positions. Yet Schmitt fails to follow this path—mostly, I suspect, because in

his mind this secular solution took the form of international liberalism, a solution that historically favored the Western maritime
powers. His thought thus leads to an aporia: On the one hand,
Schmitt realizes that the older European *nomos* has lost its relevance and has to be replaced by a new, global *nomos*. On the other
hand, facing the threat of universal liberalism as a form of global
domination by a hegemon, he looks to a new regionalism that goes
beyond a realist power equilibrium. However, such an arrangement
demands a shared ethics that it cannot provide on its own.

4

REVOLUTIONARY WAR AND ABSOLUTE ENEMY

Rereading Theory of the Partisan

The publication of *The Nomos of the Earth* in 1950 marked an important transition, not only in Schmitt's life but also in his oeuvre. This shift was expressed in the dual focus of the study. It looks back at the older European political and legal order (with some nostalgia and considerable idealization) and critically faces the rise of a new global political order of the twentieth century, an order propagated and embraced primarily by Britain and the United States. Its dogma—liberal internationalism—promises world peace through a ban on war and general prosperity through free international trade.

Schmitt's critical engagement with liberal internationalism in *The Nomos* follows a peculiar strategy of both opposing and affirming the global historical process. He affirms the desirable and even necessary transition from a plurality of national states to a smaller number of great powers defined in terms of their *Großraum* (expanded territory) by foregrounding the importance of the European colonial powers for the *ius publicum Europaeum*—a move that would exclude Germany from a central role in European and global modern history. But he sharply opposes international liberalism as a dogma that, in his mind, is responsible for an increase in international conflicts. In particular, he emphasizes the actual radicalization of war as a result of the very program to eliminate war. In *The Nomos,* Schmitt resolutely affirms a spatial and regional European order that could be globally expanded through colonial appropriations, resisting an abstract internationalism that would actually result in greater political and economic inequality, while promising equality. Moreover, Schmitt questions what he considers to be the criminalization of war as a justified instrument for solving political conflicts. In the context of international relations, he insists on the need for a legitimate military option.

Schmitt's focus in *The Nomos* on the historical fate of European colonialism sheds more light on the sharp and significant distinction between wars fought in Europe and those fought outside the European territory; that is, colonial wars. These differ in strategy as well as intensity by adopting their own rules. The distinction becomes crucial for Schmitt's later work when his emphasis shifts from the colonial context to the character and function of war itself. While Schmitt understands World War I, notwithstanding its radical changes in the use of advanced technology, as a classic interstate war and therefore as the closing chapter of the older European order, he examines later twentieth-century wars in a different context. Broadly speaking, for Schmitt interstate wars were replaced by civil wars, frequently fought on the margins of the new global order. Because of their nature, they were harder to control than traditional wars and had a greater tendency to destabilize the region. There is no longer a clear distinction between war and peace. Of course, Schmitt was not the only one who recognized this transformation, but he had a keen eye for the political aspect of the shift. Unlike the military experts, who focused on the tactical and strategic side of the new wars, Schmitt explored their political meaning and reconnected his findings with the broader question of the new global order. In brief, the questions left unanswered in *The*

Nomos return in Schmitt's later work, especially in the short mono-graph *Theory of the Partisan* (1963).

Among Schmitt's late writings, *Theory of the Partisan* stands out in more than one respect. The short monograph is the only work that deals explicitly with military strategy and tactics. Moreover, it deals with problems that were, at least for Schmitt's German audience, not of immediate relevance. The German discourse on security and defense of the early 1960s was primarily focused on the use of atomic weapons in the struggle against the Soviet Union and its allies. Although Schmitt is clearly aware of this and at the end of his essay refers to the atomic stalemate between the superpowers, he foregrounds a very different type of warfare; namely, guerilla wars that were fought outside of Europe and for which the army of the Federal Republic (*Bundeswehr*) was neither equipped nor trained. Even if we grant that for Schmitt's legal theory, and especially for his understanding of international law, the concept of war was an essential element, the detailed interest in the history of warfare and the evolution of small wars comes as a surprise. This interest goes beyond the broad distinction between classic European interstate wars (the duels between states) and colonial wars, or the distinction between contained (*gehegt*) and unrestricted war.

In his theory of the partisan Schmitt turns his attention to a very specific type of war with its own rules and aims that subvert conventional notions of warfare and the distinction between war and peace. The latter aspect is of great importance to Schmitt, because it allows him to rethink and redefine the concept of war. In this respect Schmitt's monograph picks up and develops ideas that were part of the contemporary international discourse on guerilla warfare but that remained somewhat underdeveloped in the context of discussions about military strategy. In this discussion the uncertainty in regard to the distinction between war and peace in the arena of small wars was frequently stated as a military problem but seldom reflected as a fundamental problem of international law.[1]

It is in this area that Schmitt makes his contribution.[2] Schmitt delves into and makes use of an extensive and rich contemporary discourse on guerilla warfare to construct his own historical narrative and, more importantly, his own understanding of the partisan as part of a new global order in which customary categories have lost their relevance. Tentatively we can therefore say that the engagement with this international body of literature enables Schmitt to reexamine the themes that he developed in *Land und Meer* (1942) and *The Nomos of the Earth*, the transition from an older Eurocentric order to a new order ushered in after World War I. However, in *Theory of the Partisan* Schmitt acknowledges a significant shift. Now the transition is not only accelerated but also driven by different forces. The major force (and opponent) is no longer the liberal democracy of the West but communist and national independence movements in Asia, Latin America, and Africa. Schmitt's own perspective remains fiercely Eurocentric, but now the West European colonial powers are seen in a different light. Especially France, or at least certain parts of the French political and military regime, are perceived as defenders of legitimate concerns. For Schmitt, comprehending the contemporary international partisan is the key to an adequate understanding of the new *nomos,* an order in which the changed definition of war is more than an aspect of international relations as which it is typically treated in the critical literature on strategy. For this reason, Schmitt can make use of the military theory he finds but must at the same time transcend it and move to another level in order to grasp the new structure. Whether this attempt is successful is a question for a later point.

First, we should examine Schmitt's position within the military discourse of the 1950s and early 1960s and subsequently look more closely at the political aspect of the essay. Then we can address the position of *Theory of the Partisan* in Schmitt's late work and its relation to Schmitt's return to political theology in 1970. If it can be shown that the theory of the partisan anticipates some of the major themes of *Political Theology II,* the evaluation of war articulated in 1963 takes on a different and somewhat unexpected meaning. Put differently, as long as *Theory of the Partisan* is interpreted as an extension of *The Nomos of the Earth,* the focus falls primarily on the problem of the containment of war. If emphasis is placed on the link to the definition of political theology, different aspects come to the foreground. It would change, among other things, the understanding of the political function of the partisan and guerilla warfare.[3]

The Military Discourse of the 1950s and 1960s

Carl Schmitt was by no means the first theorist to focus on partisan warfare. In this respect he could not and did not claim originality. In fact, he draws heavily on the existing critical literature. In Germany he draws on the writings of Gerhard Nebel, Rolf Schroers, Hans Joachim Sell, and Hellmuth Rentsch.[4] Among the Spanish and French experts he cites are Luis Garcia Arias, Raymond Aron, and Roger Trinquier. He is equally familiar with the Anglo-American literature, for instance the works of Peter Paret and John Shy.[5] As much as their perspective and evaluation of irregular wars may differ, these authors share the insight that these so-called small wars changed the geopolitical situation after 1945. Therefore the analysis and political assessment of these wars were of equal if not greater importance than the discussion of nuclear strategy. Mao's victory in China in 1949 after an extended period of civil war, the defeat of the French Army in Indonesia in 1954, and the Cuban Revolution and the civil war in Algeria between 1954 and 1962, which ended with the independence of Algeria, were the most visible examples of the effectiveness of subversive warfare.

Why were the insights of these authors of interest to Schmitt? For one thing, they confirmed Schmitt's fear that the age of contained interstate wars was a thing of the past, that the nuclear stalemate between the superpowers shifted political conflicts to parts of the globe where they would not trigger a completely destructive nuclear exchange. However, on closer inspection it turns out that Schmitt, especially following the lead of his French sources, advances a more radical interpretation of guerilla warfare. For him, it has become *the* major threat to the existing global political order, a threat that cannot be contained. Therefore his theory is concerned with the logic of this threat, which is ultimately political and, by extension, theological rather than military. This becomes apparent in the way Schmitt constructs the history of partisan warfare with his peculiar emphases and selection of wars.

When we look at the debates over the foreign policy of the Federal Republic of the early 1960s, it becomes very clear that Schmitt's theory offered a counterprogram, a sharp deviation from the concerns of public opinion and the political parties. These debates focused on what might be called national survival strategies under the conditions of the East-West conflict and the military threat of nuclear annihilation of the civilian population. We have to recall that in the early 1960s, with the incoming Kennedy administration, tensions were rising after the international discussion on arms control had failed. From a West German perspective the erection of the Berlin Wall in August of 1961 demonstrated again the vulnerability of the West and especially of West Germany's own borders; and the problem of the defense of Berlin raised the question of the potential use of nuclear weapons and the fear that the civilian population of West Germany, as the border state, might not survive the exchange. But the idea of containing the crisis in Central Europe by decoupling nuclear and conventional strategies was not necessarily more comforting because it potentially exposed the Federal Republic to a massive conventional Soviet attack that could not be stopped at the border. In this context the Federal Republic faced the question of whether the *Bundeswehr* should have nuclear weapons as well. And who would ultimately control the use of these weapons? Franz Josef Strauß, the minister of defense, strongly favored and pushed for West German nuclear armament after 1957 as part of the new NATO strategy.[6] The argument offered was that only a combined conventional and nuclear strategy could provide adequate security for the Federal Republic. In these scenarios the partisan option did not play a significant role. The new West German army was defined and trained as a conventional army within the context of NATO.

Schmitt's theory must also be understood and evaluated against this background. His essay radically shifted the focus of the debate by discussing a type of warfare that would be useful mostly after the occupation of West German territory by Soviet and East German armies. This option is not explicitly mentioned in *Theory of the Partisan*—only an attentive reader might draw this conclusion. However, there were, it seems, not many attentive readers who seriously considered a return to Carl von Clausewitz and his plans of a subversive war against a powerful and victorious invader as a viable option.

Clausewitz, Schmitt, and Guerilla Warfare

In general, the structure of Schmitt's essay does not fully disclose the author's intent.[7] He develops a historical narrative that begins with the Spanish guerillas of 1808 after the defeat of the regular army and concludes with the wars in Indochina and Algeria, in particular with a detailed discussion of Raoul Salan, the former commander-in-chief of the French Army in Algeria and subsequent leader of the putsch against the Fifth Republic. While some of the elements of this narrative are shared with the literature on which Schmitt relied, others stand decisively outside that story. His emphasis on Clausewitz and the Prussian army reform after 1806, as well as the detailed examination of the fate of General Salan, is notable in this regard. By comparison, the attention devoted to Che Guevara and Latin America is considerably more limited. In broader terms, Schmitt completely disregards older forms of partisan warfare such as that employed during the Thirty Years' War or the American Revolution. In other words, he excludes small wars that are not connected, directly or indirectly, with modern interstate warfare. Private wars, as well as early colonial wars, therefore remain outside his theory.

For Schmitt, the most important characteristic of partisan warfare is the thrust against regular interstate war. "War was waged between states, between regular state armies, and between sovereign bearers of a *jus belli,* who also in war respected each other as enemies, and did not discriminate against each other as criminals."[8] This definition of war, which is more fully developed in *The Nomos of the Earth,*[9] includes the sharp distinction between combatants and noncombatants and the possibility of a nondiscriminatory peace treaty. It defines partisan warfare as taking place outside of conventional boundaries and leading to a different definition of the enemy. The modern partisan "has moved away from the conventional enmity of controlled and bracketed (*gehegt*) war, and into the realm of another, real enmity, which intensifies through terror and counter-terror until it ends in extermination" (*TP* 11).

If Schmitt's aim is to emphasize the need for contained (*gehegt*) warfare, then an analysis of the partisan does not look like a promising avenue. Schmitt's agenda is more complicated and ultimately conflicted. In his discussion of Spanish partisans and Prussian plans of a popular uprising, Schmitt clearly discovers rightful goals in that the partisan means to defeat a foreign intruder. But even in the case of the contemporary revolutionary partisan, where we can speak of an absolute enemy, Schmitt recognizes legitimate aspects in organizing the defense against the outside enemy in the form of guerilla warfare instead of a doomed conventional strategy. This is the case of the French military officers in Indochina and Algeria, whose situation is extensively and sympathetically discussed. As it turns out, the distinction between a negative and a positive partisan is more difficult to draw than we would expect, if we take Schmitt's position in *The Nomos* as the standard. Schmitt's fundamental typological distinction between an earth-bound regional and a mobile, technologically advanced international guerilla throws light on this ambiguity, since this divide does not coincide with the left-right divide of the Cold War. For Schmitt the strength of Mao's struggle in China was linked to its regional and telluric character.

At the same time, Schmitt distances himself from Rolf Schroers' attempt (1961) to define the partisan as "the last resistance against the nihilism of a thoroughly *technological* world, the last defender of species and soil, and ultimately, the last man" (*TP* 19n28). He is not celebrating the partisan as an anthropolitical opponent to advanced technology and bureaucratic organization. Instead, Schmitt's point of departure, in the wake of *The Nomos*, is the problem of the just war that allows one side to discriminate against the other. As he explains in the introduction, partisan warfare is an extreme case of a mutually discriminating war with a tendency to accelerate toward absolute war.

While Schmitt acknowledges the Spanish guerilla war as the first major example of modern subversive warfare that successfully challenged the occupation by a powerful regular army, he devotes more space and energy to the situation of Prussia between 1806 and 1813 and especially to the theoretical reflections of Clausewitz. This is somewhat surprising because the partisan did not play a significant role in the Prussian war of liberation. There are two reasons for Schmitt's interest. First, it is precisely the very marginal character of the partisan in 1813 that confirms the strategic military as well as political priority of interstate warfare as the legal and ethical standard. Second, Clausewitz's thoughts on guerilla war are theoretically highly relevant because of their later impact on Marx/Engels and Lenin. This impact demonstrates the possible exchange of ideas between the conservative and the revolutionary side. Put differently, Clausewitz's writings contain a revolutionary moment that could be appropriated and used by the revolutionary Left.[10]

Schmitt's assessment of the later official Prussian position vis-à-vis partisans and irregular warfare amounts to little more than a defense of the German Army in 1870/71 and World War I, underlining the adherence of the German military to international law and a lack of comprehension with regard to the effectiveness of guerilla warfare. Small wars were not taken seriously, an observation that shows Schmitt's ambivalence toward the subversive potential of the guerilla. This ambiguity is also reflected in Schmitt's analysis of the Prussian *Edikt über den Landsturm* of April 21, 1813. He calls the edict "the unleashing of total disorder" (*TP* 43), the declaration of a popular war against the enemy without regard for military and legal boundaries. Schmitt's apparent sympathies for this decision obviously contradict the concept of interstate war otherwise used as the standard by Schmitt. How do we explain this contradiction?

First of all, the Prussian engagement with and excitement about partisan warfare in 1813 was primarily theoretical, the result of ideas that had circulated among the educated elite. Schmitt calls it

the philosophical discovery of the partisan. Clausewitz provided
the theory of the partisan, a theory without immediate consequences.
Second, the edict is part of the Prussian reform and as such a com-
ponent of German nation building, in Schmitt's perspective the
precondition for modern interstate war. Both arguments make
Schmitt's position more plausible, but they do not remove the
contradiction.

Clausewitz's analysis of irregular warfare is an essential piece of
Schmitt's overall argument because it provides the foundation for
later, more radical theories of guerilla warfare, notably those of Engels and Lenin on the Left. Schmitt's narrative, in other words,
stresses the logic of a theoretical development that becomes more
radical in each subsequent phase. Therefore we have to ask: What
are the elements of Clausewitz's thought that Schmitt emphasizes?
He notes: "Guerilla warfare became for him [Clausewitz], as for
other reformers of his circle, 'above all, a political matter in the
highest sense, meaning precisely of a revolutionary character. Acknowledgement of armed civilians, of insurrection, of revolutionary
war, resistance, and rebellion against the existing order, even when
embodied in a foreign regime of occupation'" (*TP* 45, quoting the
historian Werner Hahlweg). The key terms in this passage are "insurrection" (*Aufstand*) and "revolution." For Schmitt, Clausewitz's
plans mark a radical break with the Prussian tradition and the centrality of the legitimate monarchy. They question the very foundations of his personal and professional commitment. The Prussian
monarchy had good reasons to be apprehensive about this development because it contained—and this is not articulated by Clausewitz but clearly on the mind of Schmitt—the breakdown of the
given social and political order. Clausewitz unleashed, as Schmitt
puts it, "a new, formerly unrecognized figure of the world-spirit"
(*TP* 47), in contradistinction to the Spanish guerilla war that was
merely "the will of resistance of valiant, bellicose people" (*TP* 47).
The future of the partisan in the global historical process depended
on his philosophical articulation. By establishing a link between
Clausewitz and Hegel, Schmitt can argue that the conservative political and military theory of Prussia (here he follows the Hegel

reading of Joachim Ritter)[11] contained the revolutionary seed that would come to fruition in Marx, Engels, Lenin, and Mao Zedong.

When Schmitt emphasizes the theoretical nature of Clausewitz's contribution he does not mean to belittle its importance. On the contrary, he brings to the foreground the fact that the deeper meaning of the partisan is not limited to the level of military action (tactical or strategic). Those who make use of Clausewitz's theory fully understand, and more deeply than the Prussian officer himself, the connection between the military and the political aspect of partisan warfare. In fact, they look at this type of warfare primarily from the political side, while military tactics and strategy become secondary functions. In the writings of Lenin and Mao the subversive nature of guerilla war merges with the idea of political revolution. As Schmitt explains, it is precisely this synthesis that the French colonial officers in Indochina did not fully grasp. Schmitt devotes an entire chapter to Lenin's conception of the partisan, a discussion that is based on Lenin's 1906 essay "Partisan Warfare" and his notes on Clausewitz's *Vom Krieg* (*On War*), written in 1915. While Schmitt refers to the early essay to clarify Lenin's focus on civil war and the inevitability of partisan warfare in the revolutionary struggle (in contrast to the notion of a peaceful takeover), he pays more detailed attention to Lenin's notebooks, since they make use of a concept of the enemy that is compatible with Schmitt's own use. Lenin's distinction between war (*Woina*) and play (*Igra*) is turned into the distinction between contained and unhedged, potentially absolute war. Lenin's revolutionary war is without *Hegung* (restraint). As Schmitt notes, Lenin's "concrete absolute enemy was the class enemy—the bourgeois, the essential capitalist, and the social order in countries where this bourgeois capitalist was dominant" (*TP* 52). What makes Lenin in Schmitt's eyes superior to the statesmen and military leaders of his time is his conception of social revolution as a necessarily violent struggle for which the form of guerilla warfare is more suitable than regular war. Lenin's understanding of the partisan is first and foremost political in the sense of Clausewitz that war is the (violent) extension of the political struggle with different means. Since the political struggle between the classes becomes for the revolution a question of absolute hostility, the civil war would become absolute as well.[12] What Lenin would bring to the table in 1917 would be a synthesis of Western theory and the force of the Russian masses in rebellion against the czarist regime. It is worth noting that Schmitt at this point does not raise the question of the potential response of Western liberal and capitalist democracies. Would they just crumble or could they develop their own form of revolutionary war? He postpones this discussion until he deals with colonial warfare in Indochina and Algeria. Instead, the narrative moves from Lenin to Mao Zedong with a rather brief discussion of Stalin's use of partisan warfare in World War II.

For Schmitt, Mao is the most sophisticated and radical theorist of guerilla war and, at the same time, its most accomplished practitioner. It is hard to overlook Schmitt's distant admiration for the Chinese leader and his concept of the revolution. Of course, Mao could build on Lenin's work, which means that the absolute nature of the revolutionary war was already firmly in place and could be taken for granted in theoretical terms. By comparing Mao with Clausewitz, Schmitt can point to a moment of intensification of the revolutionary struggle that was beyond Clausewitz's imagination, which was influenced by the French Revolution and Napoleon's wars. Although Lenin and Mao are both described as *Berufsrevolutionäre* (professional revolutionaries), Mao stands out in Schmitt's mind for merging the two basic types of guerilla war: the telluric, regional, and defensive type, and the international revolutionary type. As Schmitt explains, "Mao's revolution was more tellurically based than was Lenin's" (*TP* 57), and continues, "In 1949, the Chinese Communists under Mao and his friends had struggled for two decades on their own national soil with a national opponent (the Kuomintang) in an enormous partisan war" (*TP* 57). This is for Schmitt a fundamental breakthrough. By bringing together a violent struggle against the Japanese invaders, the national rival and the colonial Western powers, Mao arrives at a new *nomos*. At the same time, Schmitt leaves no doubt that this *nomos* is still incomplete, without the intrinsic possibility of peace: "For Mao . . . peace today is only a manifestation of real enmity. Enmity also does not cease in so-called 'cold war'" (*TP* 60). Thus Mao's 1949 victory defines the international constellation of the early 1960s as a form of protracted global civil war with an uncertain outcome.

Schmitt's interpretation of Mao does not pay much attention to the details of strategic and tactical guerilla warfare; instead, he places the emphasis decidedly on the political side. For him, Mao's theoretical as well as material achievements on the ground are due to his persistent focus on the concept of the radical, uncompromising enemy. In this struggle, as Schmitt recognizes, the Chinese peasants played an essential role as the mass of the people. However, the precise nature of the relationship between the people and the leader, which is clearly crucial for Mao, seems to escape him—he views the development of guerilla warfare primarily from the perspective of the professional revolutionary rather than the concrete situation of the oppressed or invaded people. As Mao argues, "Because guerilla warfare basically derives from the masses and is supported by them, it can neither exist nor flourish if it separates itself from their sympathies and cooperation."[13] Mao defends the superiority of partisan warfare against those who favor the use of the regular army in the revolutionary struggle not only on military grounds. He claims that well-organized partisan war succeeds because it is and remains the war of the Chinese people, who are fighting under specific conditions that Mao describes as "a country half colonial and half feudal ... a country that is politically, militarily, and economically backward."[14] Its revolutionary war must be based on these conditions in order to succeed. Although Schmitt emphasizes and admires the concreteness of the Chinese revolutionary struggle in comparison with Lenin's more top-down approach in 1917, he remains attached to the immanent logic of an ultimate intensification (*Verschärfung*) of global import.

The Political Relevance of Guerilla Warfare

This brings us back to the political meaning and relevance of guerilla warfare in Schmitt's monograph: its subversive nature that cannot be contained within the limits of interstate warfare, its close link to social and political revolution, and its emphasis on the real or absolute enemy. For Schmitt, who follows Mao Zedong, the use of guerilla bands instead of regular armies is a function of the political struggle. Mao's theory stresses the priority of political consciousness and political schooling over military action. Partisans must know why they fight the enemy.[15] For Schmitt the political is more than a question of consciousness and discipline from within; rather, for Schmitt the partisan redefines the political in the twentieth century. His question is: Given the expansion of revolutionary strife after 1945 (either in the form of communist revolutions or anticolonial national movements), how can the combatants arrive at peace? Is peace possible? In the wake of *The Nomos of the Earth,* the answer is not unexpected: Peace in the sense of older European international law has become impossible once we have moved from regulated interstate war to revolutionary guerilla war. This is the lesson of Lenin and Mao. According to Schmitt, for them only complete victory of the revolution can be accepted as the basis for a lasting peace and as part of a new *nomos.* As long as this victory has not been achieved, the condition is that of "true enmity" (*wirkliche Feindschaft; TP* 61). From the perspective of a communist revolutionary this may be a satisfactory answer, but does it also apply to Schmitt's own position?

It is important to recall that Schmitt's narrative up to this point chooses the point of view of the partisan, respectively that of the theorist of guerilla warfare, and highlights the revolutionary character of the partisan in military and political terms. Other forms of small warfare that do not fit this profile are carefully left out or marginalized. Therefore Schmitt's narrative creates the effect of a teleology from the era of the French Revolution (Napoleon) and early modern nationalism to late modernity and the end of European colonialism. It is a teleological development that undermines European international law as it dominated international relations between 1648 and 1918. In *The Nomos of the Earth* Schmitt developed a similar narrative, however, with a significant difference. Here the destruction of the older European *Völkerrecht* was attributed to the dialectic of Western liberalism that turned interstate war into a potentially criminal activity. After World War II these two narratives do not merge or even run parallel because the constellation of the Cold War pits the Western powers, organized in NATO, against the Communist bloc. Must we assume therefore that Schmitt has switched his sympathies and allegiance to Mao and similar revolutionary movements?

To answer this question we have to look closely at Schmitt's analysis of the strategy developed by the French Army in Indochina and Algeria. In particular, we have to examine Schmitt's evaluation of the fate of General Raoul Salan, who organized the failed putsch of the generals against de Gaulle when the latter decided to end the war in Algeria as ultimately detrimental to the future of France. For Schmitt Salan is not simply a misguided French officer on the Far Right who committed high treason and therefore deserved the death penalty but a tragic figure who has his sympathy because he was consistent in his military defense of the French position in Algeria and was forced to oppose the legal French government in order to carry out this defense. The legitimacy of this war against the Algerian rebels is at the heart of the problem.[16]

This matter of legitimacy has two aspects: First, there is the problem of the nature of the war—that is, the use of counterinsurgency to deal with guerillas; second, there is the larger issue of European colonialism. Can it be constructed as a legitimate form of *Herrschaft* (rule), as the French Right claimed? It is worth noting that Schmitt has very little to say about the second aspect. He does not question the position of the French officers. His analysis is focused on partisan warfare carried out by government troops. The defeat of the French Army by the rebels of General Giap and Ho Chi Minh taught the French officers that conventional military strategy could not succeed against an opponent who relied on the methods of guerilla warfare. They had to adapt their own strategy by studying and learning from Giap and Ho Chi Minh. This learning process is what Schmitt is interested in. He wants to assess the plausibility of a subversive war that could stop revolutionary wars organized by communists and their allies.

Again, the military aspect of the new French strategy of a *guerre révolutionnaire* is treated only very briefly with reference to the existing literature on the subject (*TP* 62n73). Instead, Schmitt means to highlight the situation of the commanding officer, who has to deal with a subversive revolutionary enemy. Schmitt's focus is the "inexorable logic of partisan warfare" (*PT* 63) and Salan's role in it. This role consists of two decisive phases: first, that of the leading officer in North Vietnam and later as the commander-in-chief of the French Army in Algeria, and second, the phase of the rebellion against de Gaulle and the use of terrorist warfare against the French government and the French population. While Schmitt is almost silent about the first phase, he offers a relatively extensive assessment of the trial and especially of Salan's defense. In the context of a theory of guerilla warfare, this is a somewhat peculiar but telling emphasis. Schmitt's investment in the case of Salan becomes meaningful only if we understand Salan's involvement in the concept of counterrevolutionary war and its application in Algeria.

The formation of a counterguerilla theory by the French military and its application first in Indochina and later in Algeria did not occur in a political vacuum. It was designed to stabilize the colonies under attack and, in broader terms, to secure the French empire, a goal, by the way, that was not necessarily shared by the majority of the French population. Given this uncertainty, counterrevolutionary war in Indochina and Algeria was in need of a broader ideological framework that would justify the more extreme measures taken by the army to defeat the enemy completely. This is the logic of revolutionary warfare that Schmitt evokes in his discussion of Salan. Long-term military success depended on an ideological framework for two reasons: first, regular forces involved in counterinsurgency need more than the abstract goal of restoring the status quo ante (colonialism); second, to legitimize this kind of warfare, which includes torture, the international community needs ideological arguments that create sympathy and diplomatic support. Schmitt suggests that the French officers in command did not fully understand this aspect of counterguerilla warfare and therefore remained too much engaged at the level of military actions in their approach.

Looking at the Algerian war from the perspective of its outcome may have encouraged this assessment, but it clearly downplays the ideological commitments of the French colonial officers, who were in more than one way a separate group inside the army with their own career patterns (Salan's career is typical in this respect). The older generation of officers (among them Salan), for instance, served under the Vichy regime and continued to supervise French colonies in this context between 1940 and 1944. They did not automatically transfer their loyalty to the new French Republic. The subsequent instability of the Fourth Republic did not improve the relationship between the political center and the colonial army, which felt that it did not always receive the political and moral support it needed to fight a determined enemy. But they could draw on the constellation of the Cold War by claiming that the military struggle against liberation movements in the colonies was at the same time a struggle against communist expansion. In other words, they identified insurgency with the evil of communist revolution. This perception brought them much closer to the political Far Right than the metropolitan army. It also influenced their conception of colonial warfare as fundamentally different from traditional war, including the use of torture and terror as necessary means to defeat a ruthless enemy. War in the colonies becomes the ultimate battle between good and evil in which the side that can persuade the civilian population of the justness of its cause will win. As Roger Trinquier, one of the officers and theorists of the new warfare, writes, "In seeking a solution, it is essential to realize that in *modern warfare* we are not up against just a few armed bands spread across a given territory, but rather against an *armed clandestine organization* whose essential role is to impose its will upon the population. Victory will be obtained only through the complete destruction of that organization."[17]

Although Schmitt remains silent about the nature of antiguerilla warfare in Algeria, he is clearly familiar with its methods, since he makes reference to the critical literature on the subject. Moreover, his interpretation of Salan's decision to resist de Gaulle's determination to withdraw from Algeria leaves little doubt where his personal sympathies lie, yet without open support for the Organisation armée secrète (Secret Army Organization).[18] In theoretical terms, this positive evaluation comes as a surprise because the new French conception of modern warfare (Trinquier) rejects the notion of a contained war (*gehegter Krieg*) as much as did Lenin and Mao.

Peace can be accomplished only by the complete destruction of the enemy and successful indoctrination of the civilian population. What are we to make of this turn?

Revolution, Counterrevolution, and Political Theology

The last chapter of the monograph, entitled "Aspects and Concepts of the Last Stage" (*PT* 68), provides the key for an answer. Here the author draws the conclusion of his analysis by moving to a higher and more abstract level. He defines partisan warfare as a global phenomenon that has fundamentally transformed not only the concept of war (which many military theorists had already recognized at that time) but also political and social structures. Put differently, the return to the older European order becomes less and less likely. Among the four aspects of transformation that Schmitt mentions (social structures, global political links, space, and technology), only the first two concern us here because Schmitt has to address his understanding of radical social revolution (communism, the possibility of opposing this revolution, and the status of older European international law). Schmitt understands partisan warfare as part of a revolutionary logic that culminates in Mao and his disciples. At the same time, he is not involved in but sympathetic to the logic of counterinsurgency, which attempts (desperately) to oppose and stop the logic of social revolution by using the same military means. Finally, he argues in favor of contained interstate war that allows for peace treaties acceptable to both sides. However, neither revolutionary war nor antirevolutionary war can be nondiscriminatory. Therefore they should be equally rejected as normal types of war; yet Schmitt's conclusions are less unequivocal. Schmitt's analysis of the social consequences of guerilla warfare (he uses the example of Indochina) emphasizes the destructive effect in a spiral of violence and counterviolence to which the civilian population is subjected. As Schmitt explains, "One need only to think this logic of terror and counterterror through to the end, and then to apply it to every type of civil war in order to see the destruction of social structures at work today" (*TP* 73). What

Schmitt describes is a vicious cycle in which neither side can win, a fateful and horrible deviation from European international law insofar as civil war has replaced interstate war.

The perspective of this interpretation is the older system of international law described in *The Nomos of the Earth*. However, when it comes to international relations, and specifically global policies, the perspective shifts remarkably, for reexamined in this new context the partisan turns into a piece on the chessboard of world politics. Now guerilla warfare serves a purpose that is no longer defined locally but at the headquarters of the superpowers. Here Schmitt returns to the logic of revolution and counterrevolution and argues: "Only revolutionary war made him [the partisan] a key figure of world history" (*TP* 77). He does not foresee a positive solution to this conflict and explicitly rejects any expectation that advanced technology will make war superfluous and therefore lead to the extinction of the partisan. Instead, he offers two opposite theoretical solutions. Either it would be possible to make room again for a type of limited conventional war outside of the total destruction of nuclear warfare or to anticipate the devastating nuclear exchange with its predictable outcome of complete destruction on both sides, opening up the possibility of postnuclear partisan warfare. While the first solution retrieves conventional war under the umbrella of a nuclear stalemate, the second solution takes us to what Schmitt defines as "the last stage" (*TP* 81); it is, as Schmitt stresses, precisely the "stage" that Salan, the soldier in uniform, did not fully understand. Unlike the revolutionary, Salan, trained as a regular soldier, was ultimately unable to completely recognize the real enemy. By returning to the question of the enemy, Schmitt can finally focus on the symbolic and at the same time essential meaning of the partisan in contrast to his military function in modern warfare. Therefore the discussion of the military problematic ultimately turns out to be a detour that will lead us to Schmitt's concept of the political in its most radical form; namely, its theological version.

For Schmitt conventional war between sovereign states is defined as a duel determined by a set of rules observed by both sides. In this sense the enemy is a formal but not a real enemy. By contrast,

guerilla warfare, especially in the context of civil war, is understood as a war between real enemies who recognize themselves in
the enemy. As Schmitt notes, "Der Feind ist unsere eigene Frage als
Gestalt" (*TP* 85)—the enemy is our own problem embodied in
another person. Thus counterrevolutionary war recognizes and
acknowledges the character of revolutionary war, and the impossi-
bility of a conventional peace. Here Schmitt speaks of an absolute
enemy. While Clausewitz's theory of small wars against an invader
remains at the level of the real enemy (Napoleon), Lenin's definition of revolutionary war creates the absolute enemy, a constellation that a priori denies the possibility of reconciliation. When
Schmitt radicalizes the concept of the enemy to the level of the
absolute enemy, the notion of a conventional war with clear de-
marcations is no longer mentioned because it belongs to a past that
was, as Schmitt argues, undermined and then destroyed in the revolution of 1917. It seems that, given the logic of revolutionary war,
a return to traditional warfare is no longer possible. This outcome,
we have to note, leaves the reader with considerable uncertainty.

What, then, are the lessons of *Theory of the Partisan*? Some of
them are more obvious than others. Schmitt agrees with authors
such as Rolf Schroers, Hellmut Rentsch, H. Hogard, and Peter Paret about the centrality of guerilla warfare in our time, but he seems
to be more extreme in his conclusions when he questions the possibility of traditional interstate war. Second, Schmitt also draws
attention to the revolutionary function of guerilla warfare, an assessment that is influenced by French military theorists such as
Lacheroy, Hogard, and Trinquier. Third, he bemoans the loss of
older European international law without clearly stating what
could take its place. Finally, it appears that Schmitt interprets the
constellation of the Cold War as the final stage, the ultimate threat
of complete mutual destruction. However, these aspects do not
exhaust the meaning of Schmitt's essay because they mainly articulate what Schmitt has learned from the existing critical discourse.
His own approach might be called a second-order theory, although
not in the strict sense of Niklas Luhmann. Schmitt's narrative reflects on and presents different and incompatible positions by shifting back and forth between them. He can speak with equal force of

the revolutionary logic that leads from Clausewitz to Lenin, Mao, and Guevara, and of the compelling reasons to develop counter-revolutionary strategies to defend colonial French territories. He can also, as we have seen, argue against the destruction of European international law as it happens by intensifying war to the level of absolute enmity (*Feindschaft*).

This is what the communist revolutionaries and the French officers on the Far Right have in common: the fixation on the absolute enemy. To understand this symmetry we have to grasp the ideological ground of these officers. "The prescriptions offered by *guerre révolutionnaire* mirrored the diagnosis; both reflected this French military vision of Communism in the contemporary world."[19] Their theories perceive communism as a secular form of religion that has taken the place of traditional religion. While they can appreciate the commitment and discipline of the revolutionary, they have no doubt about the evil nature of their enemy. The struggle against the revolutionary partisan is a fight against evil. This stark dualism operates with the presupposition that "nationalism, anti-colonialism, and demands for social justice were regarded as no more than limited, superficial attitudes that Communism was exploiting in order to bring all non-Western, underdeveloped areas into a global Communist-led coalition against the Christian West."[20] Thus the war against the rebels becomes a crusade against the forces of evil.

This theological interpretation is of great relevance for Schmitt's theory as well, although he does not foreground it in his own discussion of French counterguerilla theory. But Schmitt's admiration for Salan, who did not give up the struggle when the politician de Gaulle looked for a prudent compromise, is telling. It is not accidental that Schmitt compares Salan to Jeanne d'Arc (*die Heilige Johanna von Orleans*), who died for her commitment to God and the nation. Do we have to conclude that Schmitt ultimately identifies with Salan and the French Far Right?

There cannot be much doubt about his affinities to this group, to their defense of a European colonial order, their nationalism, and above all their Christian faith. What he shares with the rebellious officers is their refusal of political compromise, their firm belief in an either-or. Schmitt's dictum "der Feind ist unsere eigene Frage als

Gestalt" would equally apply to the French theorists of revolutionary war, since their enemy (Mao and Ho Chi-Minh) "is on the same
level as (they are)" (*TP* 85). But these affinities do not lead to complete identification on Schmitt's part. Rather, they result in a theory
of absolute and unconditional enmity that operates at a higher
level, which includes both the revolutionary and the counterrevolutionary.

In the final section of the essay, devoted to the concept of the
absolute enemy, Schmitt tries to come to grips with the ultimate
consequences of partisan warfare as a global phenomenon. By
creating a tight link between the partisan and the revolutionary,
Schmitt describes the rise of the partisan as the rise of the revolutionary above the state. He argues that the mere existence of the
state (as a sovereign) was a guarantee of the limitation of war. In
the age of Clausewitz one could define a real enemy but not yet an
absolute enemy. But the rise of the revolutionary party above the
state creates an absolute enemy who is ultimately evil. There seems
to be, in Schmitt's mind, no return to the status quo ante. This reading has unexpected consequences, for it means that not only the
Soviet Union and China are seen as revolutionary powers but also
the West, especially the anticommunism of the United States. Nuclear war as a war of total destruction is described as a war between absolute enemies. The moral or revolutionary commitment
leaves no room for negotiations. The surprising move of the last
section is the way in which Schmitt now merges partisan warfare
and interstate nuclear warfare, which he had kept apart before.

In terms of military strategy this move clearly makes no sense
because the political function of guerilla warfare is precisely that it
weakens the immediate enemy as well as his allies (the interested
third party) without triggering a nuclear exchange. But we have to
realize that the conclusion of *Theory of the Partisan* has ultimately
little to do with the actual irregular wars of the 1950s and 1960s.
Instead, the emphasis is placed on the ultimate historical catastrophe to which the partisan contributes because of his revolutionary
zeal. To insist, as Schmitt does, on the inevitability of this logic is a
religious rather than a political perspective. What is needed, then,
is a katechon, a person or a force that can at least slow down the

accelerating course of history. The figure of the katechon, however, is part of Schmitt's late political theology articulated in *Political Theology II*.

In terms of military strategy, Schmitt's position lies far outside the mainstream of his time. There was no consensus, for instance, that conventional war was outdated by the mere presence of nuclear weapons. In fact, some theorists, among them B. H. Liddell Hart, argued that the wars of the future would still be carried out primarily by conventional forces, although not armed and deployed like those of World War II. The issue was rarely the ultimate nuclear exchange but the potential of conventional war or the combination of conventional and nuclear war.[21] Michael Carver describes the spectrum of opinions as follows:

> General Maxwell Taylor, chief of staff of the U.S. Army, and the American writer Robert Osgood took the lead in demanding that reliance should no longer be placed on nuclear weapons. André Beaufre and Raymond Aron in France, unwilling to reject them entirely, sought a solution in terms of "very limited nuclear use." In Britain Lidell Hart . . . [took] the line that Kissinger, on second thought, had taken: that the only possible forms of limiting war to avoid mutual suicide were either to limit the geographical area in which operations took place . . . or to refrain from using nuclear weapons.[22]

In short, the efforts of the theorists and strategists alike were concentrated on containing the specter of absolute war. They could do this because they stayed away from the logic of revolutionary war, which preoccupies Schmitt. They hold on to a rational framework of survival that was accepted and respected by both sides. In Schmittian terms, they think of the opponent as a rival but not as an absolute enemy.

When Schmitt returns to the question of political theology in 1970 and asserts its viability, he claims more than an analogy between theology and legal concepts. He underscores the reality of the theological in metaphysical and historical terms. The fundamental claim in his argument against Hans Blumenberg is that modernity has never successfully emancipated itself from Christian theology. History cannot be thought about without theological dogma and commitments, among them the belief in the Second Coming of Christ as the end of history. In this context the autonomy of the political as the arena of human decisions and actions is restricted by the fundamental recognition of human failure (sin) and dependence. It seems that especially the conclusion of *Theory of the Partisan* moves in this direction by underlining the catastrophic development of recent human history and the inability of the political leaders to break out of the logic of absolute enmity and absolute, self-destructive war. Unlike the French theorists of counterinsurgency, Schmitt ultimately did not believe that a strategy of counterrevolutionary war could overcome the vicious logic. He could only hope for a force that would slow down the terrifying motion of history.

It is worth noting that these deeper theological questions have only rarely played a role in the heated discussion of Carl Schmitt's conception of warfare. Instead, the debate has underscored Schmitt's opposition to the liberal theory of the just war as a potentially destructive kind of war and the war on terror launched by the United States and its allies since 9/11, since they are driven by ideological concerns that in the final analysis eliminate all restraints. His advocates have praised Schmitt as a thinker who consciously returns to the notion of a spatial political order that allows for limited (*gehegte*) wars. In other words, the lesson to be learned from Schmitt is the need to focus on the idea of restraint (*Hegung*) as opposed to modern "just" wars and the destructive guerilla wars of the international terrorist, whose bloody intentions are based on revolutionary dogma.[23] By and large, readers sympathetic to Schmitt's theory have interpreted *The Theory of the Partisan* as a call to a more peaceful world order, precisely by rejecting the demands of liberal internationalism to ban war in principle.

The United States' second Iraq War, under President George W. Bush, has repeatedly been used as the classic example of liberal overreach and the self-contradiction of radical moral liberalism. This approach has overlooked, or at least downplayed, the ambiguities of Schmitt's essay. Schmitt's disciples have done what they held against their liberal opponents: They have constructed a firm but rigid conceptual position that can be used deftly in contemporary discussion. In terms of methodology, it can be best described as a formalized approach that becomes detached from specific historical and spatial moments in order to be redeployed across the terrain. As Benno Gerhard Teschke notes in his critique of Schmitt's theory: "This process of abstraction leads to conceptual reification as the authorial definition of concepts forms the given a priori for 'application.' . . . Schmittian concepts are lifted from their original context of formation and application and grafted onto radically different sociopolitical contexts."[24] In this view Schmitt becomes a (moderate) realist who justly critiques the dangerous dogma of pure liberalism. Yet Schmitt's intellectual acceptance of the revolutionary logic that leads from Clausewitz to Mao, as well as his counterrevolutionary sympathies, which are expressed in his emotional defense of general Salan, are not acknowledged. Neither side, of course, argues in favor of a limited war. But—and this is significant—neither side isolates the partisan or the terrorist from concrete historical contexts. Both sides anticipate a return to a "normal" situation when victory is accomplished and the partisan becomes a regular soldier again.

The Theory of the Partisan cannot and should not be reduced to a political message. The text is more than a critique of liberal internationalism and its understanding of defensible or indefensible wars. It cannot be summarized as the dogma that a return to a spatial model of international relations will sustain a more peaceful world. As David Chandler has pointed out, the readings of Schmitt's disciples "have been based on selective descriptive appropriations of his work with very little regard to the underlying ontological focus on the relation between power and meaning, the legal form and the underlying power-political content."[25] The essay's relevance today is precisely its ambiguity, its tension between conflicting political and military options that will not bring us back to the golden age of the *ius publicum Europaeum*. It is not accidental that later theorists have been able to use Schmitt's writings on war for very different positions. It is obvious that in the 1960s, Carl Schmitt was especially interested in and concerned about the link between revolutionary movements and irregular warfare, a concern that was connected to the political and military divide of the Cold War, whereas today's concerns are primarily fed by spreading religious radicalism in the Middle East that threatens Europe and the United States directly as well as indirectly. This kind of irregular war, including acts of terror carried out in Western countries, is built on the belief in a radical war that an individual or a group of fighters has to carry out against the (liberal) state.

5

THE RETURN OF POLITICAL THEOLOGY

Carl Schmitt's more recent international visibility, especially in the UK and the United States, has been shaped by those aspects of his late work that focus on international relations and the military consequences of the post-European world order. As it turns out, both conservative thinkers and left theorists could claim Schmitt's late writings for their cause. This surprising fact actually implies that Schmitt has been read selectively and forcefully placed into contradictory contexts. Thus, Schmitt's more recent ubiquity presupposes a significant amount of dehistoricization, not only by turning Schmitt's close connection with National Socialism into a theoretically unimportant episode, but also by a growing resistance to the author's fundamental commitments, among them his religious beliefs and his longstanding, complicated relationship with the Roman Catholic Church. It is not accidental therefore that Schmitt's last major essay, *Political Theology II* (1970), has not received a great deal of attention in the anglophone world, although this work returns to crucial questions that Schmitt raised in the 1920s in *Political Theology* and *Roman Catholicism and Political Form.*

The unstated consensus among Schmitt's English-speaking readers, foremost interested in international relations, seems to be that this small monograph, written when Schmitt was eighty years old, has nothing new and relevant to say. This approach is encouraged by the format of the work, which spends a great deal of energy and space on a long-forgotten controversy with an obscure German theologian. Yet this seemingly antiquarian interest is deceptive. In this essay, Schmitt returns with zeal and commitment to foundational concerns that he kept in the background in *The Nomos of the Earth* and the partisan essay. While the rhetoric in these works is clearly more secular, the fundamental assumptions, though not necessarily openly stated, remain committed to a theological perspective. It was the provocation of Hans Blumenberg's polemic against the idea of a political theology in general that motivated Schmitt to assert himself by restating his position in emphatic terms. That the outcome of this reappraisal turned out to be more ambiguous than the author intended, that Schmitt's theological arguments did not necessarily bring him into the fold of the Roman Catholic Church, is a different matter.

In the present discourse on Carl Schmitt, the importance of the theological aspect of his work is still controversial.[1] We could even speak of a divide. While Continental critics, especially German scholars, have by and large acknowledged the significance of Schmitt's theological thought, the Anglo-American discourse has mostly deemphasized this aspect as a minor part of his political theory. After all, in *Political Theology* (1922) Schmitt speaks of analogies between theological and political concepts and reminds his readers of the historical dimension of modern political theory that is ultimately rooted in theological thought. Moreover, Schmitt later informs his readers that he always understood himself to be a legal theorist without any ambition to intrude into the discipline of theologians. In short, we could treat the theological aspect of Schmitt's early theory as an interesting extension of his legal and political theory without paying too much attention to it. In 2003 William

Rasch defended this position by pointing to the essentially modern, postmetaphysical character of Schmitt's theory.[2] However, this approach overlooks other statements of Schmitt's in which the significance of the theological aspect of political theory in general is presented in an entirely different light. In those, Schmitt, although admitting that he is not a (professional) theologian himself, emphasizes the seriousness of his engagement with theology as well as the foundational nature of theology for the political realm.[3] The fact that modern politics is seen as an autonomous sphere (as Schmitt is aware) does not mean that he considers this development, beginning with Hobbes and Spinoza, as a positive turn. Rather, Schmitt is close to Karl Löwith, who considers secularization as a fundamental loss. It is not surprising, therefore, that he felt challenged by Hans Blumenberg's serious critique, in his *The Legitimacy of the Modern Age* (1966), of the prevailing understanding of secularization.

The importance of the theological aspect is most clearly stated in Schmitt's late work, not only *Political Theology II* but also his posthumous *Glossarium: Aufzeichnungen der Jahre 1947–1951*. After 1945, Schmitt was careful with public statements, since he felt that he was being scrutinized and hounded by his opponents. In *Glossarium*, though, he was extremely candid because these writings were not meant for immediate publication. They show Schmitt in a very different light. Among other things, they demonstrate his stubborn refusal to admit any responsibility for his political involvement between 1933 and 1945, his continued fierce anti-Judaism, and his search for a theological position that would ground and legitimize his concept of the political. Looking back from *Glossarium* and *Political Theology II*, specific elements of his earlier theory— for example his understanding of sovereignty and the political— appear in a different light. They reveal a meaning that was not immediately accessible in the 1920s. For this reason, those critics who take Schmitt's theology seriously, like Heinrich Meier, Günter Meuter, Ruth Groh, and Jürgen Manemann, have opened up a new dimension of meaning that allows us to uncover hitherto unseen but important connections in Schmitt's writings. Of course, the fact that Schmitt, like Heidegger, was raised in a Catholic milieu was well known but mostly interpreted in terms of its social and political implications. Schmitt was seen as a member of a religious minority in Germany that was denied equal status in Imperial Germany. For this group the Catholic Church had a special relevance, one that Schmitt himself described and celebrated in *Roman Catholicism and Political Form* (1923). But a more rigorous reading of Schmitt's theological statements reveals a much more complicated picture. Although Schmitt claimed to speak from a Catholic position, his own readings of the New Testament deviate significantly from an orthodox Catholic position. Indeed, both before 1933 and after 1945 the Catholic Church kept its distance from Schmitt's writings.

While in his late work Schmitt wants his readers to believe that his commitment to the concept of political theology has remained more or less constant during the decades between the publication of *Political Theology* in 1922 and *Political Theology II* in 1970, a closer look at his original definition of the relationship between theology and the sphere of politics reveals that the situation is actually more complicated. The common denominator—the concept of secularization—is only briefly mentioned in the chapter on political theology in the 1922 publication. Instead, Schmitt approaches the question from a different angle, an angle that played a central role in the discussion about the ultimate foundation of the legal order in the 1920s. It is the issue of sovereignty that guides the search for and explication of a political theology. In this context, the question of secularization remains mostly in the background, although it is of course of critical importance for Schmitt's answer. Schmitt's model of the perfect sovereign is the absolutist monarch of the seventeenth century. While his real interest in 1922 is of course the precarious situation of the Weimar Republic; namely, the challenges coming from the Far Right and Far Left to liberal democracy, moving to an earlier phase of the modern state has the advantage of allowing him to demonstrate with superior clarity the need for a clearly marked subject position. What makes the absolutist ruler ideal for the demonstration of sovereignty is the historical fact that he or she occupies a position of power that cannot be derived from any higher norm. In other words, the ruler precedes the laws that he or she makes. Therefore, according to Schmitt, it is not the law but the decision that defines sovereignty, leading him to the famous definition: "Sovereign is he who decides on the exception."[4] The crucial point of this argument is the reversal between norm and decision. It is not the decision that is derived from the norm but the norm that is grounded in the decision of the ruler.

The theological aspect enters this discussion indirectly when Schmitt claims an analogy between political ruler and God and, more broadly, that all significant concepts of modern constitutional law (*Staatsrecht*) are secularized theological terms. One example would be the state of exception as a secularized version of the theological miracle. The core of the analogy is a comparison of a ruler to an all-powerful God. As the process of secularization eliminates the miracle in the transition from theism in the seventeenth century to deism in the eighteenth century, the emerging rationalist conception of the state rejects the idea of the state of exception and insists on the centrality of the legal order (*Rechtsordnung*), which even the sovereign ruler has to obey. This means the evolution of European metaphysics is reflected in the changes occurring simultaneously in the interpretation of fundamental political concepts.

But what is the precise nature of the proposed analogy? Is it just an interesting phenomenon that historians might appreciate? For Schmitt it is crucial to establish that the idea of analogy is more than a game. Rather, he claims that our deeper understanding of the analogy between theological and legal/political concepts reveals the structural foundations of the political order. In this assumption, he is in agreement with Catholic political philosophers of the nineteenth-century counterrevolution—figures like Louis de Bonald, Joseph de Maistre, and Donoso Cortés—who returned to an older version of metaphysics in order to oppose the rising liberal order by insisting on the unlimited sovereignty of the monarch. While Schmitt does not believe in the restoration of the monarchy, he is looking for some form of transcendence. It is in this context that the decision as the primary concept takes on critical importance. For the Catholic theorists (and for Schmitt, who feels very close to them), the analogy between theological and legal concepts demonstrates a critical structural correspondence.

Schmitt's central task is to demonstrate the validity of this correspondence in the context of the heated debate of the 1920s about the sociology of concepts and theories, which is connected with names such as Marx and Engels, Max Weber, and Karl Mannheim. Schmitt rejects the version proposed by Marx and Engels as a crude and reductive form of materialism. Although he is more sympathetic to Weber's explanation of modern capitalism as rooted in radical Protestantism, his own version opposes the notion of a causal relationship between theology and law, in which either law becomes a reflection of theology or theology a derivative of the legal order. As much as Schmitt is prepared to accept Weber's sociology of legal institutions, he insists on the separation between institutional and conceptual sociology. The latter focuses on the structural similarity between different parts of a larger (historical) order. He uses the seventeenth-century concept of sovereignty to demonstrate his case:

> But it is a sociology of the concept of sovereignty when the historical-political status of the monarch of that epoch is shown to correspond to the general state of consciousness that was the characteristic of western Europeans at that time, and when the juristic construction of the historical-political reality can find a concept whose structure is in accord with the structure of metaphysical concepts. Monarchy thus becomes as self-evident in the consciousness of that period as democracy does in the later epoch. (*PT* 45–46)

The example demonstrates Schmitt's opposition to any form of reduction and his emphasis on the structural correspondence that defines an historical era. Political theology as a theory therefore underscores a conceptual and theoretical interconnectedness that illuminates the totality of a period. In the larger context of the assumed process of secularization this means that for a later stage the presumed link between the sovereignty of God and the sovereignty of the monarch is no longer available. This becomes very clear when Schmitt discusses the legal theory of Austrian jurist Hans Kelsen. Here Schmitt links Kelsen's concept of democracy to modern science: "Today, on the contrary, such a well-known legal and political philosopher of the state as Kelsen can conceive of democracy as the expression of a relativistic and impersonal scientism. This notion is in accord with the development of political theology and metaphysics in the nineteenth century" (*PT* 49). This example makes clear that in 1922, political theology is historically defined; it represents an early stage of modernity and will be replaced by a very different structure in the nineteenth und twentieth centuries. At the same time, there can be no doubt that Schmitt views this transformation with skepticism and anxiety. Even in his very early writings, the process of secularization entails loss of meaning and security rather than progress or human emancipation. This assessment means that there is a tension between the idea of a structural equivalence, which is neutral, and the concept of modern history as a process of secularization, which contains the notion of the irretrievable loss of transcendence as well as the rise of a modern state that has the power to contain violence. But this loss can possibly be cancelled or turned around by rediscovering the importance of political theology. In 1922, this tension is not resolved, since Schmitt stresses the importance of theological concepts by drawing an analogy with legal concepts but not their genealogical priority.

In brief, *Political Theology* is primarily a study of constitutional law, whereas *Political Theology II* focuses on theology. While there is clearly continuity between 1922 and 1970, there is a noticeable shift in emphasis that stresses the genealogical side. The later study raises the question of political theology in a more radical manner by going back to an older debate in which the possibility of a political theology was denied in principle. By strongly affirming the possibility of and need for political theology Schmitt also asserts the continued validity of his older, more limited argument.

Erik Peterson's Critique of Political Theology

Political Theology II has not yet seriously entered the Anglo-American discourse on Schmitt. The specific nature of the text makes this attitude understandable. The reader is confronted with a long polemical essay that means to refute a work by the theologian Erik Peterson published in 1935 under the title *Der Monotheismus als politisches Problem* (*Monotheism as a Political Problem*). Until his conversion to Roman Catholicism in 1935, Erik Peterson was a member of the Protestant theological faculty at the University of Bonn and held a chair in church history and the New Testament. During the late 1920s and early 1930s he and Schmitt, who also taught at the University of Bonn, were close friends.[5] Therefore Peterson's negative verdict concerning the theological legitimacy of any political theology may have come as a surprise to Schmitt, in particular the fact that Schmitt was explicitly mentioned as a proponent of the condemned position. But why should the reader of 1970 be interested in a half-forgotten disagreement between a legal scholar and a church historian? Of more relevance was clearly the extensive afterword that deals with Hans Blumenberg's path-breaking study, *The Legitimacy of the Modern Age* (1966). But again: What is the connection between Peterson's treatise, which focuses on late antiquity, and Blumenberg's revisionist understanding of modernity? For Schmitt, the link between Peterson and Blumenberg was apparent. Blumenberg renewed the challenge by questioning Schmitt's conception of history and the relevance of the theological within the historical process. While Peterson challenged Schmitt's reading of the Bible and theological dogma, Blumenberg challenged Schmitt's understanding of the connection between the concept of God and the concept of history, specifically Schmitt's eschatology. Through his polemical responses Schmitt reveals that the question of a political theology could not be contained as a strictly legal problem without any serious investment in the underlying theological issues. In other words, the critique of the theologian and the philosopher forced Schmitt to account for his own conceptual framework.

The time lag of thirty-five years in Schmitt's response to Peterson is curious indeed.[6] It seems that Schmitt initially either did not recognize the fundamental character of Peterson's critique or decided to ignore it in 1935 for personal or political reasons. In any case, their friendship continued for a number of years. What may have influenced Schmitt's late decision to answer Peterson was the fact that after the war Peterson's critique found general acceptance among theologians and political theorists in West Germany: It was agreed that a political theology based on Christian dogma was impossible.[7] To put it another way, after the collapse of the Third

Reich, the link between religion and politics was interrupted. The efforts of Protestant and Catholic theologians to legitimize Hitler's regime in the name of Christ was clearly a strong reason to resist any form of political theology. However, when Schmitt returned to the question of political theology in the late 1960s, there was a new wave of political theology, but now the efforts came from the Left. Johann Baptist Metz and Jürgen Moltmann argued for the involvement of theology in political and social issues as part of a progressive inter-vention of the church.[8] Schmitt's own approach followed, as we might expect, an entirely different path. Schmitt argued for the ne-cessity of a political theology in order to deal with anarchy and apocalyptic dangers. The biblical concept of the katechon—the one who delays the coming of the Antichrist—is the answer. The ultimate reason for political theology in the modern world is its *Verlorenheit,* which cannot be compensated by philosophy. For Schmitt the philos-ophy of history as an immanent approach cannot offer a convincing solution.

Political Theology II is dedicated to Hans Barion, a Catholic legal scholar who, like Schmitt, lost his academic appointment after 1945.[9] He was one of the few scholars whom the state barred from employment because he had joined the Nazi Party and strongly favored the alliance of Roman Catholicism and the National So-cialists. His fate, in other words, is very similar to that of Schmitt. Peterson, on the other hand, while initially sympathetic to fascism and certainly no admirer of liberalism, had drawn the line. His monograph *Der Monotheismus als politisches Problem* therefore argues against a specific form of political theology that he recognized in the alliance between the early Church and the Roman Empire (*Reichstheologie*). While the argument of the work is mostly his-torical, the conclusion is by no means restricted to the era of the late Roman Empire, as Peterson's preliminary remarks make quite clear. Here he argues against the development of modern post-Enlightenment monotheism (*Deismus*), a belief system without commitment to the Trinity of God the father, Christ the son, and the Holy Spirit. "For a Christian, political action is possible only under the condition of the faith in God's trinity."[10] In his critical review of the relationship between the metaphysical realm (God) and the political realm (the human community), Peterson tries to demonstrate that the concept of God as a monarch can be found in both the Aristotelian and the Jewish traditions (Philo). Here God is conceived as a monarch whose power (*potestas*) is the cause for both the cosmos and the human community. The decisive point of Peterson's argument is the close link between monotheism and monarchy. Both Greek philosophy and Jewish theology arrive at the same solution of the political: A close conceptual exchange between God and monarch means that either the political is an extension of the theological or the theological is an analogy of the political structure. In short, according to Peterson, monotheism, either in the form of Greek philosophy or in the form of Judaism, encourages a specific version of political theology: the identification of God and monarch as divine monarchy (*Göttliche Monarchie*).[11]

For Peterson the crucial question is to what extent the concept of God as monarch could be taken over by the early Christian tradition. If one could prove that the theologians of the early Christian church were familiar with and actually made use of this concept, one could speak of a Christian political theology. While Peterson is willing to entertain this interpretation with regard to early Jewish-Christian traditions, he ultimately rejects the notion of a Christian political theology as dogmatically impossible. It is important for Peterson to show in detail that the church fathers rejected the concept of *Göttliche Monarchie* as heretical. However, there is the case of the jurist and church leader Tertullian (155–240 A.D.), who explicitly uses the concept of the monarch to define God and contends that the Trinity of Father, Son, and Holy Spirit is not an argument against the conceptual construct. In Tertullian, Peterson finds a defender of Christianity who is too close to the Roman Empire for political reasons and therefore unable or unwilling to comprehend the dogmatic problem involved in comparing the political structure of the empire with the theological concept of the Trinity. After presenting the full range of the argument Peterson concludes: "We have shown that the first attempts to connect the received conception of a divine monarchy with the idea of the trinity had failed."[12]

The second part of the essay focuses on those later church fathers who made a more serious attempt to link orthodox Christian dogma and the notion of God as monarch, specifically on Origenes, who defends the Christian faith against the pagan argument (by Celsus) of its subversive and politically dangerous character, and Eusebius, the bishop of Caesarea and close adviser of Constantine. In this argument the emphasis is placed on the politically ambitious bishop and (problematic) church historian Eusebius. He becomes the real target of Peterson's polemic, since he combines in his person questionable theological concepts and a dubious role as a political adviser. To what extent was the *Pax Romana,* as it was first established by Augustus, useful for the expansion of Christianity beyond Israel, as Origenes and others had argued? For Peterson this argument is problematic because it potentially contains the notion of the priority of the Roman Empire and the idea of a unified world state. These are the very ideas that Peterson wants to push back against in 1935 when the autonomy of the Catholic Church is at stake. It is therefore the close link that Eusebius constructs between the development of a transnational Roman Empire and the development of Christianity within this empire that Peterson understands as Eusebius's fundamental failure to grasp the theological essence of Christianity. What Eusebius foregrounds—namely the overcoming of civil wars and the establishment of lasting peace under the Roman emperors, an obvious political argument—is precisely what Peterson, looking at his own world, cannot accept. In Peterson's reading, "in principle therefore [for Eusebius] monotheism began with the monarchy of Augustus."[13] Eusebius thus turns the church over to the emperor.

Why is Peterson so concerned about Eusebius's interpretation of the link between church and state? Because "Euebius's thoughts have had a major historical impact. One finds them everywhere in the writings of the later church fathers."[14] What concerns Peterson about this tradition is the mutual intertwinement of Christian Church and pagan state, the fact that Augustus is turned into a Christian statesman *avant la lettre* and Christ into a (loyal) Roman citizen (under Roman law). The key word in this context is *Reichspolitik* (imperial politics) as a specific strategy of the Church toward the Roman Empire during the fourth century. But theologically speaking, this type of politics is based on the heretical understanding of the Trinity by Arius and his followers. For Peterson the heretical nature of Christian political theology is sufficient proof that a political theology based on the Bible is impossible because it fails to account for the Trinity. Only a monotheism without proper recognition of Christ and the Holy Spirit as part of the unity of God can be extended into a political theology, moving ultimately toward a unity of church and state. Peterson's conclusion is that orthodox Christian dogma, represented for instance by Augustine, prohibits the construct of political theology. Only a footnote reveals that this thesis expresses a critique of Schmitt,[15] since the refutation of Eusebius's political theology also amounts to a fundamental attack on him.

It is necessary to explore the character and the aim of this critique. Toward the end of his study Peterson moves further and further away from a descriptive historical account, focusing instead on normative aspects. The final argument of the monograph points to the importance of eternal theological truth. A rigorous reading of Peterson's argument could not deny the fundamental thrust of the critique. Schmitt's political theology is described as illegitimate and heretical. In 1935, the indictment of *Reichstheologie* (imperial theology) had a specific political meaning: It attacked the alliance of the Church (both Catholic and Protestant) with Nazi Germany, the very alliance that Schmitt favored. To be sure, in Schmitt's polemical response, this alliance is not mentioned or even alluded to.[16] Instead, Schmitt, for reasons that we will have to discuss, means to reestablish the legitimacy of political theology, specifically in the wake of Vatican II and its reformulation of the Catholic Church's political and social stance. Apart from Schmitt's personal hostility toward Peterson, which is still apparent, the connection with Vatican II should be kept in mind.

Schmitt's Response to Peterson

In his response to Peterson, Schmitt himself chooses a different emphasis to frame the debate. He invokes the crisis of Protestant and (to a lesser extent) Catholic theology in the early twentieth century and Peterson's role in this crisis as a stern defender of Christian dogma and critic of liberal, historically inflected versions of theology. He reads *Der Monotheismus als politisches Problem* as an extension of the theological crisis caused by the rise of National Socialism in 1933. Schmitt refers to the *"Totalitätsansprüche"* (absolute claim) of Hitler's regime and suggests that the work must be interpreted as a response to an extreme situation. But what kind of intervention is it? To answer this question, Schmitt carefully prepares the ground for his rejoinder by stressing the traditional dualism of state and church, politics and religion, and its dissolution after 1918. The fact that the state lost "its monopoly on the political" (*PT II* 44) created the need for a new, a more fundamental definition of the political, a definition that Schmitt offered in 1927 in *The Concept of the Political* by making the basic distinction between friend and enemy. In separating the state and the political, Schmitt also, at least implicitly, suggests a political element in the religious sphere, since the political has become a free-floating concept. Quoting Ernst-Wolfgang Bockenförde, Schmitt makes this political moment more concrete: "Therefore one cannot circumvent the political by retreating to a neutral position, to some prepolitical natural law or to the pure proclamation of the Christian gospel" (*PT II* 46). The fact that Bockenförde functioned as one of Schmitt's important disciples in postwar Germany makes it sufficiently clear that through this quotation Schmitt reinstates his own position as correct and true. A more serious challenge to this position, but now linked to the 1960s and the arrival of Pope John XXIII, is Barion's insistence that the new teaching of the church developed in the wake of Vatican II does not have a foundation in the dogma. In order to reject the progressive theological stance of Pope John, Barion (like Peterson before him) denies the legitimacy of a specific political doctrine as derived from the dogma. Again, the writings of Augustine become crucial testimony to support Barion's intervention.[17]

Schmitt's return to the question of political theology occurred at a specific time, one critical to the fate of the Roman Catholic

Church. Vatican II raised the question of a necessary political involvement of the Church on the progressive side. Johann Baptist Metz developed the idea of a politically and socially committed Catholic Church, while Jürgen Moltmann spoke in a similar vein for the Protestant (Lutheran) Church. Those who disagreed with this development, like the conservative political scientist Hans Maier, referred back to Peterson in order to reject the political theology of Vatican II. In the discussion of the late 1960s, in which Schmitt found himself involved as a defender of political theology, he does not really question the theoretical possibility of a political use of the Christian faith or, to put it more cautiously, the political implications of theological positions. At the center of the debate (as Schmitt certainly realizes in his polemic against the Catholic theologian Ernst Feil) we find the disagreement over the political goals—a progressive or conservative commitment, democracy or authority. In Schmitt's eyes, Feil is inconsistent when he calls for a new form of political theology along the lines of Metz, but attacks conservative versions under the heading of "divine monarchy" and "caesaro-papists" (*PT II* 54). Schmitt's own defense of political theology would clearly not include a theology of revolution proposed by the radical left wing of the Church. Still, both Schmitt and Feil are involved in what the Egyptologist Jan Assmann has called active political theology, as distinct from a merely descriptive version that explores different ways of connecting or separating state and church or the political and the theological.[18] It is difficult, if not impossible, for Schmitt to relate to a descriptive concept of political theology, as can be gleaned from his critique of Ernst Topitsch, who proposed a sociological approach to the problem. For Schmitt, Topitsch's method amounts to neutralization and positivism, since it excludes the moments of commitment and action.

Still, it has to be noted that Schmitt makes a serious attempt to reconstruct Peterson's essay, both in terms of its history and place within his oeuvre and in its argument. At the same time, he discusses its function in 1935 as a possible analogy between Constantine and Hitler or Stalin, suggesting that the historical material does not sufficiently support this analogy. But Schmitt's real aim transcends this skeptical argument; he means to demonstrate not only the feasibility of political theology but its inevitability given the public role of the Church in the world (*Sichtbarkeit der Kirche*). Basically, he does this by reorganizing and reinterpreting the historical material that Peterson had used to demonstrate the incompatibility of political theology and Christianity. Here, it is important to remember that Peterson's early work, especially his monograph *Heis Theos* (1926), was an important text for Schmitt, since it seemed to confirm Max Weber's concept of the charismatic leader (*PT II* 66–67). On the whole, Schmitt's strategy is to broaden the discussion by including non-Christian forms of political theology and stressing sovereignty rather than monarchy. The aim is to deflect the interest of the reader from the theological point that Peterson wants to make; that is, the significance of the concept of Christian Trinity for political theology, to a discussion of the imprecision of Peterson's concept of the charismatic leader (*PT II* 74–75). If Peterson cannot, as Schmitt suggests, distinguish between a legitimate king and a charismatic leader, his entire argument is too simplistic to be of any use.

Obviously this strategy does not get to the core of Peterson's argument, as Schmitt realizes when he finally squarely focuses on Peterson's theological reservations. He rightly emphasizes that Peterson's negative verdict is exclusively directed against a Christian form of political theology, and he correctly notes that the historical evidence Peterson presents is more ambiguous than the conclusion Peterson finally draws. The most apparent case would be that of Eusebius, the friend and counselor of Emperor Constantine, whom Peterson, following Jacob Burckhardt, describes as a dubious politician. The crucial issue here is, as Schmitt knows, not the good or bad reputation of the bishop of Caesaria but his theological position. In other words, the question is: Can we derive a valid form of political theology from his theological statements on the Trinity? Or was he a secret supporter of Arius, who had denied the similarity of God the father and Christ the son?

Schmitt's defense of Eusebius uses both historical (political) and theological arguments. By placing the bishop in the context of the Council of Nicea (AD 325), he stresses the inseparable unity of the political and the theological aspect. It is interesting and important to observe how Schmitt changes the character of the problem when he suggests that there is ultimately no position outside of the political that even a completely orthodox theologian would turn into a political theologian as soon as he participates in the public debate. We have to remind ourselves that this is not Peterson's problem. Peterson wants to demonstrate that a legitimate form of political theology cannot be derived from Christian dogma because of the essential category of the Trinity. Schmitt does not respond to this challenge by giving evidence for Eusebius's correct interpretation of the Trinity and a correct deduction of the political monarchy from this dogma. Instead, he shifts the argument to an assessment of the Roman Empire in the light of the eschatological expectations (*heilsgeschichtliche Endzeiterwartung*) of the Church. Eusebius, according to Schmitt, was really condemned because of "his exaggerated view of the Roman Empire in the history of salvation" (*PT II* 86). Schmitt shrewdly points out that Peterson himself, in a 1929 lecture on the Church, emphasized the ambiguous nature of the early Catholic Church: "The intrinsic ambiguity of the church can be clarified through the interpretation of empire and church" (quoted in *PT II* 86–87). Obviously this statement is not normative but descriptive and historical. And this is, it seems, the level where Schmitt wants to situate the question of political theology. The assumed ubiquity of the political extends into the theological realm and becomes the public space of the Church. It is the political mission of the Church that he wants to defend, while Peterson wants to restrict this mission. Therefore the question of whether one can devise a valid form of political theology from a specific theological dogma is not the crucial issue for Schmitt. For him, the mere fact that a theological argument extends into the realm of praxis makes it political.

Rethinking the question of political theology after the war and in particular his disagreement with his former friend Peterson, Schmitt realized that Peterson meant to send him a message about the consequences of the recent alliance between state and church in Germany and the role of those who favored this alliance—for example, Schmitt himself. The polemic against the "infamous Caesaro-Papist Eusebius" (*PT II* 80) has, at least in Schmitt's eyes, a personal angle, although neither he nor Peterson openly state the analogy. The defense of Eusebius uses the familiar argument of the ubiquity of the political. Peterson's retreat from the political to the theological sphere cannot solve the problem because this move is as much a political decision as the support of the alliance. This argument undermines the very distinction that Peterson made to save the church. With some justification Schmitt points out that Peterson's 1935 text is itself a political intervention in the name of pure theology against political corruption, here personified by Eusebius's support for Constantine.

The ground for this defense is explicated in the following paragraph when Schmitt shifts the argument from the theological to the political sphere and suggests (going back to his concept of the political) that in a period of crisis clear distinctions between state and church are no longer effective. "The categorical distinctions between the two kingdoms and spheres . . . do not work any longer when the religious cannot be clearly differentiated from the church and the political from the empire or state" (*PT II* 97). The point Schmitt wants to make is that in a period of crisis (like 1933) the pretension of absolute purity cannot be upheld. The politicization of religion and its institutions becomes as inevitable as the transfer of religious concepts into the political realm. To be sure, Schmitt's approach misrepresents Peterson's position, since the latter, by insisting on the absolute priority of the theological dogma, means to block the intrusion of forms of political actions that are not legitimized by the Church's theology and its institutions. The example of this kind of corruption is Heidegger, who, according to Peterson, transferred the commitment to God and Christ into a commitment to the charismatic leader (i.e., Hitler; *PT II* 97).

Schmitt's Catholic Commitment and the Interpretation of History

Ultimately, Schmitt's refutation of Peterson never quite focuses on the most basic disagreement, which involves the theological interpretation of history. While Schmitt's final polemic against Peterson foregrounds the limitations of a pure theology and claims the relevance of jurisprudence for the conception of political theology, his real disagreement with Peterson concerns the problem of eschatology—notwithstanding his claim that he understands *Political Theology* (1922) as "the statement of the jurist about a systematic structural analogy between theological and legal concepts that offers itself both in theoretical and practical terms" (*PT II* 148n2, translation altered). What is the meaning of history? For Peterson its meaning can be defined only and exclusively in theological/religious terms; for Schmitt, on the other hand, the time between the first and the Second Coming of Christ is given its own specific meaning in the realm of political action. This aspect becomes much clearer in Schmitt's response to Hans Blumenberg, which is added to the essay as a postscript.

Before we turn to the postscript, it is important to emphasize the nature of Schmitt's religious and/or theological commitment because his own statements are contradictory. His attempt to create a legitimate space for himself as a nontheologian who moves into the field of theology by demarcating his own position as strictly defined in legal terms (*juristisch*) has to cover the fact that Schmitt makes theological claims, claims that transcend the safe method of stating analogies and pointing to the fate of theological concepts and ideas in a process of secularization. For Schmitt, "secularization" is not a neutral term. In a letter to his friend Helmut Rumpf (May 23, 1948), Schmitt states his own Catholicism in strong terms: "I am a Catholic, not only in terms of my beliefs but also in terms of my historical background."[19] His almost simultaneous critique of Jünger's use of the Bible in his diaries (*G* 130) underlines the seriousness of his own commitment. It does not suffice therefore to emphasize Schmitt's definition of political categories as secularized theological concepts; we have to understand and acknowledge the concept of secularization in Schmitt's late work as a theological conception of history.

In his study of Donoso Cortés, published in 1950, Schmitt offers a reading of history that operates with the concept of the Christian historical period and its possible end: "This raises the question whether the Christian era has come to an end or not."[20] At the same time, the Catholic commitment and consequently the belief in the coexistence of a spiritual and a worldly realm has not prevented Schmitt from favoring a political solution of the conception of the Catholic Church; that is, an emphasis on Christianity as the religion of the state as promoted by Eusebius.[21] In this respect he was and remained part of the New Catholicism in Germany, together with Catholic intellectuals such as Theodor Haecker, Hugo Ball, and Georg Moenius. Especially for Father Moenius the connection between Roman Empire and Catholic Church was crucial.[22] Given the basic pattern, it did not matter whether one supported or rejected the National Socialists. In either case the priority of the Church would be preserved, which means that the support of the National Socialism is seen as a secondary commitment only. In *Political Theology II*, Schmitt, now removed from his involvement in 1933, reiterates the need for a political theology based on the needs of the Roman Catholic Church. The much-quoted testimony for this self-understanding is this statement in *Glossarium*: "This is the secret key of my entire intellectual and public existence: the struggle for the true Catholic intensification" (G 165). This *Verschärfung* (intensification), part of a quotation in a text of the Catholic poet Konrad Weiß on Theodor Haecker, marks a radical turn against liberalism, modernity, humanism, and pacifism—a decisive step beyond traditional Catholicism.

One of the areas in which this *Verschärfung* would have significant implications is the concept of history, specifically the definition of the period before the end of history and the Second Coming of Christ. In *Political Theology* this question was already a focus of Schmitt's attempt to define the relationship between theological and legal concepts. For Schmitt legal concepts were secularized theological concepts. However, in 1922 Schmitt did not fill out the theological frame by referring to the end of history. In *Political Theology II,* through the discussion of the function of the Roman Empire for the Church, this topic comes into the foreground. This was probably the reason why Schmitt added his response to Hans Blumenberg's *Legitimacy of the Modern Age* (1966) as a postscript, although Blumenberg's and Peterson's positions were clearly not compatible. While Peterson's theology denied validity to the realm of secular history, Blumenberg's aim was primarily to rescue the secular human sphere from the absolute demands of theology. While disagreeing with Schmitt, Blumenberg raised the very questions that challenge the legitimacy of absolute theological claims. For this reason, Schmitt was justified in his assessment that Blumenberg's critique of his work, in particular of his understanding of the process of secularization, appears as an appropriate continuation of the old debate. He notes: "In this book, the non-absolute is declared absolute and an attempt is made to negate *scientifically* any political theology—scientifically in the sense of an understanding of science which does not accept any validity for a continuing influence of, or transposition from, the history of salvation stemming from a religion which claims to be absolute" (*PT II* 117). These remarks, while they seem only to summarize the book, already anticipate the strategy of Schmitt's response. By emphasizing the scientific nature of Blumenberg's approach, he suggests that Blumenberg ultimately cannot do justice to the metaphysical aspects of the problem. It is interesting to note that he takes over Blumenberg's key concept to describe historical changes in the field of theology and philosophy but seems to be uncertain how to use it. In Schmitt's use, transposition (*Umbesetzung*) is a term that denotes loss rather than reorientation and rethinking.

Blumenberg's Intervention

But what precisely is the nature of the disagreement? Schmitt presents his own position as that of a legal scholar who accepts and supports Western rationalism as it was developed (against religious and theological claims) in the field of law and politics. The state, he reminds us, is a specifically modern institution. Only recourse to Blumenberg's critique in *The Legitimacy of the Modern Age* can clarify Schmitt's response. Blumenberg's central theme is the necessary reinterpretation of the category of secularization to explain the modern age (*Neuzeit*) as a qualitatively distinct period of history, a period that overcame a theological Christian interpretation of the world. Secularization, Blumenberg argues, is used in different areas and ways to demonstrate the dependence of the modern age on previous historical formations. The concept of secularization thereby undermines the legitimacy of modernity and the Enlightenment.

In this context Blumenberg briefly mentions Schmitt's *Political Theology* as an example of the typical and problematic use of secularization, but Blumenberg's critique mainly focuses on Karl Löwith's study *Meaning in History: The Theological Implications of the Philosophy of History* (1949), which offers a rereading of German idealism, especially of Hegel, that stresses the moment of transformation from theological to modern philosophical thought. In this context Christian teleological understanding of history (*Heilsgeschichte*) becomes philosophical progress. Where Löwith assumes continuity, Blumenberg objects and argues that "between eschatology and the idea of progress are critical differences that block the transfer. These differences problematize the criterion of an identification of the theological moments in history."[23] The shift from a transcendent to an immanent interpretation of the world cannot be explained by the concept of secularization. Blumenberg suggests that the persuasive force of the secularization thesis is largely a linguistic phenomenon—the similarity of linguistic formulations where the actual historical processes and actions are quite dissimilar.

Schmitt's political theology would be a case in point: "The statement 'All meaningful concepts of modern political theory are secularized theological concepts' has not become more persuasive since it was uttered in 1922, because we have learned to doubt that this modernity has ever been modern."[24] The criticism comes from an unexpected angle, since Blumenberg emphasizes the slowness and inadequacy of the process of modernization in Europe. What Schmitt reads as a specifically modern secularization of theological concepts may well be the belated status of basic legal and political concepts. It is, in other words, the incompleteness of the process of the Enlightenment that Blumenberg holds against Schmitt's thesis. It is also apparent that he does not, as in the case of Löwith, charge that Schmitt did not grasp the character of the *Umbesetzung*. The specific angle of Blumenberg's critique offers Schmitt the opportunity to answer the criticism by focusing on the legal aspect while down-playing the theological and by foregrounding the problem of modernity that Blumenberg himself had stressed.

Schmitt's Critique of Blumenberg

The postscript of *Political Theology II* proves that Schmitt fully understood the challenge of Blumenberg's thesis, far beyond the specific criticism of his early work. Therefore his response aims to radicalize this thesis to the point where its problematic nature will become apparent. According to Schmitt, Blumenberg's goal is the detheologization (*Enttheologisierung; PT II* 117) of the world. "In the end, Blumenberg is interested in the self-empowerment of human beings and in the human thirst for knowledge. . . . Autism is inherent in this argument. Its immanence, directed polemically against a theological transcendence, is nothing but self-empowerment" (*PT II* 120). The choice of words makes it clear that Schmitt is, to say the least, uncomfortable with Blumenberg's claim. But he does not close the door by simply restating the need for transcendence and the limitation of human knowledge and planning. Instead, he opens a dialogue by suggesting to Blumenberg that the theological debate between him and Peterson, including a serious reassessment of gnosis, might be the way to understand his concept of the political.

As it turns out, the assessment and evolution of gnostic thought patterns becomes central in the dialogue with Blumenberg. We have to remember that for Blumenberg gnostic dualism and the need for redemption of the world because of its basic imperfection is the unresolved problem of medieval theology, a problem that only the modern age can overcome. This position is clearly stated in *The Legitimacy of the Modern Age*. In his dialog with Blumenberg, Schmitt acknowledges this position without accepting it. In fact, he reintroduces the gnostic dualism between a bad creator God and the God of redemption to ground his own political theology. "The main structural problem with gnostic dualism, that is, with the problem of the God of creation and the God of salvation, dominates not only *every* religion of salvation and redemption. It exists inescapably in every world in need of change and renewal, and it is both immanent and ineradicable" (*PT II* 125, my emphasis).

By claiming to uncover a universal pattern, Schmitt also includes the Christian faith. He does this by underlining the proximity of Augustine and gnosis with the distinction, of course, that for Augustine human beings are to blame for the evil in the world. As Schmitt puts it, "Humans . . . prove their freedom not through the good they do but through their wicked acts" (*PT II* 124). Whether we follow the gnostic or the Augustinian argument makes no fundamental difference: We have to accept the presence of evil in the world and the fundamental enmity between men (*Feindschaft zwischen Menschen*). As a result, there can be no basic change or improvement of the human condition. Neither reforms nor revolutions can accomplish this. In other words, Blumenberg's thesis is forcefully rejected. When Blumenberg argues in favor of human emancipation from the oppression of absolute theology (God is unknowable and humans completely dependent), Schmitt returns to what he calls a *Stasiologie* (*PT II* 126) that cannot be overcome. It is the function of the state to limit the political implication of *stasis* (civil war). Not surprisingly, therefore, Schmitt defends the need for a political theology in a strict sense of the term, since in secularized modern versions of the political the older patterns remain intact. Without mentioning Blumenberg, at the end Schmitt restates his position in strong terms. It is no less than a complete rejection of modernity; that is, of human emancipation, progress, and the development of knowledge independent of theological foundations. The final statement also illuminates the importance and range of Blumenberg's provocation, which is much more fundamental than the critique of Peterson. The disagreement concerns the historical role of Christianity, especially in the transition from the Middle Ages to modernity, a form of radical questioning that was equally alien to medieval theologians and the legal theorists.

Blumenberg forced Schmitt to rethink the theological foundations of his position and, at the same time, enabled him to sharpen his theological argument. Now he can do what Peterson denied: He can anchor his own position in the concept of the Christian Trinity by arguing that the unity of God includes the hostility between God the father and God the son.[25] We have to realize that Schmitt is developing a private theology that would not be acceptable to the Catholic Church. If we separate the two persons of God in such a way that Christ the redeemer must turn against his father, then Christ takes on the character of a rebel who endangers the work of God. Only by dividing Christ into a divine and a human side can Schmitt control the explosive outcome of his own private theology.[26] It is the human, the Promethean side that has to be checked. Christ the rebel is responsible for the division within God, which in turn is responsible for the origin of the political, in Schmitt's sense. The reality of the enemy as the organizing principle of the world can therefore always be retraced to its theological origins.

The Dialogue between Blumenberg and Schmitt

Despite the conciliatory rhetoric of the postscript, Blumenberg could not overlook the severity of Schmitt's rebuttal, including Schmitt's implied claim that a solution could be found only within the theological framework offered by Schmitt. Still, Blumenberg decided to approach Schmitt and enter a dialogue. The publication of the letters exchanged between 1971 and 1978 throws much more light on Blumenberg's formal response in the second, significantly revised edition of *The Legitimacy of the Modern Age* and later monograph *Work on Myth* (1979). Among other things, Blumenberg had to persuade Schmitt that his own project could not be properly described as "scientific," as a form of positivism, quite apart from the fact that his own biography as a "half-Jew," who was put into a concentration camp, escaped and went into hiding until 1945, created a personal challenge.[27] In the exchange of letters, the personal aspect is consistently left out. Instead, it is the difference between their positions (theologically, philosophically, and anthropologically) that defines the nature and direction of their dialogue.

A detailed analysis of this dialogue cannot be offered here. It must suffice to follow the process of the (mutual) clarification of their respective positions, a process in which the younger partner was more interested than the older one. Blumenberg takes up the challenge by explicitly questioning his own solution to the problem of secularization. In this process he maintains his goal: a reassessment of the concept of secularization that does not include the notion of illegitimacy. However, he is not satisfied with his own understanding of detheologization through the concept of *Umbesetzung* and *Selbstbehauptung* (self-assertion).[28] At the same time, he tries to define the methodological difference between Schmitt's assessment and his own. It is tentatively described as the difference between Schmitt's interest in the question, "Where is the extreme situation/state located?" (*"wo liegt der extreme Zustand?"*)[29] and his own interest in the question "how can this be preserved?" (*"wie kann sich dies erhalten?"*).[30] But the explication does not go beyond this brief statement.

Schmitt's response (on March 31, 1971) makes clear that he fully understands the tentative nature of Blumenberg's first letter as an invitation to explore the difference, although he politely declines the offer. Instead, he suggests that Blumenberg's approach is indebted to Ernst Troeltsch and Max Weber (i.e., to a sociology of religion), while his own conception of secularization is based on canonical law. Of course, this seemingly neutral assessment of the difference is anything but neutral, since it places Blumenberg within a scientific tradition that tries to neutralize theological concepts. Furthermore, Schmitt refers to his study, *The Nomos of the Earth* (1950), to demonstrate his own understanding of the difference between a theological and a secular, juridical approach to the question of war. In this context Schmitt emphasizes the danger of an absolute, theological understanding of war. In other words, he makes room for a positive and legitimate conception of secularization, while holding on to a theological frame.

There remains a tension, which becomes evident in two contradictory claims. On the one hand, Schmitt, especially in *The Nomos of the Earth*, argues for the more humane quality of a strictly legal politics over absolute theological politics; on the other, he stresses the inevitable theological origin of the political in the notion of an original divine conflict. It seems that Schmitt was unable to extricate himself from this tension, and Blumenberg's intervention in his

Säkularisierung und Selbstbehauptung (1974), the revised first two parts of *Legitimität,* as much as it did more justice to Schmitt's theory than the first edition, ultimately did not help Schmitt, since it rigorously reinterpreted the theological claim and its insistence on a historical grounding of the political in theology as an extended metaphor: "'Political theology' is a metaphorical theology."[31] As a metaphorical construct it becomes plausible insofar it operates with persons, rather than laws that can be applied mechanically. The distinction between a rational and a voluntaristic theory enables Blumenberg to define Schmitt's political theology. Schmitt represents the second type that needs a subject at its center: "Voluntarism is necessarily dependent on a subject, be it only a fictional one. Hence, it requires 'persons,' be they only 'legal persons.' Decisionism cannot function without a 'sovereign,' be it only a metaphorical one."[32] For Schmitt God is needed to legitimize the political sovereign, but this need is, according to Blumenberg, no more than a need for an analogy. In other words, Blumenberg reads Schmitt backward: The structure of modern political theory, beginning with Hobbes, suggests a theological background that can be invoked to legitimize its existence and its structure. This reading allows for a connection between the old theological and the new secular construct, but it is not perceived as a deduction or a substantive continuation, nor as a loss of substance. Instead, Blumenberg stresses the need for human intervention to leave the cage of theological absolutism: "It is not a secularized theology but rather the selection from theology of what will be tolerable in the world, which then in its turn can be given out as the norm governing the content of what is decreed."[33] Theological terminology becomes a vehicle for the explication of the political; as such it is useful and legitimate, but it is not the process of secularization that Schmitt wants to claim.

As Blumenberg acknowledges, Schmitt did not concede the use of legitimacy in the context of his study. Instead, he spoke of the legality of the modern age, thereby suggesting a lack of legitimacy. This critique of modernity is of course a central element of Schmitt's work, as much as Blumenberg affirms the justification of modernity in historical terms. In the face of this critique, Blumenberg must defend himself against the accusation of arguing in favor of human *Selbstermächtigung* (self-empowerment) as the defining moment of modernity. He does this by pointing to specific historically conditioned functions of reason in early modernity. Reason accepts the challenge created by the absolutism of late scholastic theology; namely, the complete dependence of humans on the will of an unknowable God. It is therefore not the autonomy of reason that is the problem but its interpretation as the unruly and illegitimate child of theology. "Self-assertion determines the radicalness of reason, not its logic."[34]

Schmitt's Gnosticism

There is no indication that Schmitt ever accepted Blumenberg's interpretation of his political theology, although the exchange of letters continued. For Schmitt, in particular in the later years, political theology was not a question of metaphors but a question of religious commitment. He remained convinced that history after the first coming of Christ moved toward the Second Coming of the Redeemer. In this eschatological view, the figure of the katechon mentioned in Paul's letter to the Thessalonians plays an increasingly important role for Schmitt (2 Thess. 2:1–8). The katechon is the person (or power) who holds back the coming of the Antichrist at the end of history.[35] While a strictly eschatological orientation (that of the early Church) devalued history, the work of the katechon gives meaning to history. For Schmitt, the emperors of the Roman Empire and the German medieval empire can be seen in this light. By establishing a political order in the secular realm they postpone the arrival of the Antichrist. We might say that the significance of legal theory depends on this model, for pure eschatology would make it superfluous. At the same time, theology and law cannot be separated.

As Heinrich Meier observes, the central element in Schmitt's theory that secures the connection between revelation and politics is the idea of grounding the political in a triadic constellation, which can occur any time and everywhere. Where we have three persons (natural or metaphysical) the political becomes possible. It is precisely the distinction between friend and enemy that makes the political and the theological sphere compatible.[36] Meier points to the struggle between Christ and Antichrist as the ultimate political constellation. But in the end it is the concept of the divided God—the tension between father and son—that provides the theological model. It is therefore not only the rebellion of Satan that demonstrates the metaphysical character of the political but the Schmittian concept of the Trinity (ultimately turned against Peterson). Schmitt's *"eigentlich katholische Verschärfung,"* the emphatic insistence on the Catholic ground of political concepts, turns out to be less Catholic than Schmitt believed.

The deviation from orthodox dogma can either be interpreted as a private mythology (Ruth Groh) or in theological terms as a form of gnosis (Jürgen Manemann). Schmitt's unrelenting insistence on the evil of man in metaphysical rather than moral terms and the loneliness and depravity of the world in general should be read as indicators of his proximity to gnostic thought.[37] In this respect, he is by no means an isolated figure in the early twentieth century.[38] Still, the question that has to be answered is the compatibility of Schmittian theory and gnostic thought as well as the place that gnosis has in Schmitt's writings. The fact that Schmitt considered himself a Roman Catholic does not exclude gnostic affinities because these were already present in the early Church. For this reason the theologian Metz refers to the *"gnostische Dauerversuchung"* (permanent gnostic temptation) of the church.[39] Still, it is not sufficient simply to point to the moment of deviation from orthodox Catholic dogma—for instance Schmitt's emphasis on evil, his interpretation of Christ as a promethean rebel figure, and his emphasis on the role of the katechon (which is minor in the dogma)—to demonstrate gnostic structures; it is his deemphasizing of the Christian belief in redemption through Christ and the belief in the permanent conflict between good and evil as an irresolvable dualism that highlights the deep affinity. The lonely and contingent individual, desperate in its need for redemption because of its own contamination with evil, represents the gnostic version of the Christian constellation. Most revealing is Schmitt's note in *Glossarium*: "God is the completely Other? This is what the theologians tell us. Okay, theologians with Christian customers, state officials who claim to be victims of fascism. Over-privileged and potential winners of the Nobel Prize. God the completely Other? God is the completely identical. God is I" (July 5, 1950, G 307). The knowledge of the God within, the gnostic version, is clearly different from the Christian dogma. Even the typical gnostic constellation is modified in this statement, insofar as the gnostic system saw God the redeemer as the complete "Other" that Schmitt denies. With some justification Jürgen Manemann speaks of Schmitt's gnosis as "*kupierte Gnosis*," since it remains immanent but retains a strict dualism.[40] However, this dualism places the emphasis on the radically sinful nature of man and therefore the need for redemption. Moreover— and here Schmitt is closer to Calvin than Catholic orthodoxy—he underlines the divide between those who are chosen and those who are not (G 63).

If the world, as Schmitt claims, is fundamentally depraved and lost, there are two possible responses: either we strive for redemption or we try to give order to the chaotic world through the law. As Jacob Taubes suggests, this is Schmitt's perspective as legal theorist.[41] Any order is better than chaos.[42] It is not surprising therefore that Schmitt understood himself as a katechon whose actions postpone the end of history. The katechon counters the utopian drive, the problematic confidence to fundamentally change the world as a secularized form of the eschatological constellation of the New Testament. For Schmitt's political theology this counterforce is of crucial importance. It defines the state as an interim formation between the first and the Second Coming of Christ. The state itself does not have sacramental power; it cannot by itself carry out or even bring closer the redemption promised by Christ.[43] Hence the history of the state and *Heilsgeschichte* remain separate, although they are of course part of the same overarching constellation.

The fact that Schmitt sometimes insists that his own discourse is exclusively juridical and on other occasions claims a theological role for himself may be related to this dual history and its dialectic. The full and ultimate meaning of the worldly order can be grasped only from a theological perspective, but this does not mean that it is a mere extension of *Heilsgeschichte*. Especially in a gnostic version, as Schmitt puts it in *Political Theology II*, the divide between God the redeemer (*Heilsgeschichte*) and God the creator of an evil world (secular history and the state)—the objective dualism—cannot be overcome. This assumption throws light on the specific character of Schmitt's political theology: Its political perspective is not Christ the redeemer but the opposition of imperfect creation and redemption. Yet even this definition of the *complexio oppositorum* is not the final word. By splitting the figure of Christ into a Promethean (rebellious) and an Epimethean (obedient) part, Schmitt forcefully undercuts all utopian aspects of the political.[44] In this context, Schmitt's reference to Dostoevsky's novel *The Brothers Karamazov* is revealing. According to Dostoevsky, the true aim of the Roman Catholic Church is to neutralize the impact of Christ the redeemer, to block the anarchist tendencies inherent in Christianity without openly showing the anti-Christian commitment of the Church (*G* 243). Establishing order in the world is more important than Jesus the redeemer. It is telling that Schmitt cannot find a fundamental distinction between the *ecclesia militans* of the Counter-Reformation and Hobbes's modern sovereign. For both sides the constitution of political and social order is the foremost goal.

Reasserting Political Theology

This raises a fundamental question: What does Schmitt mean when he reasserts the viability of political theology in 1970? Only in *Political Theology II* do the radical theological implications of his position come into full view. There is significantly more involved than the analogy between theological and legal concepts. Against Blumenberg, who suggests that we should understand Schmitt's theory metaphorically, Schmitt underscores the reality of the theological aspect both in historical and metaphysical terms. Modernity has not emancipated itself from the grasp of a theological past. The conciliatory tone of his letters to Blumenberg can only mask the radical disagreements when it comes to the interpretation of secu-

larization. For Schmitt secularization did not change the fundamental structure of the world; it made it only less visible. His claim
against Peterson that political theology does not dissolve itself
because of a particular Christian dogma (here the structure of the
concept of Trinity) is not only meant as a specific historical argument.
Instead Schmitt maintains the relevance of theology for political
thought in much more general terms. However, his own reflections
were focused on Christianity and indirectly on Judaism. To what
extent all forms of monotheism either contain or at least allow a
political theology remained outside of his horizon, since he looks
at political theory from a Catholic position that is in polemical
disagreement with secular definition of the law. Hence his idea
brings to the foreground "the opposition between authority and
anarchy, faith in revelation and atheism, obedience to and rebellion against the supreme sovereign."[45]

To put it another way, for Schmitt political theology always had
a strategic and polemical function and reflected deeply held personal convictions. This may be the reason that Schmitt did not
open a dialogue with younger theologians—such as Jürgen Moltmann
on the protestant side and Johann Baptist Metz on the catholic
side—who explicitly renewed the tradition of political theology
from a Left perspective, although he shares their belief that Christianity implies a political commitment. Given the radically conservative nature of his commitment, which finds its ideal expression in
the admiration of Donoso Cortés, Schmitt must either ignore or
attack the reactivation of political theology in the wake of Vatican II.
Schmitt insists on the concept of the sovereign God as the ultimate ground of the political and thereby rejects the possibility of
a purely immanent approach through philosophical reason, a position that sets limits to his dialogue with Blumenberg, for whom
political theology in the Christian tradition is a strictly historical
moment whose present relevance only philosophical reflection can
adequately explore.

The renewed interest in the link between religion and politics,
partly inspired by the revival of religion after the exhaustion of secular ideologies and partly imposed on the West by radical Islamic
fundamentalism, has also increased the interest in Carl Schmitt's

version of political theology. At the same time, this twenty-first-century discussion has demonstrated the limits of a debate within the parameters of Schmittian thought. Jan Assmann's work, for example, has shown that the concept of political theology is by no means limited to the Christian and/or Judaic tradition by focusing on Ancient Egypt. Even Heinrich Meier's suggestion that a mono-theistic religious structure would be needed to develop a political theology turned out to be too narrow, for the connection between religion and political institutions in the older kingdom of Egypt can be interpreted in terms of a political theology. Of course, with his reconstruction of this constellation in *Herrschaft und Heil* Assmann does not mean to revitalize ancient forms of political theology. In contrast to Schmitt, he understands his project as descriptive rather than prescriptive *(betreibend)*.[46] When he characterizes Schmitt's political theology as polemical and strategic, he also defines Schmitt's self-understanding. Although Schmitt avoids the term, his project is normative. However, we have to realize that Schmitt's discourse cannot easily be defined within the opposition descriptive vs. normative, since Schmitt blends historical elements and normative aspects with performative moments in which the act of writing itself becomes a political act.

After 1945, Schmitt preferred to downplay or deny the performative moment because it reflected his involvement in the NS regime. The private political implications of his theological position are not spelled out in concrete terms. In this respect, *Political Theology II,* although highly polemical with regard to the fundamental theological issues, remains aloof and refrains from any direct political criticism This ambiguity has confused Schmitt's readers. They were not always certain how to interpret his statements. Are these serious polemical and praxis-oriented claims or merely historical and conceptual descriptions? More recently, there has been a growing consensus among Schmitt's critics that both the theological and the political claims have to be taken seriously. If there had been any doubt, his polemical responses to Peterson and Blumenberg confirms this reading. Schmitt presents himself as a political theologian who invokes scripture and dogma (although heretically) to assert his political position. Consequently, it would depend on the social and political context whether the theological invocation turns into political decisions or not. These decisions, however, as we have to remind ourselves, are framed by the fundamental divide between friend and enemy.

As a political theologian, Schmitt remains an enigmatic and ambiguous figure, capable of shifting positions and contradictory claims. It seems that only in his later years, particularly in his *Political Theology II,* did he engage in a sustained theological discussion, which was imposed on him by his adversaries Peterson and Blumenberg. In defense of the position he outlined in 1922, in *Political Theology II* he looks carefully at scripture and (Christian) dogma as well as the theological discussion surrounding them. A specific theological position, which is distinct from that of the Roman Catholic Church, becomes discernable. It is based on Paul's interpretation of the Christian faith but is by no means limited to Paul's position. In addition, gnostic ideas seem to influence his understanding of the New Testament and, by extension, his truly pessimistic interpretation of world history—an interpretation that the Church could hardly endorse.

This approach to political theology differs from the type of political theology put forth in *Political Theology* (1922) and especially *Roman Catholicism and Political Form* (1923), where the agent of the political is the Church with its consistent neutrality vis-à-vis the ideological positions of external secular powers. However, this neutrality of the Church, its willingness to form alliances with both progressive and reactionary governments, contains, as Schmitt shows much later in his discussion of Bishop Eusebius in *Political Theology II,* the ultimate claim that, supported by its theological dogma, the Church was called on and empowered by God to rule over the world, either directly or indirectly. While the medieval Church could maintain this position, the Christian schism in the sixteenth century turned this position into an intractable political problem; namely, the spread of civil war caused by the rivalry and hostility of competing Christian churches. Under these conditions, Schmitt argues, modern legal theorists looked for a lasting solution to the religions conflict by separating the state from the churches and turning it into a neutral arbiter that resolves the threat of civil war.

The early Schmitt clearly sides with the jurists (and Hobbes) and in *The Concept of the Political* favors a secularized concept of the political. Even in *The Nomos of the Earth* (1950), the political as part of the modern state is still seen as a postreligious sphere structured by legal terms and norms to which the Europeans agreed in order to contain war. On the other hand, Schmitt underscores the crucial role of the Church and thereby a theological grounding of the political during the Middle Ages. The late Schmitt, however, returns to the radical question posed decades before. But now, forced by his opponents, he uses a theological discourse based on the New Testament and the history of Christian dogma to find a theologically grounded answer. This twofold answer is ambiguous and ultimately contradictory: On the one hand, Schmitt affirms the historical claim of the Church to be the final arbiter not only in spiritual but also in secular questions (including political issues); on the other hand, closer to gnosticism he posits the unredeemable nature of the secular world, which can be sustained only by a katechon, a power that arrests or slows down history and thereby prevents the Second Coming of Christ. In either case, the concept of secularization is taken back. Theology has returned to the center.

The later Schmitt forcefully renewed his commitment to political theology with the claim that ultimately the most basic concept of the political—the distinction between friend and enemy—is grounded in the Christian conception of the Trinity. It is the distinction between God the creator and God (the son) the redeemer that enables Schmitt to introduce a powerful transcendent anchor. At no point in his extensive correspondence with Hans Blumenberg is he willing to reconsider and accept political theology as a metaphorical theory. In this emphatic claim he was not alone. After all, the late 1960s and early 1970s witnessed the return of political theology within Catholic and Protestant theology in Germany. This resurgence was driven by a left political message that Schmitt could only reject. It was also provoked by the heated debate around the progressive political theology of Vatican II, a position with which

Schmitt hardly agreed. By restating his position in *Political Theology II,* he also restated his rejection of secular liberalism and its potential utopian dimensions. We should note, too, that Schmitt's last work, while confirming the Christian perspective and the priority of the theological moment over the moment of secular politics, did not significantly alter the political application of his theory.

6

Final Reflections

Is There a Usable Schmitt?

The previous chapters examined Carl Schmitt's late writings with a two-fold interest. On the one hand, they carefully retraced the historical horizon of these works, bringing to the fore the concrete circumstances in which they were composed and paying attention to the author's original intention. This approach reminds us that after 1945 Schmitt was not an author whose narratives and arguments would receive neutral attention. He came, as he was aware, with heavy baggage from the years of the Third Reich, a burden that made him persona non grata not only in the new, democratic Germany but in Europe and the Americas as well. On the other hand, these chapters placed Schmitt's late work into the contemporary context, which differs so much from the mid-twentieth century that these writings come across as novel and unexpected, urging today's reader to reexamine them within a starkly different horizon that gives them potentially new meaning and function.

It appears that this moment of refunctioning in the Brechtian sense has played an important role in the more recent reception of Schmitt, especially in the English-speaking world. With only some exaggeration, we could argue that the Anglo-American discussion has created a distinct and novel author who is removed from the historical Carl Schmitt. We can observe a process of translation in the literal and metaphorical sense that was deeply impacted by the interests and needs of those participating in the transmission. The emphatic discovery of Schmitt's late work went hand in hand with the latent crisis of Western liberal democracies, beginning in the 1990s and intensifying after September 11, 2001. Again, Schmitt's writings proved their power in a period of crisis. Schmitt turns out to be the crisis theorist par excellence.

Linguistically, the Anglo-American Schmitt is largely based on the existence of translations. It seems that the majority of the participants in the debate are less interested in studying the fine points of the original German texts, which also means that they are less inclined to make use of the extensive critical literature on Schmitt in German, unless it is available in translation. Hence, after 2000, references to German Schmitt scholarship decrease. Now the point of departure for the anglophone discussion is the translation. For instance, it was only with the availability of the translation of *Der Nomos der Erde* (*The Nomos of the Earth*) in 2003 that a broader discussion of this 1950 work took off.

Yet it would be reductive to explain the Anglo-American discourse on Schmitt simply as the result of a direct theory transfer. While this may have been correct in the 1980s and early 1990s, when much of the labor of translation and transmission was done by the journal *Telos*, it does not accurately describe the situation in the late 1990s and the first decade of the new century. Strong impulses came from France and Italy, notably from authors like Chantal Mouffe and Georgio Agamben.[1] Mouffe argues that Schmitt had to be taken seriously despite his flaws as an adversary of remarkable intellectual quality and urges her readers to engage Schmitt as a critic of contemporary postpolitical liberalism. It is precisely Schmitt's fierce opposition to the liberal emphasis on norms and procedures that she stresses as Schmitt's valuable contribution to the contemporary debate. For Mouffe the repression of conflict in the liberal conception of the political in particular makes the return to Schmitt imperative. At the same time, she does not want to be misunderstood as a proponent of a radical Schmittian Left, which defines her own position as a left-liberal critic of liberal models.

Hence, it was an already mediated reception that broadened and intensified the debate in the United States and Great Britain. Put differently, it was a Europeanized Schmitt, largely freed from his German political baggage, that influenced the still mostly academic discussion in the anglophone world. This change was by no means accidental, for it was the European turn in Schmitt's late work, so clearly stated in *The Nomos of the Earth,* where Germany is mostly absent, that prepared the shift in his reception as well. Two issues in particular were now moved from a German to a European and potentially global discussion: first, the critique of liberalism as the dominant ideology of the West, and second, the problem of a new international order after the demise of the Soviet Union and the Communist Bloc. With the rediscovery of the spatial Schmitt, his work was, by and large, no longer seen as connected to German international policies of the late 1930s and early 1940s. The indirect appropriation of Schmitt's late work by way of Italian and French critics helped to sanitize Carl Schmitt by pushing the darker aspects of his thought into the background. Moreover—and this may be even more significant—the indirect reception in which Schmitt's original agenda was already modified has encouraged readings that increasingly move away from Schmitt's texts and establish new levels of meaning and use. It is safe to say that Schmitt's German postwar critics, whether they attacked or defended him, would not recognize the author in the more recent Anglo-American debate.

The Reconfiguration of Schmitt in the English-Speaking World

This Anglo-American Schmitt deserves closer scrutiny, since he has moved more and more to the center of the international debate, especially the debate over the fate of contemporary (American) liberalism and the feasibility of a new, post-European and post-American world order. This discourse is definitely driven by contemporary political concerns beyond Carl Schmitt's own horizon. We are dealing, therefore, with a mode of theory transfer that ultimately underscores refunctioning and application rather than interpretation of meaning, although these political moments are not always openly stated. The attention that Schmitt's work has received during the last two decades marks a phenomenal shift in his standing in anglophone academic discussions. It describes a process of normalization that has led to an understanding of Schmitt's political theory as classic and his work as essential in a number of fields.

To a large extent, this process was facilitated by the need to find an oppositional theory after the demise of state socialism in Eastern and Central Europe and the subsequent marginalization of the Marxist tradition. Schmitt was discovered as a fierce critic of liberalism when the victorious West claimed that liberal capitalism was the final answer to the world's problems.[2] Consequently, broadly speaking, the anglophone Schmitt reception of the 1990s focused on the critique of liberalism in Schmitt's writings during the Weimar years, dealing with fundamental but unresolved questions of democratic constitutionalism that the dominant neoliberal agenda repressed. In the following decade, clearly and brutally marked by the terrorist attack of September 11, 2001, the interest in Schmitt shifted to his later work, a shift that was motivated by the violent challenges to the imperial power of the United States and its European allies. A critical reassessment of the unique status of the United States as a world leader went hand in hand with the discovery of Schmitt's *The Nomos of the Earth* and the concept of *Großraum* (expanded territory). The more it turned out that the new world order proclaimed by the West was flawed because of its social and political contradictions, the more Schmitt's oeuvre became the focus of keen analysis. As strange as it may sound, in the theoretical constellation of the first decade of this century Schmitt's theory moved into the place of the oppositional voice formerly occupied by Western Marxism and Critical Theory.[3]

As we might expect, this exchange would not occur without some violence to Schmitt's texts and most of all with a noticeable disregard of the intentions of the historical Schmitt during the turbulent Weimar years and the even more disturbing Nazi period. Critics as different as David Dyzenhaus, John McCormick, and William Scheuerman agreed that, selectively read, Schmitt's harsh critique of liberalism could be used to strengthen liberalism. Because Schmitt had posed a series of provocative and pertinent questions to persistent problems in the liberal rule of law, they believed it would be wrong to disregard his work on the basis of his complicity with the NS regime.[4] This move, fruitful as it turned out to be, also had the unwanted consequence of normalizing Schmitt by bringing him closer, albeit through negation, to the liberal mainstream. The devil's advocate slowly became a canonical figure.

This can be shown especially in the second wave of reception after 2000, when problems of international law and the question of American hegemony became the center of the appropriation. At this point the disoriented Left, especially in the United States, turned to Schmitt as a theorist who could supply an oppositional voice with which to attack the dominant neoliberal or neoconservative agenda of the Bush administration. While the appropriation of Schmitt by the Left (Chantal Mouffe, Slavoj Žižek) was still articulated within the confines of an academic sphere, its urgency was clearly politically motivated. By this time, liberal theory (Jürgen Habermas, John Rawls) had become the primary enemy, seen as responsible for the disastrous turn of global politics, beginning with the wars in Iraq and Afghanistan.

What these critics seem not to notice was the fact that their own political protest, using selective readings of Schmitt, simultaneously increased the process of normalization. Schmitt, the outlaw of the early postwar years, had now become the savior of the Left opposition. As Jan-Werner Müller observed in 2003, the Left, without an alternative social model after 1990, retreated to anti-liberal critique.[5] As a consequence, at least rhetorically, Carl Schmitt turned into a patron of international relations as a subdiscipline of political theory. This meant that Schmitt could be treated in the anglophone academic world as a canonical theorist, even by scholars who did not share the beliefs and commitments of the Left or the Right. The discovery of the spatial Schmitt[6]—of the analysis of *nomos* as a critical European and later global concept during the second decade of this century—could continue and expand the critique of American neoliberalism, but its proponents were not necessarily part of the Left. Schmitt's thought entered the discipline of international relations as a (valuable) contribution to the discipline. As William Hooker explains, "We should welcome the gradual reduction of knee-jerk hostility to the use of Schmittian categories in the debate."[7] For Hooker, Carl Schmitt was already part of the history that Schmitt had defined. He had become a major character in the narrative of the end of the modern nation-state.

The reconfiguration of Carl Schmitt in the English-speaking world, especially in the United States, confronts us with a theory that is largely dehistoricized, removed from the specific moments of its genesis and its former functions. If Carl Schmitt essentially claimed to reject abstract forms of theorizing in favor of concrete, historically grounded thought, the outcome of the Anglo-American reception is the opposite; namely, a theoretical construct that is more or less self-contained and therefore applicable to a variety of temporal and spatial configurations. In short, the Anglo-American Schmitt has morphed into a more systematic theory that, precisely because of this more systematic shape, can be used as a tool to confront opponents, among them international liberalism and Western imperialism. While some of the proponents of this process are quite aware that the historical Schmitt does not match his new incarnation, the force of the internal dynamic of the discussion has been so strong that its participants either entirely dismiss the historical Schmitt as merely of biographical interest and no longer relevant to the present discussion or carefully differentiate between the (bad) historical Schmitt, who was involved with German fascism, and the valuable essence of his thought, which can be abstracted from history, thereby becoming morally neutral and useful as a critical tool for the contemporary confrontation of other positions. In any case, the result of this process has been a streamlined Schmitt with sharper and harder theoretical contours, which now serves a theoretical and political purpose that the historical Schmitt would not have imagined. Left behind is the daunting question of why and how Schmitt's theoretical interventions of the 1930s and 1940s could and did support the NS regime. Was the ideological proximity no more than an accident? One of the amazing features of this revision is the almost complete occlusion of the theological element, which was clearly crucial to the historical Schmitt. Accordingly, the new American Schmitt is as secular as his liberal and socialist opponents.

Of course, the writings of Carl Schmitt have frequently been used for specific political purposes. In fact, its author thought of some of his texts as political interventions in concrete temporal and spatial constellations. More specifically, Schmitt understood himself as the theorist of an age that was fundamentally in crisis. This self-understanding he shared, by the way, with several theorists of his generation, among them Eric Voegelin, Gershom Scholem, Ernst Bloch, and Walter Benjamin, although these thinkers occupied very different and conflicting theoretical as well as political positions. But the more recent revisions and appropriations of Schmitt's work, particularly of his late writings, are strongly shaped by the polemical nature of their purpose. They enhance the force of the argument at the expense of a careful examination of the text's structure. The more Schmitt's oeuvre has been integrated into the field of international relations, the more it has been restructured as a set of coherent arguments to be applied in the contemporary debate. Accordingly, what does not fit the overall argument is pushed to the margins or left out. In this development the moment of close reading and interpretation of Schmitt's texts has been shortchanged. Tensions and ambiguities are not acknowledged and discussed, because they would only undermine the ultimate purpose of the argument. This approach therefore is ultimately in danger of reducing Schmitt's writings to useful formulas that support specific positions and agendas.

Even in those instances where there is no identification with Carl Schmitt, where the authors clearly differentiate between Schmitt's own agenda and the role of his theory in the contemporary debate, there is a noticeable shift toward an affirmative reading of the texts. Schmitt's interpretations of European history, for instance, are rarely problematized. His accounts of the development of modern

Europe from the sixteenth to the twentieth century as well as his assessment of European colonialism are more or less accepted as historical truth instead of being discussed as peculiar constructs. His distinction between land and sea powers, first developed in *Land and Sea* in 1942, has become an unquestioned standard dichotomy. Hans Blumenberg's fundamental critique of Schmitt's interpretation of the modern age, first formulated in *The Legitimacy of the Modern Age* in 1966, has not yet impacted Anglo-American Schmitt scholarship, although Blumenberg's intervention is critical for Schmitt's polemic against the Enlightenment and modern liberalism.[8]

The American Schmitt, unlike the historical Schmitt, is explicitly modern and secular, freeing his theory from the entanglement with premodern religious concerns. This containment also reduces the complexity of his theory, turning it into a mere opposition to the dominant voice of Western liberalism. Repressing Schmitt's Catholic roots and his repeated insistence on the centrality of theology, both as the point of departure and as the ultimate perspective of his thought, turns his political theology invisible. Schmitt's concept of history, with its peculiar gnostic elements, which come into the foreground especially in *Political Theology II*, is removed from the record as inessential. This turns Schmitt into a political realist like Hans Morgenthau, making it impossible to understand and appreciate the persistent, deeper anthropological commitments that determine not only Schmitt's ill-fated personal decisions but also the conceptual structure of his theory. The ultimate rational of the friend/enemy distinction as the definition of the political reveals itself in the parallel distinction between Christ and the Anti-Christ. Without this theological frame Schmitt's fierce and persistent opposition to the Enlightenment and liberalism loses much of its rationale. For Schmitt the stakes are so high because the fate of the world and its history are under discussion. This may be difficult to appreciate for contemporary readers who face a very different cultural environment, especially for those readers who live and act outside of the Christian sphere. For them, to be sure, Schmitt's Christian beliefs and commitments have no immediate relevance. In fact, they seem to stand in the way of an updating of Schmitt's theory that would secure its contemporary global application.

Hence, there is a dialectic at work that complicates the international reception and appropriation of Schmitt. The globalization of his theory removes it from the very ground on which it was built. Its concrete German and European specificity, on which Schmitt insisted (*konkretes Denken*), stands in the way of its straightforward international appropriation and applicability.[9]

The Problem of Dehistoricization and Schmitt's Relevance for the Left

This raises a more fundamental question: Is it possible at all to distill a usable Schmitt from his writings, which after all span five decades? Of course, Schmitt himself adjusted his conceptual framework as well as his interests and topics during his lifespan. The focus of his late work, in particular the question of a new *nomos,* after World War II, reflects the actual changes and transformations on the ground, changes for which the concept of the nation-state was of limited use. And it is not accidental that the present debate in international relations frequently refers to and makes use of Schmitt, because it is faced with questions and problems that seem to resonate with Schmitt. Still, without the theological frame, Schmitt's search for a new world order, and especially his persistent resistance to the dominance of international liberalism under the umbrella of the United States, remains a strange and isolated fact. The nature of the underlying theological concepts and arguments is the reason why Schmitt's thought is attractive to the Right and the Left in a situation of fundamental crisis. These concepts provide the patterns that then determine the specificity of the proposed political theory. Fundamental for this theory is Schmitt's sense that the world as a failed creation is lost. This assessment is based on a sharp gnostic dualism, where Good stands against Evil, respectively God the father and creator opposes God the son and redeemer, who is also the rebel in *Political Theology II.* This conceptual narrative underscores the theological roots of political conflict, a conflict that mankind cannot remove or overcome as hard as it might try. The best that can be achieved under these circumstances, as Schmitt underscores again and again, is the action of the katechon of the New Testament who slows down the rapid and dangerous progression of history by imposing political order. Thus the conservative, Ordo-oriented statesman is more than a supporter of tradition and legitimacy; his or her work positively determines the process of history by keeping in check the apocalyptic crisis.

How then would this configuration be turned into a usable political theory? For the Right the fundamental crisis can be met by a sovereign who is empowered to make decisions in order to reestablish social and political order when the rule of law no longer provides security for the citizens. For the Right, Schmitt provides authoritarian or even more radical solutions to the fundamental political crisis of the present. In other words, the Right can make use of the authoritarian elements of Schmitt without hesitation, including his preferences for Catholic or even fascist solutions. The international surge of right-wing populism can draw on a selective reading of Schmitt. It shares with Schmitt a sense of doom and resentment, leading to a sharp distinction between "us" and "them." But can the Left buy into this configuration without losing its self-understanding? The Anglo-American Left has focused its appropriation of Schmitt on his critique of liberalism and liberal democracy, avoiding, by and large, contact with Schmitt's theological thought as the basis of his theory as a whole. The Left prefers a secular Schmitt. Yet this strategy limits the use of Schmitt's writings. The emphasis is clearly placed on negation, avoiding an embrace of his Catholic authoritarianism and his sympathies for a figure like General Salan.

Of course, there are good reasons why the American Left—in contrast to the German Left—represses the theological elements. Accepting this side of Schmitt would lead to the dark gnosticism of his late work, the fundamental and unchangeable struggle between the good and the evil forces as the engine driving the process of history on its way to the Second Coming, or, as *Political Theology II* contends, the conflict between God, the Creator of an imperfect world, and Jesus, the rebellious son and redeemer. In this configuration there is no space for human autonomy. But can the Left appropriate Schmitt's conception of history without damaging or even giving up its own legacy?

While there is certainly room for a critical review of the concept of human autonomy in its traditional humanistic or progressive versions, which have underscored, as Schmitt has pointed out again and again, the moments of self-empowerment and technological control of nature, the question remains whether the American Left can and should adopt Schmitt's conception of history as a process that leaves the human race at the mercy of a fundamental and uncontrollable theological conflict. Instead, the Left may have reasons to embrace the concept of human *Selbstbehauptung* (self-assertion) that Hans Blumenberg developed in *The Legitimacy of the Modern Age* (1966) in response to Schmitt's understanding of the modern age as a fundamental loss of a proper and sustainable theological grounding. What appears to be appealing today in Schmitt's polemic against the triumphalism of the Enlightenment and progressive liberalism—namely, his critique of human hubris and shallow optimism—is also its limitation; it leaves not much room for human creativity in the arena of politics. Given the critical importance of conflict in Schmitt's thought, there is a strong, almost exclusive emphasis on power as the means for defining the political. But unlike liberalism, the Left, if it counts Marx as part of its legacy, is not per se afraid of power. A revolutionary theory that recognizes social inequality and injustice as its driving elements can acknowledge the centrality of power to overcome the deficient status quo. Still, it is the function of power that deserves scrutiny. While Schmitt and the Left agree on the importance of political power, this does not mean that they agree on its role in the social sphere. For the Western Marxist tradition, revolution as a period of extreme and violent conflicts, has a beginning and an end determined by the changing material conditions. The central question then is the place of revolution in Schmitt's work and its potential appropriation by the Left.

Indeed, in his late work Carl Schmitt can and occasionally does show sympathy to the idea of social revolution as a critical moment of the historical process. Especially in the *Theory of the Partisan* he acknowledges the significance of the partisan as part of the revolutionary struggle by drawing a line from the ideas of the Prussian military resistance to Napoleon around 1812, formulated by Carl von Clausewitz, to the concept of irregular warfare in the writings of Lenin and Mao. Yet his sympathies with the logic of the revolutionary partisan remain ambiguous; they are checked by his equally strong sympathies for the cause of the European colonial powers against the irregular warfare of the liberation movements in Indochina and Algeria. As long as the American Left identifies with this struggle, there can be no easy and straightforward appropriation of Schmitt's assessment of the partisan. Only a highly selective reading of this work, focused exclusively on the theoretical development from Clausewitz to Mao, could be integrated into a Left position. In part, the belated international reception of the partisan essay in the West has weakened this identification and created a stronger link to the terrorist attacks of the early twenty-first century,[10] a link in which the connection to the idea of a legitimate social revolution, still quite visible in the 1963 essay, is increasingly lost. Yet this updating of Schmitt's theory, which shows the partisan in a new and mostly negative light, relies more on the conservative strand of the essay and overlooks its conflicted ambiguity. In short, for the Left the question of a usable Schmitt is extremely difficult to answer.

Unlike mainstream international relations theorists, who discovered and integrated Schmitt without much critical distance after 2000, the Left, broadly defined, had two choices. It could either appropriate his work selectively, always insisting that Schmitt's conservative right-wing beliefs and political commitments had to be rejected of course, or it could propose a critical reception of his entire oeuvre in which the ideological aspect is openly analyzed and discussed without treating the critique of Schmitt's highly problematic ideology as the final word. The former strategy, which has been the predominant approach, has the advantage of focusing immediately on those elements of Schmitt's writings that are supposedly useful for a Left agenda. It is taken for granted that Schmitt's commitment and decisions, even after 1945, remain unacceptable for the Left cause. On the other hand, because of Schmitt's critique of the liberal center and his (correct) analysis of the fateful contradictions of international liberalism, parts of his writings can be integrated into a Left agenda. The downside of this approach is the unaddressed ambiguity of Schmitt's conceptual apparatus—the fact that it can be employed for decidedly different political causes.

Hence the democratic Left has to deal with the question: How much of Schmitt's right-wing commitments are carried over into a critical agenda by necessity, or at least are likely to be, and will therefore encroach on the validity of the overall critical argument? Obviously there is no general answer to this question. It depends on the willingness of the individual theorist to buy into and borrow more or less extensively from Schmitt's concepts and theoretical narratives. In any case, there is in this instance a fine line between useful appropriation and maintaining one's independence.

If we choose instead the path of an overall critical assessment of Schmitt's (late) writings with an eye on a productive dialogue, the parameter as well as the nature of the encounter changes significantly. Then the appropriation of viable elements is not immediate; it is instead part of a critical process that reexamines Schmitt's concepts and arguments from a vantage point outside of Schmitt's theory, but without polemical intent. This dialogue turns the theory inside out and looks for those moments where the structure of the theory itself, not only its individual elements, elicit a critical response that opens up new and different perspectives that were not part of the author's intention. In other words, the question becomes whether Schmitt's theory can be used also against Schmitt.

Examining Schmitt's Use on the Left

In order to explore the critical potential of each approach, we can examine two individual attempts to rescue Schmitt from his historical context. The first is William Rasch's interpretation, which seeks to appropriate Schmitt for a fundamental critique of liberalism and especially its use by American administrations. The second case is the essay collection edited by Louiza Odysseos and Fabio Petito, who have marked their own position as different from and somewhat critical of Schmitt. At the same time, Odysseos and Petito have underscored the importance of Schmitt's writings for contemporary political debate.

The Secular Schmitt: William Rasch

Rasch developed his position in a number of essays published between 2000 and 2005. For the purpose of our argument his first
essay, entitled "Conflict as a Vocation: Carl Schmitt and the Possibility of Politics," is the most relevant, since in it Rasch explains
why he, who had been known as an accomplished interpreter of
Niklas Luhmann's systems theory,[11] was drawn to Schmitt's theory in the first place.[12] For Rasch the essence of Schmitt's theory is
a response to the phenomenon of political conflict. How do we best
understand conflict and how do we deal with it? For Rasch this is a
purely secular problem, the locus of which in the modern age has been
the state. He makes no attempt therefore to include Schmitt's theology in the discussion. In fact, Rasch treats Schmitt's theological reflections and commitment as a private aspect that has no relevance
for the significance and value of Schmitt's theory. Instead, he focuses his attention on the sovereign state as the key concept that
can be employed to fend off what he, following Schmitt, considers
the greatest danger of the evolution of international relations in the
twentieth century: the hidden monism of Anglo-American democracy,
which undermines the older pluralism of European nation-states.

In this Rasch follows Schmitt's narrative in two ways: First, he
sides with Schmitt (and German conservatism in general) that, with
respect to the dualism of state and civil society, the state deserves
greater attention as the stabilizing factor when dealing with conflict. Second, he shares Schmitt's suspicion of moral discussions as
they occur in civil society and penetrate the sphere of the state from
there. He takes over from Schmitt, without further discussion, the
animus against "moralism" in politics and underscores the autonomy of the political from the sphere of ethics and morality. This
means that he seeks to reserve the political for the state. The sovereign state becomes the center of the political, the locus for political
reflection, arguments, and decisions. Assuming that Schmitt is a
thorough modernist who follows Weber rather than Leo Strauss,
Rasch sees no way to anchor the law and social norms in an ultimate
ground (natural law, metaphysics, religion). As a consequence, the
sovereign (state) becomes the center of the political, the anchor for

the decision-making process, especially in a time of crisis when the weakness of the law has become apparent. In brief, Rasch accepts without hesitation the inherent decisionism of Schmitt's theory: "Three notions—sovereignty, decision and the exception—come together here to form a constellation that can do justice . . . to the particularity of the social reality, a particularity rendered invisible by the self-mystification of the liberal rule of law."[13] In the spirit of Schmitt he then defines the sovereign as the autonomous agent that can and must make a decision under conditions of emergency. Rasch is of course aware that Schmitt's definition was formulated under the conditions of the fundamental political and social crisis of the late Weimar Republic, a situation where Schmitt considered the state, as opposed to parliament and civil society, as the only guarantor of order and stability.

In this argument, by contrasting the sovereign and the (liberal) rule of law (*der Gesetzesstaat*, to use Hans Kelsen's term), the fate of democracy drops out of sight. By downplaying the importance of civil society, Schmitt and Rasch reach a point where the political decision becomes more important than the organization of the political community. In 1932, Schmitt believed that rescuing the state was more important than defending the well-being of liberal democracy. It is not clear whether Rasch follows this line of argument, but he certainly does not object to it. He buys into the Schmittian dichotomy of law and decision, of abstract norms and concrete actions by the state, of normalcy and the state of exception as the ultimately defining moment of the political. In broader terms, Rasch accepts as part of his own argument a theory that was historically defined in terms of a fundamental systemic crisis.

What does Rasch seek to get out of Schmitt? Without directly addressing the urgent questions of international relations around 2000, he focuses on the advantages of international pluralism advocated by Carl Schmitt over the mono-polar global order of the 1990s controlled by the United States. More specifically, he tries to demonstrate that the universal ideas of international liberalism promoted by the United States in order to strengthen world peace in fact had the opposite result: they destabilized the international community because of wars that are fought to punish those states that (supposedly) violate the international order. By contrasting Schmitt and Leo Strauss, Rasch *pace* Schmitt turns against the notion that the concept of a just society and a perfect moral order will lead to a sustainable peaceful world order. Instead, following Schmitt's well-known narrative, Rasch proposes a pluralism of nation-states as a more fruitful and peaceful structure. Instead of a normative approach to international relations, Rasch suggests that a balance of power, as it was maintained in Europe between 1648 and 1914, might be the more desirable solution. Of course, this argument relies on a rather streamlined and idealized version of European history in which political and social revolutions are kept out of sight and where the contingent element of interstate relations, with the always given possibility of war, is treated as a relatively minor problem.

To give this Schmittian pluralism a stronger appeal, however, Rasch shifts the argument from the advantages of pluralism to the disadvantages of normative international policies. They were imposed by the liberal powers (England and France) after World War I and by the United States after World War II and then again after the collapse of the Soviet Union. In this line of argument humanism as a dualism of the humane and the nonhumane becomes the target of the polemic. In brief, a politics built on liberal values, Schmitt and Rasch tell us, is bound to end in destructive wars fought in the name of these values. Rasch refers to Jean-François Lyotard to question the reliability of universal liberal values for the common good and draws the line from there back to Schmitt, who through this link to postmodernism and post-structuralism, is lifted from the old accusation of collaboration with National Socialism. Instead, Jürgen Habermas and Richard Wolin are explicitly chastised for criticizing Schmitt's work as protofascist. It is a critical left liberal like Habermas who is accused supporting ideologically motivated warfare, while Schmitt is seen as a theorist who speaks out in favor of controlled war (*gehegter Krieg*).

As we have shown, Rasch has to buy deeply into Schmitt in order to find a usable theory for the present. In his view this present in 2000 is American imperialism that uses liberal values to impose its economic and military power on the rest of the world. His reading

is driven by a legitimate concern, which sets him off from a normalizing academic appropriation that remains neutral with respect
to Schmitt's beliefs and commitments. At the same time, this concern makes it difficult for him to keep a critical distance from his
object of study. He identifies with Schmitt, possibly more than he
would like to, because he is aware after all that Schmitt does not
easily fit the description of a progressive left theorist. Under these
circumstances his method of reading is determined by his thematic
interests, which then can be traced in different works of Schmitt.
This approach must be relatively abstract and cannot pay much
attention to the concrete historical moment of writing and the specific intentions of the text. But if we worry about the future of
democracy, as William Rasch certainly does, is Schmitt a useful guide?
Can he be trusted to provide the framework for a plurality of democratic communities? After all, the late Schmitt does not argue in
favor of the autonomous nation-state anymore (as Rasch seems to
assume) but proposes a plurality of *Großräume* whose internal
structure is never sufficiently examined. While there is pluralism in
this new order as well, there is no internal mechanism to safeguard
against abuses by the hegemonic power at the center of the *Großraum*.
In sum, Rasch's struggle for a community of nation-states that reach
peace by way of a pluralist balance of power is not supported by
Schmitt's conception of competing *Großräume*.

Schmitt's Impact on International Relations:
Odysseos and Petito

The speed and energy with which scholarship on Schmitt's late
work developed in the English-speaking world after 2000 can be
gleaned from the volume edited by Louiza Odysseos and Fabio
Petito in 2007. In it, Rasch's emphatic appropriation has given
way to a more distant and more differentiated reception. There is
no attempt to excuse Schmitt's ill-fated decision to make his mind
available to the Nazis, but this aspect is moved to the historical
background. At the same time, the editors underscore Schmitt's relevance for the present when they note: "But it is only now that a
serious engagement with Schmitt's international political thought

is progressively seen as a useful, some might say, necessary, engagement for understanding the current international situation."[14] Yet unlike Rasch, Odysseos and Petito focus their interest more on Schmitt's contribution to international relations as a subdiscipline. The volume is expected to discover the work of a scholar whose contributions had not been fully recognized. In this context then Schmitt's *The Nomos of the Earth* is mentioned as a missing classic. Their interest in Schmitt, in other words, is less partisan, but they are in agreement with Rasch that it is the present—the rise of global terrorism and the U.S. wars on terror in Iraq and Afghanistan— that defines the renewed interest in Schmitt. As their introduction makes clear, Odysseos and Petito follow Schmitt's narrative in *The Nomos* to underscore the difference between older European international law and the present constellation. Accordingly, the theological problematic is treated as a purely historical question. For them, as for Rasch, Schmitt is primarily a secular, post-Westphalian theorist whose relevant contributions to the present treat the political as an autonomous sphere.[15]

Where then do the editors see Schmitt's major contribution to the present debate over the international crisis? If we accept Schmitt's contention that the older international law was broken in 1914 and was followed by a crisis that international liberalism could not master because it was unable and unwilling to control the use of war (*Hegung*), then Schmitt's search for a new *nomos* becomes the key issue. Summarizing the volume's essays, the editors emphasize the critical side: the influence of international liberalism as a theory that demands global attention without regard for spatial difference, the increasingly dangerous role of the United States as the dominant power that imposes its own values on the rest of the world, and the use of discriminating wars against those who do not follow the lead of the West. On the affirmative side, we find the stress on the need for greater global pluralism, the need to control the use of war (*Hegung*), and the emphasis on the critical importance of a spatial understanding of the political order.

It is worth noting, however, that their summary of the ideas and conceptions brought forward in the volume to articulate a new *nomos* in the spirit of Carl Schmitt remains rather close to Schmitt's ideas, not only the stress on pluralism (pluralist world order) but also the rejection of the *Pax Americana*. In this they replace the old liberal orthodoxy with a new orthodoxy, definitely more differentiated than that of Rasch's 2000 essay, and moving tentatively toward a new dogma, actually more so than the individual essays contained in the volume. In brief, Odysseos and Petito embrace the notion of a usable Schmitt by highlighting the core narrative of *The Nomos* and the usefulness of select concepts, among them the distinction between controlled and discriminating war, a universal and a concrete spatial political order, and universal liberalism and concrete political thought. In their new configuration these concepts, although derived from Schmitt's writings, take on their own life. In the end, it is the present relevance that defines the approach to and the use of Carl Schmitt. While their enthusiasm for Schmitt is more guarded than that of William Rasch, Odysseos and Petito clearly believe in the transformative power of Schmitt's thought and its adequacy for the present global crisis.

The Return of the Historical Context

Can this commitment be sustained? Is there a usable Schmitt who can be separated from the complicity of the author and the complexity of the historical situation in which his thought was developed, articulated, and applied? In their recent monograph two European scholars, Claudio Minca and Rory Rowan, respond to this question in the following way:

> For us, as for many others, Schmitt's work appeared to somehow speak directly to the tensions of the moment, cutting through the paralyzing ideological fog and hitting precisely on the raw mechanism of global power that neoconservative hubris had suddenly exposed. . . . Crucially, Schmitt's analysis of political space appeared to offer a conceptual key to the strange fusion of brute material force, ideological spin and technological virtuality that had come to characterize the reigning global order in the first decade of the new millennium.[16]

Yet despite this initial enthusiasm, Schmitt became less of a friend and guide the more Minca and Rowan immersed themselves in his work. "His sharp insights grew muddy in the light of his fatally compromised politics, and slipped through the fingers the harder one tried to grasp them. Concepts that first appeared as incisive critical tools became double-edged swords that conceded too much ground to the opponent."[17]

Once the deep ambiguity of Schmitt's texts has been grasped, it becomes much more difficult to distill a usable theoretical framework out of his writings. It is not only the compromised politics that impede the open and straightforward use of Schmitt for the present global crisis, it is the character of the theory itself, if we can speak of a single systematic theory in the first place. As Minca and Rowan found out, Schmitt's concepts as well as his historical narratives are open to different and conflicting readings to such an extent that a Left agenda will ultimately find itself in a self-contradictory situation. It is not accidental therefore that these authors decided "to maintain a critical distance" from their object of study,[18] while they remained committed to a rigorous investigation, without simply dismissing Schmitt because of his alliance with fascism in 1933. They see the potential for a contemporary appropriation of his work only through the use of a critical lens that brings to the fore the ambivalence of the Schmittian agenda. Differently put, there is no usable Schmitt without considering the specific historical configuration that impacted the purpose of his writing. We have to remind ourselves that Carl Schmitt did not understand himself as a recluse academic author who wrote for a small circle of colleagues. His ambition was to influence the political elite of his time. This was true even after World War II.

Similarly, the 2016 *Oxford Handbook of Carl Schmitt* presents a carefully balanced and historically differentiated view of Carl Schmitt. As one would expect from a reference work, it covers both the early and the late writings, addressing a variety of important aspects without pushing an affirmative reception. In fact, in their introduction, the editors, Jens Meierhenrich and Oliver Simon, demonstrate that they are aware of Schmitt's darker sides; accordingly, they keep a noticeable distance from their object of study. Moreover, while being international in outlook, the handbook includes important voices from German Schmitt scholarship, among them Reinhard Mehring, Friedrich Balke, and Ulrich von Preuss. Clearly, the editors were seeking a critical approach to Schmitt by including contributors who were already known to be highly skeptical of Schmitt, such as Benno Teschke and Raphael Gross. However, the most significant advance is the conviction of the editors that Schmitt's writings cannot be defined exclusively in legal and political terms. They correctly underscore the interconnection between Schmitt's legal, cultural, and political thought. This cultural turn, which should have included the theological aspect more strongly than it does, frees the reading of Schmitt's work from the one-sided perspective of emphasizing either legal or international relations studies. While the question of a usable Schmitt is raised in a number of contributions, it does not dominate the volume. In short, it appears that by 2016 the emphatic Carl Schmitt renaissance had come to an end.

The Limits of Appropriation: Schmitt on the Left and Right

The emphatic selective appropriation of Schmitt's ideas and concepts after 1990 and especially in the new millennium has given us a distorted understanding of his thought. The disregard for his late theological work, for example, makes it difficult to grasp Schmitt's pessimistic *Weltbild* (world picture), the unshakable belief that the course of human history, notwithstanding all efforts to improve the conditions, is doomed, that the best outcome can be the delay of the catastrophic end. This perspective explains Schmitt's disbelief in the moral potential of the human race, his hostility toward any form of utopian thinking and social planning. His grim realism is thus considerably darker than the position of the realists within international relations. It means, among other things, that for Schmitt any political order is better than the chaos of an unstructured human community. While in his later work Schmitt may have realized that the Roman Catholic Church, once the guarantor of political order, was no longer positioned to provide a global spiritual and political *nomos,* he held on to the close connection of theological and political structures by discovering the concept of enmity in the Christian Trinity itself. This explication overshadows any potential organization of political life. Schmitt's enduring hostility toward the unipolar global order of the United States reflects his basic rejection of the latent Christian aspirations of the American ideology to replace the older claims of the Roman Catholic Church with the belief in American exceptionalism and triumphalism. For Schmitt, after the loss of the medieval order, pluralism is the best attainable goal.

If we translate Schmitt's call for pluralism as a way of ending the global civil war of the twentieth century into the language of a secular global political structure, something significant is lost. In that case his theory can be used either as a mere description of actual tendencies of the more recent international development, where the singular status of the United States has been challenged by competing powers (e.g., China). Or it can be considered normatively as a recommendation for a better and more stable world order, because a balance of power is supposed to deliver a more peaceful order than the dominance of a single hegemonic power. In the first scenario we are dealing with an empirical assessment that reflects factual tendencies, in the second scenario we are exploring a recommendation or demand based on the belief that a plurality of power centers is structurally more successful than a single center of power. The proof for this evaluation can be given only negatively: The dominant role of the United States since 1990 has not brought the world peace that it was supposed to provide. In either application, therefore, the emphatic theological notion of the irreplaceable loss of the Church as the guide to world peace becomes invisible. If we strip away the unstated theological framework, Schmitt's claim loses much of its immediate persuasive force. Both the empirical assessment and the normative claim call for a more elaborate argument in the field of political thought or the arena of political ethics.

What minimal ethical expectations would be needed in order to establish and maintain international stability in a world dominated by a small number of Schmittian *Großräume*? For Schmitt, political ethics is primarily concerned with the obligations of the state to avert civil war. The state has to protect its subjects, who therefore owe loyalty to the government. However, these considerations do not apply to the field of international relations. In this arena one of the expectations would be the internal stability of the individual *Großraum*, which can be achieved only when the relationship between the central and the dependent powers is based on trust and mutual support. In terms of social and economic interests, the goal is to seek a sustainable compromise that satisfies both the central power and its satellite states. In the relationship between the *Großräume*, the minimum expectation would be the recognition of the right of the surrounding *Großräume* to exist. In addition, these larger units may have to recognize and confirm the territorial integrity of neighboring *Großräume* and their spheres of influence. But these minimal provisions would hardly secure a sustained global peace. It would at best provide basic ground rules for international diplomacy. This is the reason why international liberalism insists on universal values to guarantee a peaceful global order. If these values are no longer promoted, what would replace them? It appears that forms of trust and solidarity are indispensable for a more peaceful global order. They are different from feelings of loyalty and fidelity between state and citizen, proposed by Schmitt. Without trust among political units (states or *Großräume*) even formal treaties defining international relations are ultimately useless, since treaties can always be broken by sovereign states if they stand in the way of expansion. Even among political opponents, trust is needed to maintain the (peaceful) status quo. Deliberate undermining of mutual trust—that is, political gambling—increases the likelihood of instability and war.

The case for solidarity may be more difficult to make, for this concept is typically explored and applied in a social rather than political context.[19] Used either descriptively or normatively, it presupposes a social unit—a group or class—whose members share interests and values. They stand in for each other to defend these features against pressure or threats from the outside. This means that solidarity looks to the inside rather than the outside. While the members of the group share a sense of belonging together on the basis of equality and mutual obligations and benefits, those on the outside are excluded. The critical element of reciprocity, therefore, is limited to those on the inside. It seems to be precisely this restriction that strengthens the members' sense of being bonded, the readiness to struggle and fight if necessary against forces that threaten the unit as a whole. The attempt to transfer the concept of solidarity from the social to the political sphere is thus easier in the case of the nation-state than in the arena of international relations.

For the modern nation-state, solidarity among its citizens means that the conception of the nation is based on equality of the citizens in political (but not necessarily economic and social) terms. Citizens are expected to share social burdens and obligations in order to enjoy the benefits of freedom and security. It is understood that foreigners are not included and therefore are excluded from the benefits of citizenship. In other words, nationalist solidarity emphasizes the division between inside and outside, "us" and "them."[20] In the sphere of international relations this very structure seems to limit the use of solidarity. Even in the case of the *Großraum,* an immediate sense of solidarity between the citizens of the central power and those of the satellite states cannot be taken for granted. In fact, the structural power differential tends to undercut the sense of togetherness and equality.

One way of overcoming this restriction, of course, consists of invoking the concept of humanity—the claim that there is a need for human solidarity, *tout court.* This claim is of course precisely what Schmitt's understanding of international relations emphatically rejects as the dangerous dogma of international liberalism that results in war. The question then arises whether international solidarity can only be based on the framework of international liberalism. However, it appears that the notion of solidarity is also a suitable tool for defining international political ethics, because it is more fluid and flexible than a strictly universalist approach. The shortcomings of a nationalist model of solidarity can be taken as a clue to what the path to international solidarity would look like. It is the moment of rigid exclusion, the emphatic refusal to accept accountability for human problems and conflicts as political conflicts beyond the national border that decreases its value and usefulness in a globalized setting. Given the actual interconnectedness not only of the economy but also of social and cultural life, the concept of solidarity can transcend the border of the nation-state or the *Großraum*. This is clearly understood and accepted in case of natural disasters such as earthquakes and floods. There is a real sense of a global community that can be organized effectively to bring help to the victims of natural disasters. In the arena of political relations, however, this sense of a common ground, of shared responsibilities across national borders, is far less well established. Mass migration from Africa and the Middle East to Europe is a good example of serious problems with respect to solidarity. Under pressure, European nation-states have largely refused to extend solidarity to each other and foreigners in distress, although they are aware of their humane responsibility as well as the negative political consequences of not dealing with these problems. Nonetheless, it is this growing awareness, as much as it is still resisted in the name of the nation-state, that can serve as an index for the slow emergence of international solidarity, not as an abstract value or norm but as a sense of shared debts and obligations, as part of a global perspective. In the long run, without this awareness, Schmitt's plurality of *Großräume* will not be able to establish a stable global order.

These reflections have treated the concept of *Großraum* as a given. But what can be expected from a critical review of this concept, which Schmitt introduced in the late 1930s when he was no longer satisfied with the idea of the nation-state as the appropriate building block of a global political order? To be sure, the concept was introduced in connection with specific German political claims vis-à-vis the Western powers, in particular the United States. The strong opposition to American claims beyond its own hemisphere (declared in the 1823 Monroe Doctrine) replicates the structure of the new American empire, thereby also affirming the hegemonic position of the United States at the center and a loose cluster of dependent satellite states.

It is not easy therefore to remove the ideological baggage from the concept of the *Großraum*. Schmitt's use of the term in the 1940s is connected to strong political claims on the part of the Third Reich in the field of international relations. While this spatial conception leads to the idea of a pluralist world order, in the 1940s it was by no means clear that this new global order, consisting of a small number of *Großräume,* would be an improvement over the crisis of the 1920s, unless you assume along with Schmitt that *any* recognized order is better than the protracted competition for the hegemonic center as part of a global civil war.

The more recent Anglo-American appropriation of Carl Schmitt's thinking, insofar as it transcends the level of neutral academic reception, articulates a fundamental critique of the United States, especially of its foreign policies. It seeks to demonstrate that the United States, by presenting itself as the guarantor of global peace through diplomatic and military interventions, actually undermines the very possibility of a stable global order. It is this more general critique that has to be taken seriously. It has to be understood as a critique of a latent religious (Protestant Christian) agenda to impose American (secularized) religious values on the rest of the world. At the same time, it is crucial to recognize that this line of argument is secular and therefore ultimately not compatible with Schmitt's theological understanding of the new global *nomos,* which stands under the sign of an impending apocalyptic catastrophe.[21]

From the perspective of the democratic Left, Schmitt's call for international pluralism has two drawbacks. First, it relies heavily on the concept of *Großraum* without defining the interior structure of this constellation. There is no guarantee of equality or even fairness inside the *Großraum.* Second, it is largely based on the concept of power and the notion that a balance of power, while it cannot guarantee eternal peace, can and will provide international stability. Put differently, Schmitt's theoretical position leaves underdeveloped the role of political ethics to work out the interstate structure of a pluralist arrangement. The autonomy of the political (in regard to morality) cannot be reduced to the concept of power. For the historical Schmitt such a reduction did not occur, since he insisted on the persistent validity of a political theology, meaning that, beyond a mere analogy, the political is ultimately contained within the theological sphere. He was not looking for a purely secular solution, as are Schmittians on the left.

However, such a secular solution is a game changer. The rejection of or tacit withdrawal from Schmitt's gnostic theology alters the nature of the theory. It either has to defend its propositions in empirical terms or it must seek a new normative ground. In the first case, its statements cannot transcend historical experience and future probability. In the second instance, there is the question of the ultimate ground. More specifically: How can one replace the universal values of international liberalism? If the answer to this question is that after the deconstruction of liberal universalism universal values are no longer available, a new and different form of pragmatism has to be found. Still, in all of the above-mentioned scenarios we have left the sphere of Schmitt's theory. In other words, the usable Schmitt turns out to be no longer Schmitt. This also means that the distance toward Carl Schmitt is not only a question of his problematic biography—that is, his dubious personal commitments and decisions—but also a question of his theory. It appears that this theory is ultimately not compatible with the agenda of a secular democratic Left.

What are the prospects of the Right? Is there a better ground for appropriating and using Schmitt? The rise of populist movements in Europe and the United States in the new millennium has definitely changed the face of the Right, mostly by challenging traditional forms of conservatism. Donald Trump's 2016 victory in the United States was not only a defeat of the Democratic Party but of conventional Republicanism as well. Trump's white nationalism, which strongly articulated the grievances of the white working and lower middle classes, undermined the orthodoxy of the Republican Party by expressing ideas and demands that contradicted fundamental beliefs of the party elite. Especially Trump's foreign policies, as they began to take shape after the election, undercut Republican traditional support for *Pax Americana,* which is based on a belief in international free trade and the benefits of a network of international alliances dominated by the United States. Trump's aggressive nationalism, on the other hand, resonates with a widely felt sense of betrayal of the common man by the political elites.

What is Schmitt's role in this new configuration? It is unlikely that his conservative admirers recognized their own agenda in Trump and his movement—but there was at least Slavoj Žižek who came out in support of Trump. Still, there can be no doubt that Trump's style and the general direction of his ideas and policies has a Schmittian tone. Not only do Schmitt and Trump share the sense of deep crisis with apocalyptic overtones, in their understanding of the political there is an unmistakable focus on the enemy, the hard distinction between us and them, friend and enemy. Furthermore, there is the determined rejection of the belief in universal liberal norms that can be codified as international law. Instead, Trump, like Schmitt, proposes a spatial understanding of international relations, based on a plurality of nation-states. For Trump, as for Schmitt, the political world is an arena of persistent conflict ("deals" in Trump's language) where one either wins or loses. Trump's first moves in the arena of foreign policy definitely promised a radical shift that undermined the notion of maintaining global peace through international agreements. At this point, these are no more than similarities. At least so far, Trump and his circle of advisers have not yet invoked Schmitt's name and thought. But such a move cannot be excluded as logically impossible, since Schmitt's thought would resonate within the movement. A populist reading of Schmitt with a stress on the sovereignty of the nation-state and the need for a leader who identifies with a homogeneous people is definitely a possibility. Schmitt's dark gnosticism in particular would find an echo in the more radical pronouncement of the leader. In other words, a populist Schmitt can be imagined as an aspect of his American reception.

NOTES

Introduction

1. Ernst Jünger and Carl Schmitt, *Briefe 1930–1983,* ed. Helmuth Kiesel (Stuttgart: Klett-Cotta, 1999), 241–45.

2. Ernst Jünger, *Werke* (Stuttgart: Klett-Cotta, 1978), 5:495–538.

3. Walter D. Mignolo, *The Darker Side of Western Modernity: Global Future, Decolonial Options* (Durham, NC: Duke University Press, 2011), 27–35.

1. The Outlaw

1. See Carl Schmitt, *Das internationalrechtliche Verbrechen des Angriffskrieges und der Grundsatz "Nullum crimen, nulla poena sine lege,"* ed. Helmut Quaritsch (Berlin: Duncker & Humblot, 1994). Translations are mine. Subsequently cited in parentheses as *IVA*.

2. See Joseph J. Bendersky, *Carl Schmitt: Theorist for the Reich* (Princeton, NJ: Princeton University Press, 1983); Reinhard Mehring, *Carl Schmitt: A Biography,* trans. Daniel Steuer (Cambridge: Polity, 2014), 407–30.

3. See Edgar Wolfrum, *Die geglückte Demokratie: Geschichte der Bundesrepublik Deutschland von ihren Anfängen bis zur Gegenwart* (Stuttgart: Klett-Cotta,

2006); Konrad Jarausch, *Die Umkehr: Deutsche Wandlungen 1945–1995* (Munich: Deutsche Verlags-Anstalt, 2004).

4. See Jost Hermand, *Kultur im Wiederaufbau: Die Bundesrepublik Deutschland 1945–1965* (Munich: Nymphenburger Verlagshandlung, 1986), 64.

5. Carl Schmitt, *Glossarium: Aufzeichnungen aus den Jahren 1947–1951* (Berlin: Humblot & Duncker, 1991). Translations are mine. Subsequently cited in parentheses as *G*.

6. Nicolaus Sombart, "Ein Invalide des Untergangs: Carl Schmitts Aufzeichnungen aus den Nachkriegsjahren," *Die Zeit,* January 17, 1992. My translation.

7. Ibid.

8. Richard Faber, "Es gibt einen antijüdischen Affekt! Über Carl Schmitts *Glossarium*," *Zeitschrift für Religions- und Geistesgeschichte* 46, no. 1 (1994): 70. My translation.

9. Heinrich Meier, "Freund Jünger als Feind. Carl Schmitts verblüffende Nachlaß-Bekenntnisse," *Der Spiegel,* January 31, 1992, 169. Translations are mine.

10. Ibid., 172.

11. Jürgen Busche, "Carl Schmitt—der Gehilfe. Ein zersplittertes Plädoyer vor leeren Richterstühlen," *Süddeutsche Zeitung,* September 14–15, 1991. Translations are mine.

12. Ibid.

13. Ibid.

14. Henning Ritter, "Positionen in Begriffen: Carl Schmitts Aufzeichnungen 1947–1951," *Frankfurter Allgemeine Zeitung,* October 8, 1991. Translations mine.

15. Ernst Jünger, *Strahlungen* (Tübingen: Heliopolis, 1949); Thomas Mann, *Tagebücher: 28.5.1946–31.12.1948,* ed. Inge Jens (Frankfurt: Fischer, 1977).

16. Schmitt notes, for example, "The hatred that Kaete E. demonstrates and promotes against me is without limits. It is the hatred of a Jewish woman against a German man, against the Roman Catholic" (*G* 169).

17. See, for example, Ernst Jünger/Carl Schmitt, *Briefe 1930–1983,* ed. Helmuth Kiesel (Stuttgart: Klett-Cotta, 1999).

18. See, for example, his letters to Gretha Jünger in *Briefwechsel Gretha Jünger und Carl Schmitt 1934–1953,* ed. Ingeborg Villinger (Berlin: Akademie, 2007) and the exchange with Nicolaus Sombart in *Schmitt und Sombart: Der Briefwechsel von Carl Schmitt mit Nicolaus, Corina und Werner Sombart,* ed. Martin Tielke (Berlin: Duncker & Humblot, 2015).

19. For Weiß, see Wilhelm Kühlmann, "Im Schatten des Leviathan—Carl Schmitt und Konrad Weiß," in *Die eigentliche katholische Verschärfung . . . : Konfession, Theologie und Politik im Werk Carl Schmitts,* ed. Bernd Wacker (Munich: Wilhelm Fink, 1994), 89–114.

20. See Joseph W. Bendersky, "Carl Schmitt's Path to Nuremberg: A Sixty-Year Assessment," *Telos* 139 (2007): 6–34; and Robert W. Kempner, *Ankläger einer Epoche: Lebenserinnerungen* (Frankfurt/Main: Ullstein, 1983).

21. Schmitt notes on September 27, 1947, "The path of the spirit is the detour (Hegel). Distance, separation, mediation, outcome of all human activity (*Werk*). My path from Berlin, via Nuremberg to Plettenberg" (*G* 20). The time sequence is as follows: removal from office, prison, interrogation, and isolation in Plettenberg

is rewritten, following Hegel, as the dialectic of the spirit. The painful humiliation results in hope and overcoming. Following this pattern, the retreat to Plettenberg turns out to be a *refugium* where the spirit can not only rest but also progress.

22. An early entry, which discusses the legitimacy of keeping a diary, elaborates this point. The writing subject is in a position of self-contradiction: "May one carry on a diary that is written with the purpose of being read by other people? Answer: Given the demand to demonstrate humility, a Christian is not allowed, [it is justified] only when ordered by a superior in the church or a confessor, respectively motivated by God or by the need to defend oneself" (*G* 13, September 10, 1947).

23. Thus the diary sharply contrasts Schmitt's early interest in Max Stirner's ego-philosophy and the position of the Catholic theorist Juan Donoso Cortés. The diary cites his letter of June 10, 1851 in order to underscore the "satanic I" of the natural human being. This is followed by the remark that the ego-centered nihilism of Stirner was conceivable only "in the context of the failed Germanic colonization of East Germany . . . and only in the years between 1840 and 1848" (*G* 21, September 29, 1947).

24. This question is controversial in Schmitt scholarship. See Friedrich Balke, *Der Staat nach seinem Ende: Die Versuchung Carl Schmitts* (Munich: Fink, 1996), 39–47.

25. The diarist notes, "With respect to Christ, Pilate was not acting as a judge, he did not condemn him to death; pressed by the Jews, he only ordered the crucifixion as an administrative measure [*Verwaltungsmaßnahme*]" (*G* 208, December 2, 1948). Obviously, he buys into and underscores the narrative of the gospels in their attempt to exonerate the Roman governor at the expense of the Jews. On Schmitt's anti-Semitism see Raphael Gross, *Carl Schmitt und die Juden: Eine deutsche Rechtslehre* (Frankfurt: Suhrkamp, 2000).

26. See Jan-Werner Müller, *A Dangerous Mind: Carl Schmitt in Post-War European Thought* (New Haven, CT: Yale University Press, 2003), 63–75.

27. This interpretation goes back to a lecture by Max Kommerell, given on November 9, 1934, at the University of Bonn, a printed version of which appears in Max Kommerell, *Geist und Buchstabe der Dichtung: Goethe, Schiller, Kleist, Holderlin*, 6th ed. (Frankfurt/Main: Klostermann, 1991).

28. Carl Schmitt, *Ex Captivitate Salus. Erfahrungen der Zeit 1945/47*, 2nd ed. (Berlin: Duncker & Humblot, 2002). Translations are mine. Subsequently cited in parentheses as *E*.

29. Carl Schmitt, *Die Lage der europäischen Rechtswissenschaft* (Tübingen: Internationaler Universitätsverlag, 1950). Translations are mine. Subsequently cited in parentheses as *LER*.

30. See Schmitt's letter to Ernst Jünger of February, 25, 1941, in Jünger/Schmitt, *Briefe 1933–1983*, 114.

31. See Mehring, *Carl Schmitt*, 437–39.

32. See Dirk van Laak, *Gespräche in der Sicherheit des Schweigens: Carl Schmitt in der politischen Geistesgeschichte der frühen Bundesrepublik*, 2nd ed. (Berlin: Akademie-verlag, 2002), 134–35.

2. Transition

1. Carl Schmitt, *Der Nomos der Erde im Völkerrecht des Ius Publicum Europaeum 1950*, 2nd ed. (Berlin: Duncker & Humblot, 1974); translated into English by G. L. Ulmen as *The Nomos of the Earth in the International Law of the* Jus Publicum Europaeum (New York: Telos, 2006). All English translations unless noted are based on this edition and subsequently cited in parentheses as *N*.

2. Carl Schmitt, *Völkerrechtliche Großraumordnung: mit Interventionsverbot für raumfremde Mächte. Ein Beitrag zum Reichsbegriff im Völkerrecht 1939*, 4th ed. (Berlin: Duncker & Humblot, 1991); translated into English by Timothy Nunan as "The Großraum Order of International Law with a Ban on Intervention for Spatially-Foreign Powers: A Contribution to the Concept of Reich in International Law 1939–1941," in Carl Schmitt, *Writings on War*, ed. Timothy Nunan (Cambridge: Polity, 2012), 75–124. All English translations unless noted are based on this edition and subsequently cited in parentheses as *GRO*.

3. In addition to Friedrich Ratzel, Karl Haushofer most fully articulates this older conception of the geopolitical in his numerous writings from the 1920s and 1930s, including Haushofer, *Grenzen in ihrer geographischen und politischen Bedeutung* (Berlin: K. Vowinckel, 1927); Haushofer et al., *Bausteine zur Geopolitik* (Berlin: K. Vowinckel, 1928).

4. For more on German foreign policy under National Socialism, see Hans-Adolf Jacobsen, *Nationalsozialistische Außenpolitik, 1933–1938* (Frankfurt/Main: A. Metzner, 1968); Klaus Hildebrand, *Deutsche Außenpolitik 1933–1945: Kalkül oder Dogma?*, 5th ed. (Stuttgart: Kohlhammer, 1990); Christian Leitz, *Nazi Foreign Policy, 1933–1941: The Road to Global War* (London: Routledge, 2004).

5. *Völkischer Beobachter*, April 29, 1939, 5. My translation.

6. Lothar Gruchmann, *Nationalsozialistische Großraumordnung: Die Konstruktion einer "deutschen Monroe-Doktrin"* (Stuttgart: Deutsche, 1962), 11.

7. Giselher Wirsing, *Der maßlose Kontinent Roosevelts Kampf um die Weltherrschaft* (Jena: Diederichs, 1942), 177.

8. Carl Schmitt, "Die Raumrevolution: Durch den totalen Krieg zum totalen Frieden," *Das Reich* 19, September 29, 1940, 3. My translation.

9. Hildebrand, *Deutsche Außenpolitik*, 34–36.

10. Ibid., 99.

11. Schmitt was at least partially familiar with the ample U.S. literature on the Monroe Doctrine. Among others, he referred to the standard work by Dexter Perkins, *The Monroe Doctrine 1867–1907* (Baltimore: Johns Hopkins University Press, 1933), as well as Alejandro Alvarez, *The Monroe Doctrine: Its Importance in the International Life of the States of the New World* (New York: Oxford University Press, 1924). At the same time, it should be noted that prior to 1933, there was already an intensive discourse concerning the Monroe Doctrine that Schmitt could refer to.

12. Schmitt, *The Nomos of the Earth*, 253.

13. Carl Schmitt, "Großraum gegen Universalismus" in *Positionen und Begriffe: Im Kampf mit Weimar-Genf-Versailles*, 3rd ed. (Berlin: Duncker & Humblot, 1994), 337. Translated by Matthew Hannah as "Großraum versus Universalism" in *Spatiality, Sovereignty, and Carl Schmitt: Geographies of the Nomos*, ed. Stephen Legg (New York: Routledge, 2011), 48.

14. On the history of the meaning of the Monroe Doctrine and its interpretation around 1900, see Dexter Perkins, *A History of the Monroe Doctrine* (Boston: Little, Brown, 1963), 192–275.

15. Gruchmann, *Nationalsozialistische Großraumordnung*, 68–69.

16. Ibid., 69.

17. Ibid., 121–45, among others.

18. Martin Broszat, *Nationalsozialistische Polenpolitik 1939–1945* (Stuttgart: Deutsche, 1961); Hans-Ulrich Wehler, *Deutsche Gesellschaftsgeschichte*, vol. 4, *Vom Beginn des Ersten Weltkriegs bis zur Gründung der beiden deutschen Staaten, 1914–1949* (Munich: Beck, 2003), 881–902.

19. Gruchmann, *Nationalsozialistische Großraumordnung*, 95; my translation. See also Helmut Heiber, "Der Generalplan Ost," *Vierteljahrschrift für Zeitgeschichte* no. 3 (1958): 307–8.

20. See also Michael Walzer, *Just Wars and Unjust Wars: A Moral Argument with Historical Illustrations*, 2nd ed. (New York: Basic Books, 1992).

21. Carl Schmitt, *Politische Theologie II. Die Legende von der Erledigung jeder politischen Theologie*, 4th ed. (1970; Berlin: Duncker & Humblot, 1996). Translated into English by Michael Hoelzl and Graham Ward as *Political Theology 2: The Myth of the Closure of Any Political Theology* (Cambridge: Polity, 2008). See also Jürgen Manemann, *Carl Schmitt und die politische Theologie: Politischer Anti-monotheismus* (Münster: Aschendorff, 2002).

22. William Rasch, "Menschenrechte als Geopolitik: Carl Schmitt und die völkerrechtliche Form der amerikanischen Hegemonie," in *Terror im System: Der 11. September 2001 und die Folgen,* ed. Dirk Baecker, Peter Krieg, and Fritz B. Simon (Heidelberg: Carl-Auer-Systeme, 2002), 130–58.

23. By contrast, the Bush regime's distance from a liberal conception of international relations is elucidated by Richard Perle's polemic against the UN and their purportedly fantastic claims to ground a new, peaceful world order through the implementation of an international law represented by the UN itself. In their negative judgment of international institutions like the League of Nations and UN, Perle and Schmitt are entirely in agreement. See Richard Perle, "Thank God for the Death of the UN," *Guardian*, March 21, 2003.

24. Gary Dorrien, *The Neoconservative Mind: Politics, Culture, and the War of Ideology* (Philadelphia: Temple University Press, 1993); Shadia B. Drury, *Leo Strauss and the American Right* (New York: St. Martin's, 1997); Alex Callinicos, *The New Mandarins of American Power: The Bush Administration's Plans for the World* (Cambridge: Polity, 2003).

25. See also William E. Scheuerman, "Carl Schmitt and the Road to Abu Ghraib," *Constellations* 13, no. 1 (2006): 108–24.

26. Rasch, "Menschenrechte," 148.

27. Rasch's critique, if I understand correctly, is principally levied against the conception of the "American Empire" that, while not first developed under George W. Bush, at least for the first time was referred to by name by the official speakers and unofficial commentators of his government. Of course, within this government itself, not all participants were willing to admit to U.S. imperialism. They preferred instead to veil U.S. claims to hegemony in appeals to democracy and foundational Western values. See also Andrew J. Bacevich's criticism from the

conservative side, *American Empire: The Realities and Consequences of U.S. Diplomacy* (Cambridge, MA: Harvard University Press, 2002). Within the American discourse, Rasch would be placed among the realists from the school of Morgenthau, along the lines of John J. Mearsheimer.

28. Hans Blumenberg, *Die Legitimität der Neuzeit* (Frankfurt: Suhrkamp, 1966); translated into English by Robert M. Wallace as *The Legitimacy of the Modern Age* (Cambridge, MA: MIT Press, 1985).

3. The Fate of European Colonialism and Carl Schmitt's New World Order

1. See Dirk van Laak, *Gespräche in der Sicherheit des Schweigens: Carl Schmitt in der politischen Geistesgeschichte der frühen Bundesrepublik* (Berlin: Akademie, 1993); Jens Hacke, *Philosophie der Bürgerlichkeit: Die liberalkonservative Begründung der Bundesrepublik* (Göttingen: Vandenhoeck & Ruprecht, 2006).

2. Francis Brooks, "The Impact of Disease," in *Technology, Disease, and Colonial Conquests, Sixteenth to Eighteenth Centuries: Essays Reappraising the Guns and Germs Theories,* ed. George Raudzens (Leiden: Brill, 2001), 129.

3. In November of 1949 he notes, "The contemporary worldwide discussion about Vitoria and the right of the Spanish Conquista is the sad incidental music connected with the destruction of the glorious European overseas empires, the transformation of India and Indonesia into equal members of the United Nations." Carl Schmitt, *Glossarium: Aufzeichnungen aus den Jahren 1947–1951* (Berlin: Humblot & Duncker, 1991), 280.

4. William H. McNeill, *Plagues and Peoples* (New York: Anchor, 1976); Carlo M. Cipolla, *Guns and Sails in the Early Phase of European Expansion 1400–1700* (London: Collins, 1965).

5. Jared Diamond, *Guns, Germs, and Steel: The Fates of Human Societies* (New York: Norton, 1998).

6. More recent military history has also challenged the notion of a military revolution around 1500 that would account for the rapid success of the colonial project in North America and elsewhere. While the superior firepower of the Europeans cannot be denied, the notion of a causal connection between a military revolution and successful colonial occupation is no longer viewed as self-evident. "It can be suggested," Jeremy Black argues, "first, that there was no Military Revolution, and, second, that even if there was, it did not have the revolutionary effect overseas." Jeremy Black, "European Overseas Expansion and the Military Revolution," in Raudzens, *Technology, Disease, and Colonial Conquest,* 6. See also Jeremy M. Black, ed., *War in the Early Modern World* (Boulder: Westview, 1999). Once the notion of the superiority of modern European warfare has been questioned, indigenous military resistance and its success appears in a different light. "Primitive" warfare can be successful depending on the geographical circumstances. This is what Schmitt later recognizes and theorizes in his partisan study of 1963.

7. For a general assessment of decolonization see Franz Ansprenger, *The Dissolution of the Colonial Empires* (London: Routledge, 1989); D. George Boyce, *Decolonisation and the British Empire, 1775–1997* (London: MacMillan, 1999).

8. George Raudzens has shown that the military conquest by the Spanish and the British was considerably more complex than commonly assumed. In most cases it took place in the form of small confrontations that changed the relationship without a definitive victory. Raudzens underscores the growing number of settlers rather than firepower as decisive for the outcome of the colonies. See George Raudzens, "Outfiring or Outpopulating? Main Reasons for Early Colonial Conquests," in Raudzens, ed., *Technology, Disease and Colonial Conquest*, 31–57.

9. Brooks, "The Impact of Disease," 131.

10. The question of rethinking the history of decolonization has played a major role in recent scholarship, in particular, the difference between the historiography concerned with the rise and fall of European colonial empires, written from the viewpoint of the European center, and the postcolonial approach from the point of view of the former colonies. For Schmitt the latter was still simply inconceivable. For an extensive discussion of these problems see James D. Le Sueur, ed., *The Decolonization Reader* (New York: Routledge, 2003), especially 7–44. However, for the analysis of Schmitt's theory the conflict between history and postcolonial theory is ultimately less important than the fundamental break with the imperial perspective that Schmitt continues even when he proposes a new pluralistic world order of *Großräume*, since each *Großraum* is conceived as an imperial space.

11. See Raymond F. Betts, *France and Decolonization 1900–1960* (New York: St. Martin's, 1991).

12. R. F. Holland, *European Decolonization 1918–1981: An Introductory Survey* (New York: St. Martin's, 1985), 169.

13. For a discussion of the cultural and intellectual impact of the Algerian war on France after Algerian independence, see James D. Le Suer, "Decolonizing French Universalism: Reconsidering the Impact of the Algerian War on French Intellectuals," in *The Decolonization Reader*, 103–17. Le Suer argues that the internal debates among French intellectuals were motivated and guided by a normative understanding of French culture and politics, an idea that was, in their minds, compromised by the brutal suppression of the Algerian liberation movement.

14. See Carl Schmitt, "Völkerrechtliche Formen des modernen Imperialismus," in Schmitt, *Positionen und Begriffe im Kampf mit Weimar—Genf—Versailles*, 3rd ed. (Berlin: Duncker & Humblot, 1994), 184–203.

15. Carl Schmitt, "Das Rheinland als Objekt internationaler Politik," in Schmitt, *Frieden oder Pazifismus: Arbeiten zum Völkerrecht und zur internationalen Politik, 1924–1978*, ed. Günther Maschke (Berlin: Duncker & Humblot: 2005), 29.

16. Frantz Fanon, *Toward the African Revolution: Political Essays* (New York: Monthly Review, 1967), 78.

17. Ibid., 81.

18. Ibid., 43.

19. Possibly this lack of attention can be explained by when it was written. If the manuscript was partly or mostly composed before 1945, Schmitt could not be aware of the emerging liberation process after World War II. Of course, he could have updated the manuscript between 1947 and 1950.

20. "According to Vitoria, the right to appropriate land arose only indirectly, and then only by way of arguments favoring just war." Carl Schmitt, *The Nomos*

of the Earth. The International Law of the Ius Publicum Europaeum, trans. G. L. Ulmen (New York: Telos, 2003), 105. The case of a just war against the Indians can be constructed when they block Christian missionary activity in principle. As Schmitt continues, now taking over Vitoria's position, *"The papal missionary mandate* was the legal foundation of the conquista" (my italics). *The Nomos of the Earth,* 111.

21. Schmitt, *The Nomos of the Earth,* 108.

22. Ibid., 130. Still, it is worth noting that Schmitt himself falls back on the argument of mental and cultural superiority when he discusses the conquest of the American Indians. In his mind, the New World was rightly taken because of the invaders' intellectual dominance.

23. Ibid., 134.

24. Carl Schmitt, "Die Ordnung der Welt und der Zweite Weltkrieg," in *Staat, Großraum, Nomos, Arbeiten aus den Jahren 1916–1969,* ed. Günter Maschke (Berlin: Duncker & Humblot, 1995), 592–618.

25. Carl Schmitt, "Appropriation, Distribution, Production: Toward a Proper Formulation of Basic Questions of Any Social and Economic Order," *Telos* 95 (1993): 53–64. Originally published in German in 1953.

26. See Carl Schmitt, "Die Ordnung der Welt nach dem Zweiten Weltkrieg," in Maschke, *Staat, Großraum, Nomos,* 592–618.

27. For an extended discussion of *Großraum* see chapter 2 and also William Hooker, *Carl Schmitt's International Thought: Order and Orientation* (Cambridge: Cambridge University Press, 2009), 126–55.

28. For the background of Schmitt's geopolitics, see the work of the German geographer Friedrich Ratzel (1844–1904), especially his *Politische Geographie oder die Geographie der Staaten, des Verkehres und des Krieges* (Munich: R. Oldenburg, 1897) and *Der Lebensraum: Eine biogeographische Studie* (Tübingen: H. Laupp, 1901).

29. Schmitt, *The Nomos of the Earth,* 355. The title of the original German essay is "Der neue Nomos der Erde."

30. For a critique of Schmitt's position see Walter D. Mignolo, *The Darker Side of Western Modernity: Global Futures, Decolonial Options* (Durham, NC: Duke University Press, 2011), 27–35. As Mignolo points out, Schmitt's basic assumption was that the second world order was exclusively defined in European terms. While he agrees with Schmitt that the European powers dominated the world between 1500 and 1918, he stresses the moment of continuity from the first to the third order. Therefore, decolonization, which is a serious problem for Schmitt, can be conceptualized also as a revitalization of the older Nomos.

31. Carl Schmitt, "USA und die völkerrechtlichen Formen des modernen Imperialismus," in Schmitt, *Frieden oder Pazifismus,* 356.

32. See chapter 2.

33. See Schmitt, "Die Einheit der Welt," in Schmitt, *Staat, Großraum, Nomos,* 496–512, especially 500, where Schmitt insists on real pluralism.

34. For a comparative perspective on Schmitt's position, see Mika Luoma-aho, "Geopolitics and Grosspolitics: From Carl Schmitt to E. H. Carr and James Burnham," in *The International Political Thought of Carl Schmitt: Terror, Liberal War and the Crisis of Global Order,* ed. Louiza Odysseos and Fabio Petito (New York: Routledge, 2007), 36–55.

35. Niall Ferguson, *Colossus: The Price of America's Empire* (New York: Penguin, 2004), 198.

36. Niall Ferguson, *Empire: The Rise and Demise of the British World Order and the Lessons for Global Power* (New York: Basic Books, 2002).

37. Ferguson, *Colossus*, 178–79.

38. Ibid., 176.

39. Ibid., 67–68.

40. Michael Ignatieff, "The Burden," *New York Times Magazine*, January 5, 2003, 24, quoted in Jeanne Morefield, *Empires without Imperialism: Anglo-American Decline and the Politics of Deflection* (New York: Oxford University Press, 2014), 208.

41. Morefield, *Empires without Imperialism*, 208.

42. Ibid., 213–14.

43. See the cautious discussion of Danilo Zolo, "The Re-emerging Notion of Empire and the influence of Carl Schmitt's Thought," in Odysseos and Petito, *International Political Thought of Carl Schmitt*, 154–65.

44. I concur with Alessandro Colombo that Carl Schmitt cannot be treated as a straightforward realist such as Carr or Morgenthau, although there are of course realist elements in his theory. See Alessandro Colombo, "The 'Realist' Institutionalism of Carl Schmitt," in Odysseos and Petito, *International Political Thought of Carl Schmitt*, 21–35.

45. Schmitt, *The Nomos of the Earth*, 42.

46. See chapter 5.

4. Revolutionary War and Absolute Enemy

1. See Herfried Münkler, *Die neuen Kriege* (Reinbek: Rowohlt, 2002).

2. The short monograph was conceived and written as a contribution to the celebration of Ernst Forsthoff's sixtieth birthday, as Schmitt mentions in a letter to Mohler (September 14, 1962), but there is no indication why Schmitt chose this topic for his former student and friend Forsthoff. Possibly it could be an allusion to Forsthoff's role as the president of the Constitutional Court of Cyprus from 1960 to May of 1963. He resigned because of a conflict with the Greek government concerning a ruling in favor of the Turkish minority, shortly before the beginning of the civil war. In terms of content, more relevant is a later remark Schmitt made to Mohler, in a letter dated February 21, 1963, that he considers *Theorie des Partisanen* as a companion piece to *Der Begriff des Politischen*. Schmitt, *Briefwechsel mit einem seiner Schüler*, ed. Arnim Mohler (Berlin: Akademie, 1995), 328. This remark would confirm that Schmitt was more interested in the political than in the military aspect of the partisan.

3. With the premise that the political is prior to the military (war), Schmitt clearly stands in the tradition of Clausewitz, for whom the distinction between the political aim of the war and the actual war was essential. See Herfried Münkler, *Über den Krieg: Stationen der Kriegsgeschichte im Spiegel ihrer theoretischen Reflexionen* (Weilerswist: Velbrück, 2003), 75–90.

4. Gerhard Nebel, *Unter Partisanen und Kreuzfahrern* (Stuttgart: Klett, 1950); Rolf Schroers, *Der Partisan: Ein Beitrag zur politischen Anthropologie* (Cologne:

Kiepenheuer & Witsch, 1961); Hans Joachim Sell, *Partisan: Roman* (Düsseldorf: Diederichs, 1961); Hellmuth Rentsch, *Partisanenkampf: Erfahrungen und Lehren* (Frankfurt: Bernard & Graefe, 1961).

5. Luis Garcìa Arias, *La guerra moderna y la organización internacional* (Madrid: Instituto de Estudios Políticos, 1962); Raymond Aron, *La société industrielle et la guerre* (Paris: Plon, 1959); Roger Trinquier, *Modern Warfare: A French View of Counterinsurgency*, trans. Daniel Lee (New York: Praeger, 1964); Peter Paret and John W. Shy, *Guerrillas in the 1960's* (New York: Praeger, 1966).

6. In terms of West German foreign policy around 1960, Schmitt's perception of the Communist Bloc on the one hand and his interpretation of the goals of the United States on the other are much closer to those intellectuals around Franz Josef Strauß (among them Armin Mohler), who supported de Gaulle's position, than those who firmly supported NATO and U.S. leadership. Schmitt sees the Soviet Union and its allies as a continued radical threat without hope for real and sustained détente. In this constellation de Gaulle becomes the symbol of European and German resistance to U.S. leadership. De Gaulle's vision of a united Western Europe based on a close Franco-German alliance was hailed as a conservative response to the claims of a détente between the United States and the Soviet Union. However, this position on the German Right was based on a problematic reading of de Gaulle's intentions, which actually paralleled the détente policy of the United States. See Christian Hacke, *Die Außenpolitik der Bundesrepublik Deutschland: Weltmacht wider Willen?* (Berlin: Ullstein, 1993), 116–20.

7. For a detailed, historically grounded conceptual analysis of the *Theory of the Partisan*, see G. Slomp, "The Theory of the Partisan: Carl Schmitt's Neglected Legacy," *History of Political Thought* 26, no. 3 (2005): 502–19, and William Hooker, *Carl Schmitt's International Thought: Order and Orientation* (Cambridge: Cambridge University Press, 2009), 156–94.

8. Carl Schmitt, *Theory of the Partisan: Intermediate Commentary on the Concept of the Political*, trans. G. L. Ulmen (New York: Telos, 2007), 9. Subsequently cited in parentheses as *TP*. The original title in German was *Theorie des Partisanen: Zwischenbemerkung zum Begriff des Politischen*.

9. Claudius Köster, *Außenpolitik und Politikbegriff bei Carl Schmitt* (Munich: Institut der Staatswiseschaft der Universität der Bundeswehr, 1998), 86–90 and 115–119.

10. If we place an emphasis on Clausewitz's revolutionary impetus, especially in the years 1812 and 1813, he becomes a more ambiguous figure in Prussian history, an ambiguity that Schmitt could explore to reinforce the link between partisan war and national revolution. This project could ultimately lead to a national revolution against the legitimate government (monarchy) or, as in the case of Salan, to a rebellion against de Gaulle's Fifth Republic. See also Münkler, *Über den Krieg*, 108–9.

11. See Joachim Ritter, *Hegel and the French Revolution: Essays on the Philosophy of Right* (1957), trans. Richard D. Winfield (Cambridge, MA: MIT Press, 1982).

12. Although there is no proof that Schmitt was originally stimulated by Rolf Schroers's *Der Partisan* (1961), we can make the argument that *Theory of the Partisan* is a response to Schroers, a response that acknowledges the importance of

Schroers's study and, at the same time, rejects its central thesis and overall position. In his book Schroers reflects on human autonomy (*Mündigkeit*) defined in the name of reason (*Vernunft*) that motivates resistance and insurrection. This position becomes in Schmitt the negative principle of revolution and absolute war. The perspective of personal responsibility, which Schroers upholds against a purely functional concept of the political subject, is alien to Schmitt's theory, which defines the partisan in terms of the real and absolute enemy. Schroers's liberal commitment stands in clear contrast to Schmitt's interest in extreme positions on the Far Right and Left. For Schroers the partisan is a figure of opposition against the mere fact of power. The partisan therefore receives his moral importance from the resistance movement against the NS regime. Thus for Schroers the partisan is a figure of "Recht," by which he means a higher law than the positive law of the regime in power. In this struggle Schroers's partisan is involved in "autonome Selbstverwirklichung" (autonomous self-realization, Schroers, *Theory of the Partisan*, 25). Nothing could be further from Schmitt's understanding of the partisan.

13. Mao Zedong, *On Guerrilla Warfare*, trans. Samuel B. Griffith (New York: Doubleday, 1978), 41.

14. Ibid., 62.

15. Ibid., 75–83.

16. How carefully Schmitt avoids an open and clear evaluation of the political and military forces around Salan becomes apparent in a comparison with Armin Mohler's analysis of the Fifth Republic. Mohler speaks openly of the Far Right as French Fascism (Arnim Mohler, *Die fünfte Republik: Was steht hinter de Gaulle?* [Munich: Piper, 1963], 51–58) and sees the oppositional stance of the army in Algeria as part of the Fascist opposition that was ultimately unable to win against de Gaulle because it lacked the will (*Entschlossenheit*) to form a common front with the French settlers in Algeria and the Far Right in France. He notes, "Hätten die zivilen Ultras und das überwiegend antigaullistische Offizierskorps sich je zu einer entschlossenen gemeinsamen Aktion zusammengefunden, so wäre das das Ende der Fünften Republik gewesen." Mohler, *Die fünfte Republik*, 110.

17. Roger Trinquier, *Modern Warfare: A French View of Counterinsurgency*, trans. Daniel Lee (New York: Praeger, 1964), 8–9.

18. It is worth noting that Schmitt remains undecided within the French constellation between the apocalyptical version of the French colonial officers, who see their enemies as the incarnation of anti-Christian Communism, and de Gaulle, who, as the legal leader of the Fifth Republic, wants to emphasize the independence of France vis-à-vis the United States and hopes for a new international structure that overcomes the dualism of the Cold War. De Gaulle's Eurocentric conception of international pluralism was more attractive to Schmitt than the dualistic structure of the Cold War with the emphasis on NATO. See Mohler, *Die fünfte Republik*, 110.

19. John Shy and Thomas W. Collier, "Revolutionary War," in *Makers of Modern Strategy from Machiavelli to the Nuclear Age*, ed. Peter Paret (Princeton, NJ: Princeton University Press, 1986), 853.

20. Ibid.

21. The closest to Schmitt's position was possibly André Beaufre in France in his *An Introduction to Strategy: With Particular Reference to Problems of Defense, Politics, Economics, and Diplomacy in the Nuclear Age*, trans. R. H. Barr (Paris:

Colin, 1963 [French]; New York: Praeger, 1965), who favored the consistent pursuit of a total strategy that embraces economic, political, and diplomatic activities as well as military efforts to defeat the enemy. He claimed that the success of the Soviet Union in the 1940s and 1950s was due to such a strategy. But he also maintained that the strategy of long-lasting, low-intensity war embraced by Mao was not suitable to Western industrial democracies because they depend on public opinion. Unlike Schmitt, his own preference is what he called an indirect strategy where military action is only the last resort.

22. Michael Carver, "Conventional Warfare in the Nuclear Age," in Paret, *Makers of Modern Strategy*, 784–85.

23. For a nuanced discussion of the "just war" tradition and Schmitt's critique, see Chris Brown, "From Humanized War to Humanitarian Intervention: Carl Schmitt's Critique of the Just War Tradition," in *The International Political Thought of Carl Schmitt: Terror, Liberal War, and the Crisis of Global Order*, ed. Louiza Odysseos and Fabio Petito (London: Routledge, 2007), 56–69. While Brown acknowledges Schmitt's argument against the liberal justification of just wars, he ultimately opposes a return to the *jus publicum Europaeum* as insufficient for the contemporary global situation. He correctly points out that the concept of restrained war never applied to the territories beyond the European line.

24. Benno Gerhard Teschke, "Fatal Attraction: A Critique of Carl Schmitt's International Political and Legal Theory," *International Theory* 3, no. 2 (2011): 186.

25. David Chandler, "The Revival of Carl Schmitt in International Relations: The Last Refuge of Critical Theorists?," *Millennium* 37, no. 1 (2008): 47.

5. The Return of Political Theology

1. See Michael Hollerich, "Carl Schmitt," in *Political Theology: The Blackwell Companion to Political Theology*, ed. Peter Scott and William T. Canavaugh (Oxford: Blackwell, 2007), 107–22.

2. See William Rasch, "Messias oder Katechon? Carl Schmitts Stellung zur politischen Theology," in *Politische Theologie: Formen und Funktionen im 20. Jahrhundert*, ed. Jürgen Brokoff and Jürgen Fohrmann (Paderborn: Schöning, 2003), 39–54.

3. See Carl Schmitt, *Roman Catholicism and Political Form*, trans. G. L. Ulman (Westport, CT: Greenwood, 1996).

4. Carl Schmitt, *Political Theology: Four Chapters on the Concept of Sovereignty*, trans. George Schwab (Chicago: University of Chicago Press, 2005), 5. Subsequently quoted in parentheses as *PT*.

5. Barbara Nichtweiß, *Erik Peterson: Neue Sicht auf Leben und Werk* (Freiburg: Herder, 1994), 722–830.

6. Barbara Nichtweiß, "Apokalyptische Verfassungslehren: Carl Schmitt im Horizont der Theologie Erik Petersons," in *Die eigentlich katholische Verschärfung: Konfession, Theologie und Politik im Werk Carl Schmitts*, ed. Bernd Wacker (Munich: Fink, 1994), 37–63.

7. Carl Schmitt, *Political Theology II: The Myth of the Closure of Any Political Theology*, trans. Michael Hoelzl and Graham Ward (Cambridge: Polity, 2008), 49–59. Subsequently cited in parentheses as *PT II*.

8. Johann Baptist Metz, *Zum Begriff der politischen Theologie: 1967–1997* (Mainz: Matthias Grünewalt, 1997); Jürgen Moltmann, *On Human Dignity: Political Theology and Ethics* (Philadelphia: Fortress, 1984).

9. The theologian and professor of canonical law Hans Barion was among Schmitt's close friends and important intellectual contacts after World War II. Among other things, he shared the fate of being removed from his teaching position after 1945 because of his close links to the NS regime. In the 1920s Barion was impressed by Schmitt's lectures and writings, especially his monograph *Roman Catholicism and Political Form*. Under the influence of Schmitt and the Catholic theologian Karl Eschweiler, Barion joined the Nazi party in 1933. Because of his activities as a consultant to the Third Reich in matters concerning the organization of the Catholic Church, he was temporarily suspended by the Church but later reinstated under pressure from the regime. From 1939 until 1945 Barion taught at the University of Bonn, where he also served as the dean of the theological faculty. After the war the Church kept its distance from Barion; he was as isolated as Schmitt. Both were highly critical of the later development of the Church and opposed the outcome of Vatican II. In his late publications Barion became a severe critic of the new theology, a position that was shared by Schmitt.

10. Erik Peterson, "Der Monotheismus als politisches Problem," in *Theologische Traktate* (Munich: Kösel, 1951), 49. Translations are mine.

11. Ibid., 60–61.

12. Ibid., 76.

13. Ibid., 90.

14. Ibid., 93.

15. Ibid., 147n16.

16. Only the informed reader could grasp the old context, since the preface emphasizes the importance of Barion as a legal scholar and thereby indirectly acknowledges that Barion was also ousted in 1945 because he strongly favored the submission of Roman Catholicism to the NS regime.

17. It is worth noting that Hans Barion, although personally dedicated to Schmitt and possibly his closest personal friend after 1945, rejected Schmitt's concept of political theology as it was restated in *Political Theology II*, on theological grounds. While Schmitt and Barion agree on the negative consequences of political Catholicism within the structure of a pluralistic liberal state, they disagree about the appropriate involvement of the Catholic Church in political issues. According to Barion, the church was theologically not legitimized to exert political power; see Thomas Marschler, *Kirchenrecht im Bannkreis Carl Schmitts: Hans Barion vor und nach 1945* (Bonn: Nova & Vetera, 2004), 401. This means that Barion, although by no means convinced by Peterson's arguments (which he explains in a letter to Schmitt dated December 8, 1969), shares the latter's fundamental negative verdict against a Catholic political theology. Barion's criticism of Peterson, however, makes clear their agreement on the fundamental issue is motivated by very different concerns. In political terms, at least in 1933, Barion favored National Socialism (and like Schmitt the concept of the total state); in historical terms, he thinks that Peterson misreads the history of the church and especially the role of Augustine. Based on Georg Koepgen's book *Die Gnosis des Christentums* (1939), Barion argues that the theological legitimacy of political theology did depend on

the incarnation of Christ. Notwithstanding his own strong hostility toward Peterson, whom he accuses of incompetence, Barion opposes Schmitt by insisting on the exceptional role of the Church as being situated outside the political sphere. The Church cannot participate in the political sphere. For Barion, the Church has to remain indifferent to the specific nature of the political regime. As he points out, "Innerhalb eines Staates, dessen verfassungsorientiertes und als unabänderlich normiertes Religionsrecht die Kirche durch ein Ralliement anerkannt hat, verpflichten politische Weisungen der Kirche, die über das verfassungsmäßige Religionsrecht hinauszielen, nicht unter Sünde" (Within a state, whose constitutionally granted freedom of religion was recognized as unchangable and standardized by the Church via Papal decree [*Ralliement*], the political orders of the church that aim at the constitutionally valid freedom of religion are not binding in the context of sin [*unter Sünde*]). See Barion, "Kirche oder Partei? Römischer Katholizismus und politische Form," in *Kirche und Kirchenrecht*, ed. Werner Bockenförde (Paderborn: Schnöning, 1984), 506. My translation. The Church is supposed to stay away from political discourse. Barion was quite aware that his 1965 essay did not support the position of his friend. See Marschler, *Kirchenrecht im Bannkreis Carl Schmitts*, 406–407.

18. Jan Assmann, "Monotheismus als Politische Theologie" in Brockoff and Fohrmann, *Politische Theologie*, 13–27.

19. Carl Schmitt, *Glossarium: Aufzeichnungen der Jahre 1947–1951* (Berlin: Duncker & Humblot, 1991), 131. Subsequently cited in the text as G. All translations are mine.

20. Carl Schmitt, *Donoso Cortés in gesamteuropäischer Interpretation: Vier Aufsätze* (Cologne: Greven, 1950), 93. My translation.

21. See Richard Faber, "Carl Schmitt der Römer," in Wacker, *Die eigentlich katholische Verschärfung*, 272–74.

22. Ibid., 275.

23. Hans Blumenberg, *Die Legitimität der Neuzeit* (Frankfurt: Suhrkamp, 1966), 23. My translation.

24. Hans Blumenberg and Carl Schmitt, *Briefwechsel*, ed. Alexander Schmitz and Marcel Lepper (Frankfurt: Suhrkamp, 2007), 33. All translations are mine.

25. See Ruth Groh, *Arbeit an der Heillosigkeit der Welt: Zur politisch-theologischen Mythologie und Anthropologie Carl Schmitts* (Frankfurt: Suhrkamp, 1998), 160.

26. Ibid., 163.

27. A letter to Jacob Taubes dated May 24, 1977 stresses the distinction between a moral judgment of Schmitt because of his participation in the NS regime, which he explicitly and polemically (against Taubes) rejects, and a philosophical critique, which he considers as both appropriate and necessary. See Blumenberg and Schmitt, *Briefwechsel*, 260f. Taubes' description of the Schmitt-Blumenberg controversy suggests that he either did not fully understand or he misrepresented Blumenberg's approach. See Jacob Taubes, Aleida Assmann, Jan Assmann, Horst Folkers, Wolf-Daniel Hartwich, and Christoph Schulte, *Die politische Theologie des Paulus: Vorträge, Gehalten an der Forschungsstätte der Evangelischen Studiengemeinschaft in Heidelberg, 23.–27. Februar 1987* (Munich: Fink, 1993), 95.

28. Blumenberg and Schmitt, *Briefwechsel*, 105–7.

29. Ibid., 106.

30. Ibid., 106.

31. Hans Blumenberg, *The Legitimacy of the Modern Age,* trans. Robert M. Wallace (Cambridge, MA: MIT Press, 1983), 101. This translation is based on the revised second edition.

32. Ibid., 99–100.

33. Ibid., 96–97.

34. Ibid., 97.

35. See Felix Grossheutschi, *Carl Schmitt und die Lehre vom Katechon* (Berlin: Duncker & Humblot, 1996); Paul Metzger, *Katechon: II Thess 2, 1–12 im Horizont apokalyptischen Denkens* (Berlin: de Gruyter, 2005).

36. Heinrich Meier, *Die Lehre Carl Schmitts. Vier Kapitel zur Unterscheidung Politischer Theologie und Politischer Philosophie,* 2nd ed. (Stuttgart: Metzler, 2004), 111–12.

37. In this context it is curious that Blumenberg, for whom the latent gnosticism of medieval theology is the unresolved problem of the Middle Ages that could only be overcome by the Enlightenment, did not recognize or at least did not foreground the gnostic elements in Schmitt's work.

38. See Jürgen Manemann, *Carl Schmitt und die politische Theologie: Politischer Anti-monotheismus* (Münster: Aschendorff, 2002), 82–87; Harald Strohm, *Die Gnosis und die Nationalsozialismus* (Frankfurt: Suhrkamp, 1997).

39. Johann Baptist Metz, "Theologie gegen Mythologie. Kleine Apologie des biblischen Monotheismus," *Herder Korrespondenz* 42, no. 4 (1988): 187–93.

40. Manemann, *Carl Schmitt,* 180.

41. Ibid., 184.

42. See also Schmitt, *Roman Catholicism and Political Form,* 49–50, where Schmitt emphasizes the formal nature of law and its adaptability to different positions of power.

43. Günter Meuter, *Der Katechon: Zu Carl Schmitts fundamentalischer Kritik der Zeit* (Berlin: Duncker & Humblot, 1994), 213, where Meuter notes the similarity between Schmitt's view and that of the Protestant theologian Wilhelm Stapel. See Stapel, "Versuch einer Metaphysik des Staates," *Deutsches Volkstum* 6 (1931): 409–19. The affinity to certain forms of Protestant theology has to be kept in mind.

44. Groh, *Arbeit an der Heillosigkeit,* 216–43.

45. Heinrich Meier, *Was ist politische Theologie?* (Munich: Siemens Stiftung, 2006), 23.

46. Jan Assmann, *Herrschaft und Heil: Politische Theologie in Altägypten, Israel und Europa* (Frankfurt: Fischer, 2002), 16.

6. Final Reflections

1. Chantal Mouffe, ed., *The Challenge of Carl Schmitt* (London: Verso, 1999); Georgio Agamben, *Homo Sacer* (Stanford, CA: Stanford University Press, 1999); Georgio Agamben, *State of Exception,* trans. Kevin Attell (Chicago: University of Chicago Press, 2005).

2. See Francis Fukuyama, *The End of History and the Last Man* (New York: Free Press, 1992).

3. See the extensive review essay of David Chandler, "The Revival of Carl Schmitt in International Relations: The Last Refugium of Critical Theory?," *Millenium: Journal of International Studies* 37, no. 1 (2008): 27–48.

4. David Dyzenhaus, *Legality and Legitimacy: Carl Schmitt, Hans Kelsen and Herman Heller in Weimar* (Oxford: Oxford University Press, 1999); John P. McCormick, *Carl Schmitt's Critique of Liberalism: Against Politics as Technology* (Cambridge: Cambridge University Press, 1997); William E. Scheuerman, *Carl Schmitt: The End of Law* (Lanham, MD: Rowman & Littlefield, 1999).

5. Jan-Werner Müller, *A Dangerous Mind: Carl Schmitt in Post-War European Thought* (New Haven, CT: Yale University Press, 2003), 223.

6. See Claudio Minca and Rory Rowan, *On Schmitt and Space* (London: Routledge, 2016), 53–58.

7. William Hooker, *Carl Schmitt's International Thought* (New York: Cambridge University Press, 2009), 3.

8. Hans Blumenberg, *The Legitimacy of the Modern Age*, trans. Robert M. Wallace (Cambridge, MA: MIT Press, 1983).

9. A significant exception is the extensive and detailed review of Schmitt scholarship by Peter Caldwell, "Controversies over Carl Schmitt," *Journal of Modern History* 77, no. 2 (2005): 357–87. The author covers with equal thoroughness German and Anglophone publications. The reviewer is mostly interested in factual as well as interpretative accuracy rather than the question of the transfer of Schmitt's theory to the contemporary world and its application. Still, it is telling that Schmitt's late work and the question of the so-called spatial Schmitt do not play a significant role in this assessment. Instead, the focus remains on Schmitt's early writings. Looking exclusively at this review, the reader would not realize that there was a major shift in Schmitt's reception after 2000.

10. See Gary L. Ulmen, "Partisan Warfare, Terrorism and the Problem of the New *Nomos* of the Earth," in *The International Thought of Carl Schmitt: Terror, Liberal War and the Crisis of the Global Order*, ed. Louiza Odysseos and Fabio Petito (London: Routledge, 2007), 97–106.

11. William Rasch, *Niklas Luhmann's Modernity: The Paradoxes of Differentiation* (Stanford, CA: Stanford University Press, 2000).

12. At the same time, we have to note that Rasch's position evolved. In his contribution to the 2016 *Oxford Handbook of Carl Schmitt*, he provides a more historically differentiated assessment of Schmitt's concept of democracy. While still hostile to the liberal tradition, he now emphasizes the plebiscitary character of Schmitt's theory of democracy, in which representation takes on a special meaning. It requires representation to be symbolic, calling for the people's acclamation of a proposition introduced by the leadership. In fact, Rasch points out that some readers might actually be frightened by this model of democracy. See William Rasch, "Carl Schmitt's Defense of Democracy," in *The Oxford Handbook of Carl Schmitt*, ed. Jens Meierhenrich and Oliver Simon (New York: Oxford University Press, 2016), 312–37.

13. William Rasch, "Conflict as Vocation: Carl Schmitt and the Possibility of Politics," *Theory, Culture & Society* 17 (2000): 7.

14. Louiza Odysseos and Fabio Petito, eds., *The International Political Thought of Carl Schmitt: Terror, Liberal War, and the Crisis of Global Order* (London: Routledge, 2007), 1. Contributors to this volume came from numerous counties, among them the United States, England, France, Italy, Finland, Russia, Australia, and Norway.

15. In his critique of the post-structuralist Schmittians, Chandler argues that they remain idealists in their reading of Schmitt's work. Schmitt is read mostly descriptively and used as a tool against the use of moral arguments by American imperialism. But "Schmitt's ontological focus does not lead to a critique of US ethical and legal universal claims on the basis that they constitute a new US global order or nomos" (Chandler, "The Revival of Schmitt," 40).

16. Claudio Minca and Rory Rowan, *On Schmitt and Space* (Abingdon, Oxon: Routledge, 2016), 3–4.

17. Ibid., 4.

18. Ibid., 5.

19. For a discussion of the function of solidarity see Max Pensky, *The Ends of Solidarity: Discourse Theory in Ethics and Politics* (Albany: State University of New York Press, 2008), 1–31.

20. On this point see Chantal Mouffe, "Carl Schmitt and the Paradox of Liberal Democracy," in Mouffe, *The Challenge of Carl Schmitt*, 38–53.

21. Carl Schmitt, *The Nomos of the Earth in the International Law of the Jus Publicum Europaeum*, trans. G. L. Ulmen (New York: Telos, 2006), 351–55.

INDEX

Kissinger, Henry, 139
Koepgen, Georg, 219n17
Koselleck, Reinhart, 5, 88–89
Krauthammer, Charles, 84
Kristol, Irving, 84
Kristol, William, 84

"Lage der europäischen Rechtswissen-
schaft" [State of European Jurispru-
dence] (Schmitt), 10, 51
Land and Sea (Schmitt), 104, 120, 185
land appropriation (*Landnahme*), 66, 92,
100–101; ethics of, 115; modern
imperialism and, 105
Landes, David S., 108
Las Casas, Bartolomé de, 90–91
Latin America, 89, 120, 123, 137;
Spanish conquest of, 14, 90–92, 96,
99–100, 212n3, 213n8. *See also*
Monroe Doctrine
Le Suer, James D., 213n13
League of Nations, 61, 67
Lebensraum (living space), 63, 69
Legalität und Legitimität (Schmitt), 43, 168
Legitimacy of the Modern Age (Blumen-
berg), 3, 145, 150, 161–66, 185, 188
Lenin, Vladimir, 15, 125–30, 136, 189;
Clausewitz and, 127, 128; Fanon and,
97; Mao and, 128
Lessing, Gotthold Ephraim, 26
liberal democracy, 5, 45, 79, 88, 110,
187, 192
liberalism, 5–6, 116, 118, 161, 186,
192–95; Bush and, 84; contradictions
of, 189; exclusion politics and, 85;
Ignatieff on, 110; *Pax Americana* and,
7; secular, 177; theory of, 183;
universalism of, 14, 192, 201–2, 204;
Weimar and, 1, 21, 146. *See also*
neoliberalism
liberation movements, 13
Liddell Hart, B. H., 139
life world (*Lebenswelt*), 8, 53
Löwenstein, Karl, 23–24
Löwith, Karl, 145, 163
Lübbe, Hermann, 89
Luhmann, Niklas, 136, 191
Luther, Martin, 22
Lyotard, Jean-François, 193

Maier, Hans, 156
Maistre, Joseph de, 147
Manemann, Jürgen, 145, 170, 171
Mann, Thomas, 30, 37
Mannheim, Karl, 46, 148
Mao Zedong, 15–16, 97, 121, 124, 131;
Clausewitz and, 128; on guerilla
warfare, 102, 127–30, 137, 189
Marcos, Theodor Andres, 42
Maritain, Jacques, 28
Marquard, Odo, 89
Marx, Karl, 15, 125, 148, 188
Marxism, 25, 55, 181
Massu, Jacques Émile, 93
McCormick, John, 182
McNeill, William, 91
Mearsheimer, John J., 114, 212n27
Mehring, Reinhard, 198
Meier, Heinrich, 28–29, 145, 169–70,
174
Meierhenrich, Jens, 197
Merkur (journal), 58–59
Metz, Johann Baptist, 16, 151, 156,
170, 173
Meuter, Günter, 145
Mignolo, Walter D., 14, 214n30
Minca, Claudio, 196–97
modernity, 161, 169; Christianity and,
139–40; political theology and, 149,
165; postmodernism and, 193;
secularization and, 50–51, 162–64,
172–73
Moenius, Georg, 161
Mohler, Armin, 216n6, 217n16
Moltmann, Jürgen, 16, 156, 173
monarchy, 157; democracy and, 148;
divine, 82, 152, 156; monotheism and,
152, 154. *See also* sovereignty
monotheism, 173; Meier on, 174;
Peterson on, 149–55
Monroe, James, 66, 70
Monroe Doctrine, 11, 12, 82, 104, 202;
defensive/offensive uses of, 67, 106,
106; German, 24, 61–70, 75–77, 87;
global, 81–82; *Großraum* and, 61,
95–96; Italian, 69; Japanese, 63–65,
69; scholarship on, 210n11
Montesinos, Antonio de, 90–91
Morefield, Jeanne, 110